AF865305

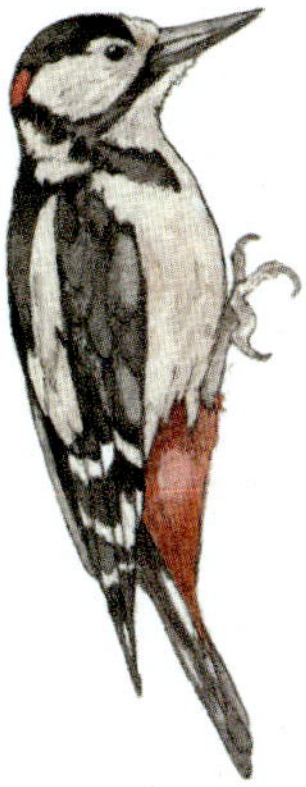
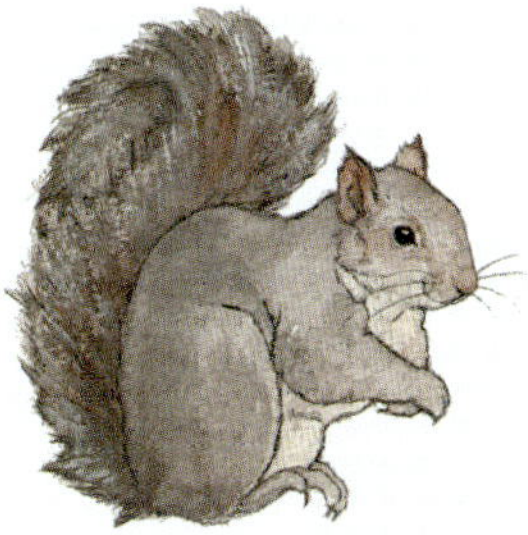
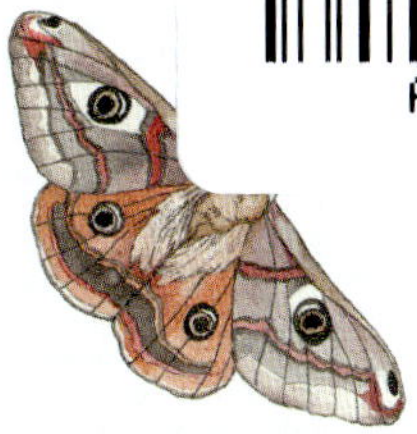

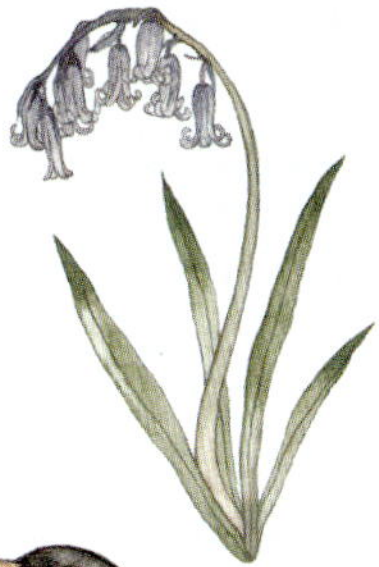

Watercolor *in the* Garden

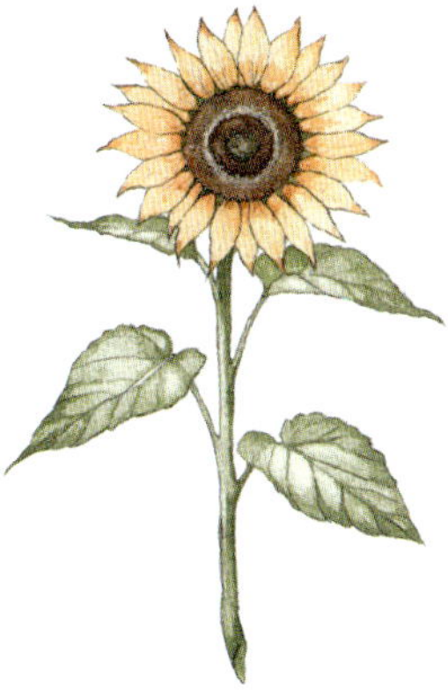
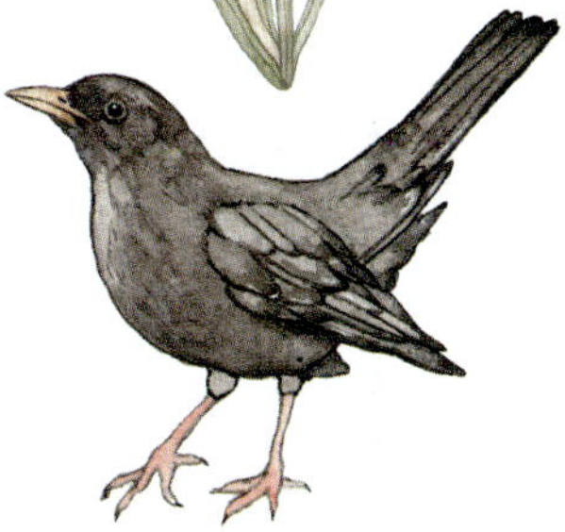

Paint a Charming World of Beautiful Songbirds, Baby Animals, Flowers and More

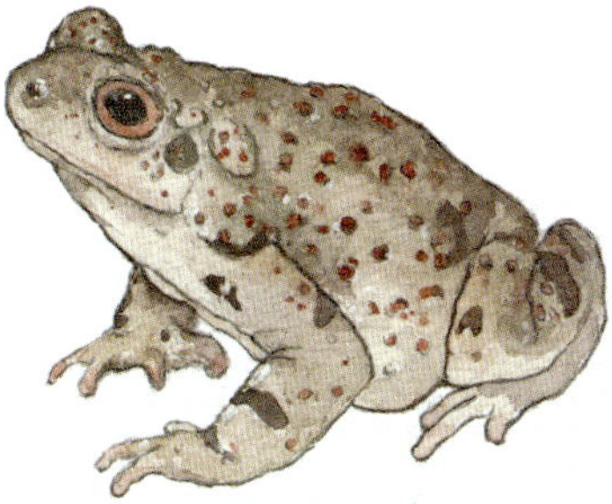
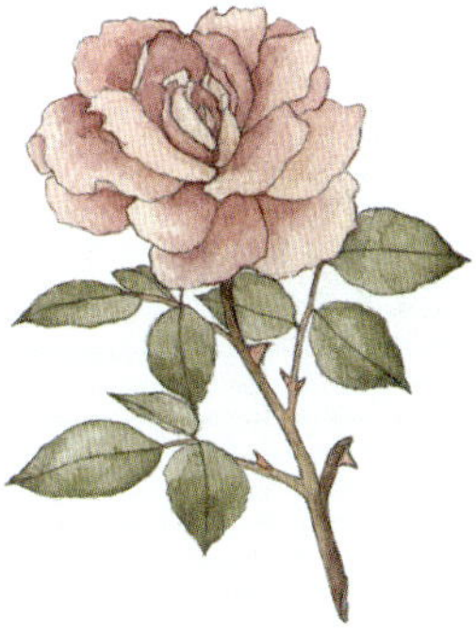

Jane Carkill

Creator of Lamblittle

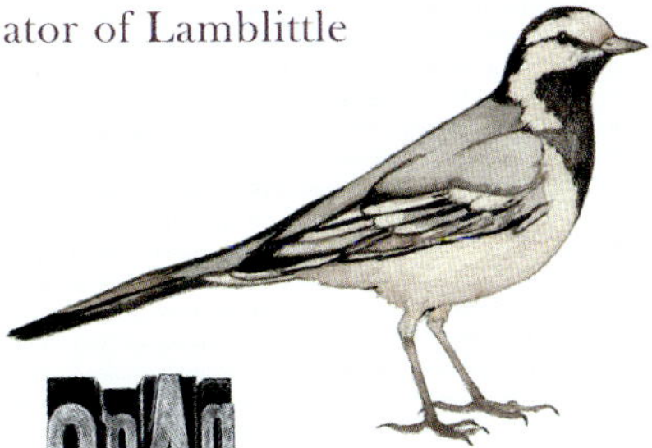
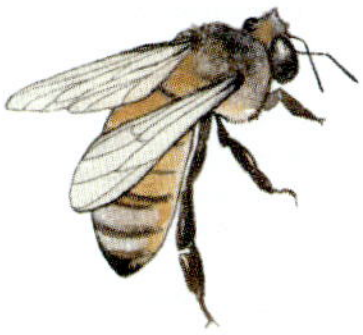

PAGE STREET PUBLISHING CO.

PAGE STREET
PUBLISHING CO.

Copyright © 2026 Jane Carkill

First published in 2026 by
Page Street Publishing Co.
27 Congress Street, Suite 1511
Salem, MA 01970
www.pagestreetpublishing.com

All rights reserved. No part of this book may be reproduced or used, in any form or by any means, electronic or mechanical, without prior permission in writing from the publisher.

Distributed by Macmillan, sales in Canada by The Canadian Manda Group.

30 29 28 27 26 1 2 3 4 5

ISBN-13: 979-8-89003-462-5

Library of Congress Control Number: 2025949493

Edited by Krystle Green
Cover and book design by Emma Hardy for Page Street Publishing Co.
Artwork by Jane Carkill

Printed and bound in China.

trustees

Page Street Publishing protects our planet by donating to nonprofits like The Trustees, which focuses on local land conservation.

To my friends and family,
whose loyal support and faith in my work
make every creation possible.

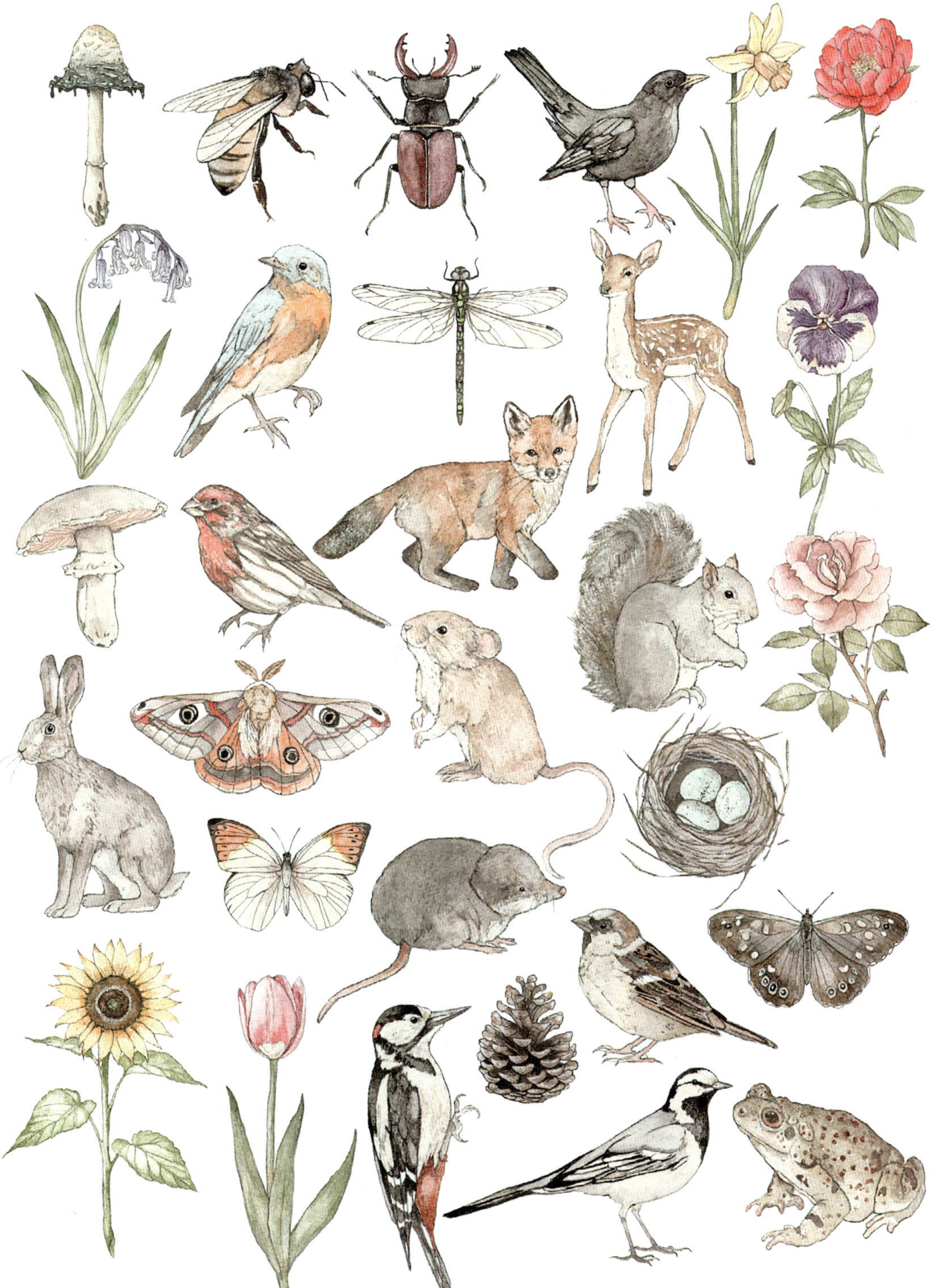

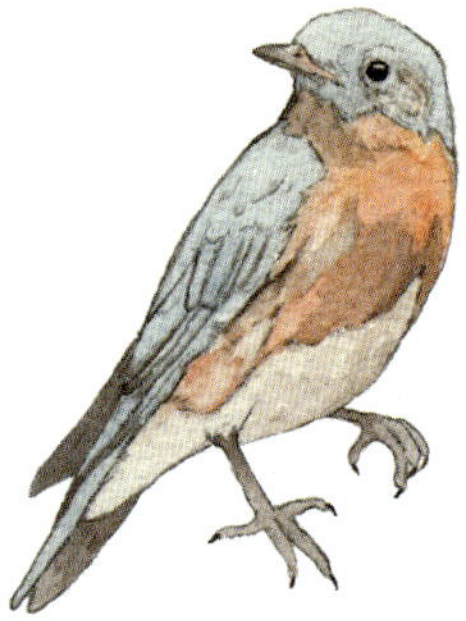

Table *of* Contents

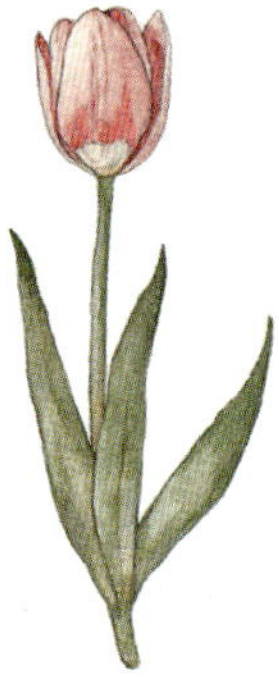

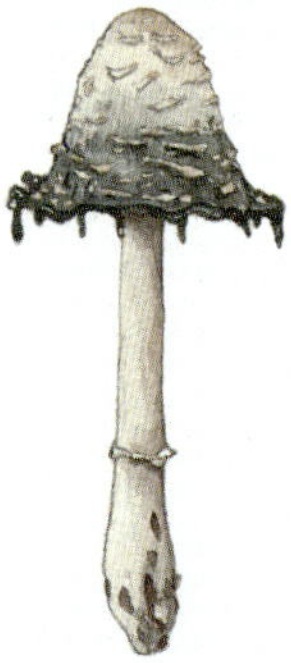

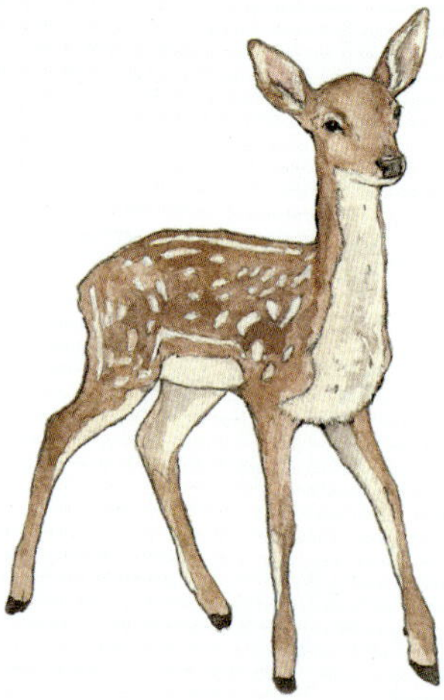

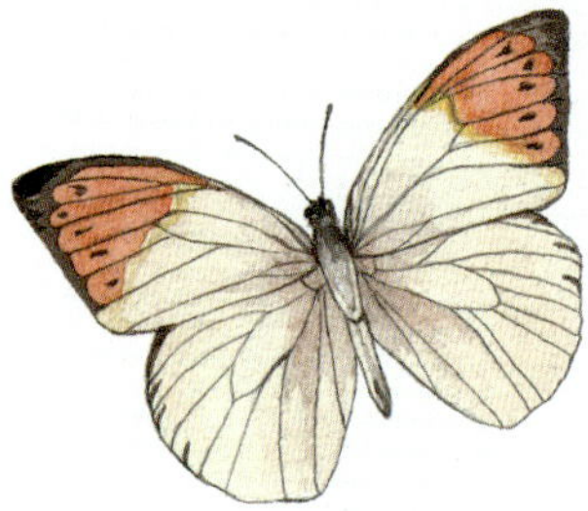

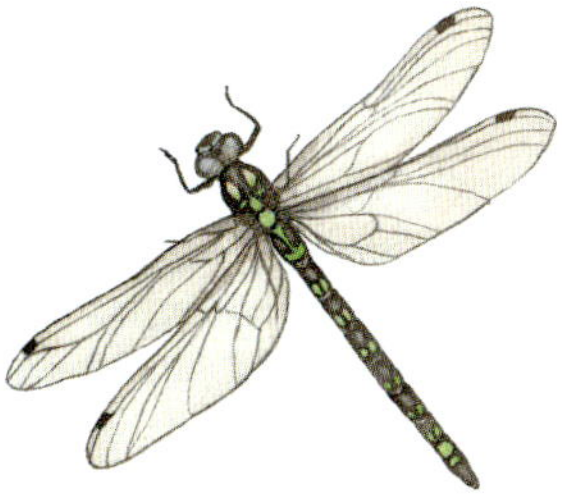
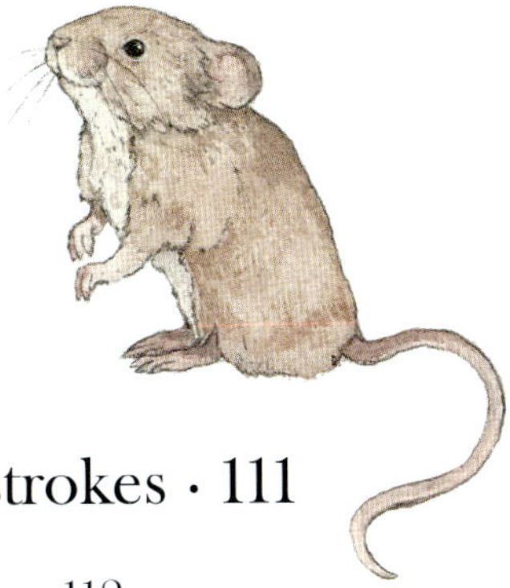
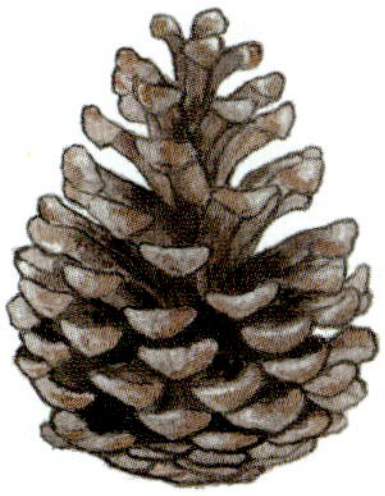
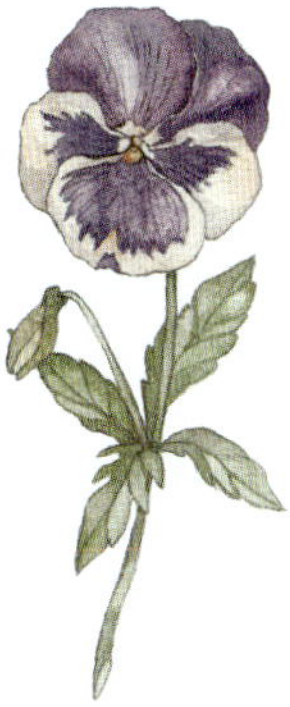

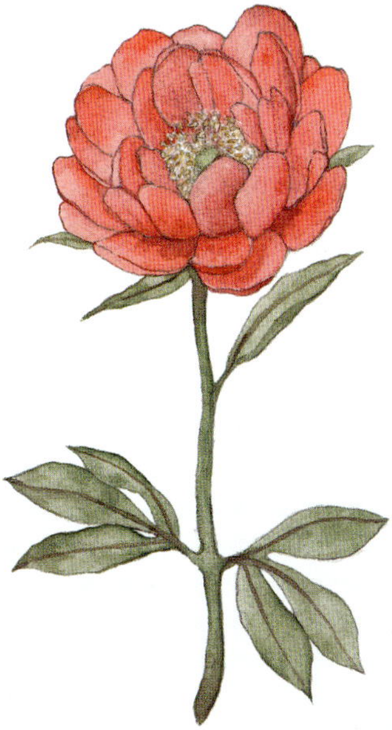
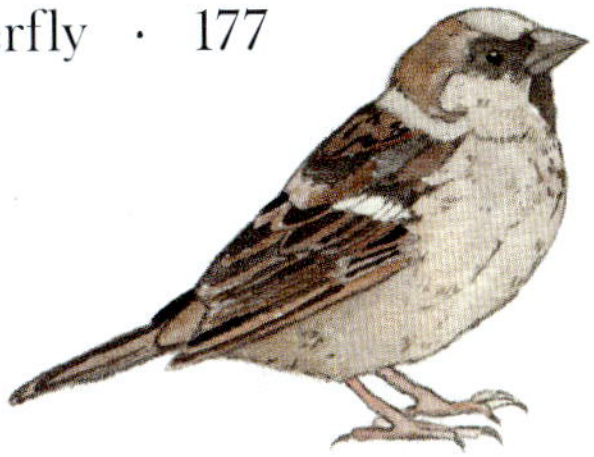
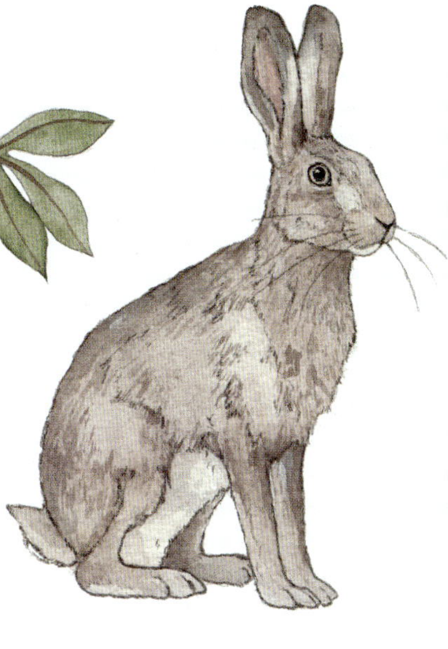

Introduction

Creating has always felt like a thread running through my life, something steady and instinctive that has brought a familiar sense of both calm and excitement. I will always hold dear the early childhood memories of what it felt like to discover meaning through the simple act of making art; watching a line become a shape, a shape becoming a creature or leaf or landscape, inevitably sparked a fascination that never truly left me. Even as my studies carried me into different areas of art and design, it was drawing and painting that continued to feel like home. Watercolor found its way into my practice gradually, then all at once. I realized how beautifully it could echo the world around me. Its soft luminosity, its gentle transparency and delicacy attracted me like no other medium had ever done before.

This sense of joy through creation is not something I've ever wanted to keep to myself. One of my deepest aims in writing and teaching is to pass along that same sense of delight and discovery, to offer others the chance to feel the familiar spark that rises when a painting begins to take on a life of its own. Sharing that joy feels like a natural extension of creating itself.

One of the reasons that I created this book was based on an observation that I have had through my many years in different art communities: Anybody who has ever picked up a brush and a set of watercolors has, at some time, attempted to paint the vast array of nature's flora and fauna yet felt overwhelmed by watercolor's grace, which is then matched by its unpredictability. Nature in all its complexities gives us an almost infinitely diverse palette to choose from, so even for beginners, it is an excellent starting point for inspiration. For example, flowers are about color, delicacy, and shape in all forms. The task of painting flowers is synonymous with color. Understanding of color and basic techniques will produce the freshness and spontaneity you need in an expressive, realistic painting. Fauna such as fox cubs and squirrels can teach a beginner all about texture as you experiment with different brushstrokes to create dense, realistic fur.

The main question you may ask is, How do I do it and do it well? The artist inside each of us wants to know the answer, and it is the pursuit of this that fuels our enthusiasm to paint. These pages invite you into a slower way of looking at nature, breaking each subject into approachable steps so you can learn how light moves across surfaces, how textures emerge through layers, and how small details breathe life into a painting. We will explore not just the flora you may find in the garden but also pay close attention to other creatures, great and small, that live among the blossoms. Welcome to *Watercolor in the Garden*.

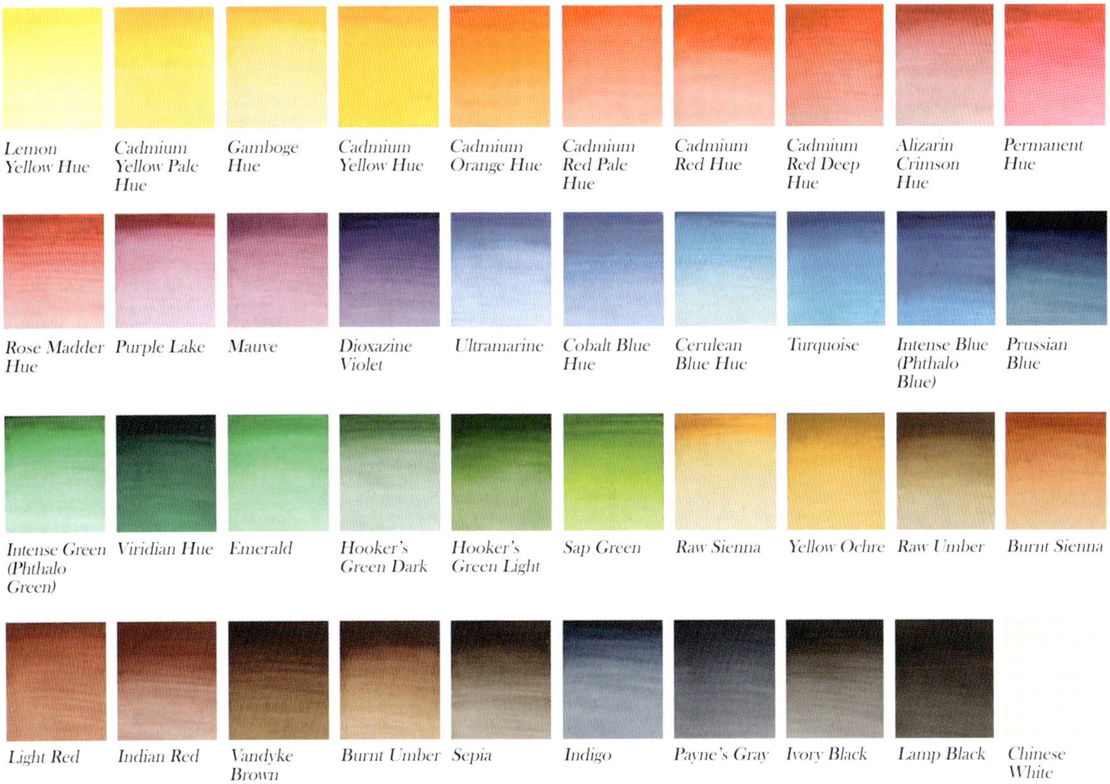

The Watercolor Toolkit
Brushes, Paper & Beyond

Analysis: Watercolor Paints

Watercolor paint consists of finely ground pigments bound together with gum arabic and mixed with glycerine, which acts like a moisturizer. Paints are sold in tubes, pans, and half pans. Pans are small blocks of semimoist color and can be bought individually as well as in specialized boxes with individual slots holding a vast array of colors. The lid opens to form a useful palette to blend and mix colors. Generally, you can buy pans complete with twelve colors or sometimes fewer. Some people prefer to choose their own colors. Every artist has their favorites, but most will favor a couple of each of the primary colors, red, blue, and yellow, and mix their own colors from these.

In my work, and for the projects in this book, a pan of color will be used. Whether you choose pans or tubes depends on your individual style and subject matter as you develop your skills and discover which techniques suit you after much experimentation and practice. I find pans very convenient as they come with wells on the lid for mixing paint and can be folded up for easy storage upon completion.

Tubes require a separate mixing palette and are wonderful to use for large-scale work since you can mix bigger quantities at strong pigmentations very easily. They are made at a standard size, which may appear very small in comparison to tubes of acrylic or oil paint, but they have a lot of longevity and are highly pigmented, so a little bit goes quite a long way!

Watercolor paints come in two varieties, artist quality and student quality. Artist quality colors are more expensive, but my perspective is when beginning watercolor or any art medium, I would invest in a small amount of the best materials; the better the tools, the better the outcome. Cheap paints are an excellent gateway if you are curious about exploring a medium, but if you find you would like to yield the most realistic results that do not have muted, dull hues, higher quality is always worth the investment. Student quality paints generally contain less pigment and may lead to disappointment. But if you are on a limited budget, perhaps for initial choices, invest in excellent quality primary colors and a less expensive quality for colors that will not be used as often.

For the projects in this book, the color chart referenced is from the Winsor & Newton™ Cotman Watercolor™ palette. You do not have to have the exact matching palette; just try your best to source colors as close as you can.

All About Brushes

Brushes are the quiet heroes of a watercolor toolkit. Many beginners start out by buying large sets of inexpensive brushes only to find they wear out quickly and don't handle paint well. A small selection of well-made brushes with resilient, springy bristles that naturally form a fine point will serve you far better over time. A good brush should have a certain resilience. You can test the spring of the bristles on your brush by wetting it to a point and dragging it over your thumbnail.

For my own work, and for the projects in this book, I rely on round brushes. Each one has a wooden handle, a metal ferrule that secures the bristles, and a tapered head that allows for both broad strokes and delicate details, like fur or leaf veins. Reliable options include the Winsor & Newton Sable series brushes, Arteza® brushes, Richard J Oliver brushes, Da Vinci Colineo brushes, and Isabey® brushes.

The larger the brush head, the more paint it will hold, so my advice is when picking a first set of brushes to have as staples in your toolkit, have a good range of brush sizes for different functions and applications, whether it be for tracing fine lines, dry brushing bushy fur, or glazing large areas with colored washes.

The brushes pictured on the opposite page are the brushes that I use often and appear in the projects of this book.

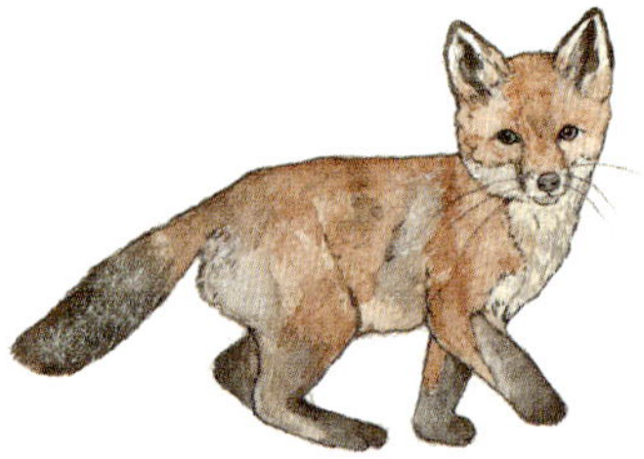

How to Care for Your Brushes

At the end of a painting session, rinse your brushes thoroughly in clean water. This helps them last longer and keeps them in excellent condition. Ensure that all paint is removed from the bristles, including the area inside the ferrule. After washing, reshape the bristles to their natural point and allow the brushes to dry fully by standing them upright in a jar or another container. Never place them downward on the bristles, as this will bend and damage the tip.

Water is a vital ingredient in producing a good painting, as you will discover quickly when your water becomes dirty. Ensure that you are replacing your water pot as you paint if you find it getting very murky or muddy with sediment. Fresh water, in turn, keeps your brushes clean and healthy and in pristine condition, therefore producing crisp, clear colors.

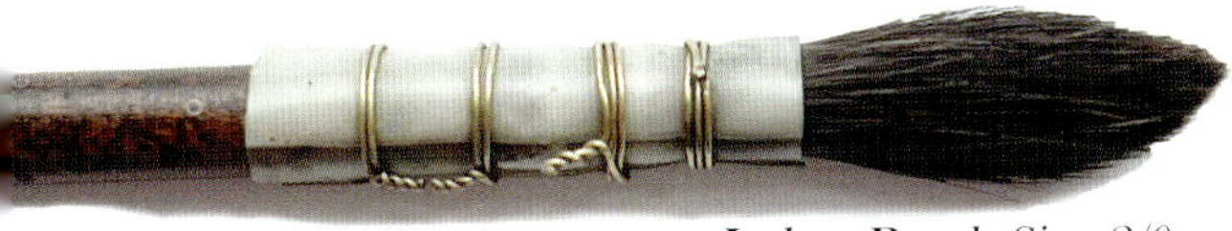

Isabey Brush Size 2/0

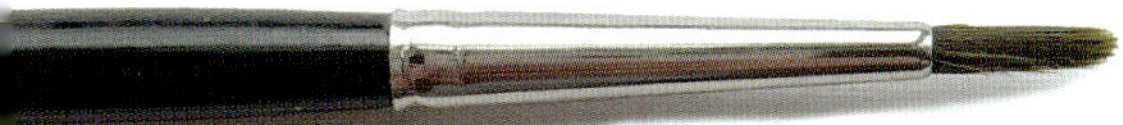

Richard Oliver Brush Size 4

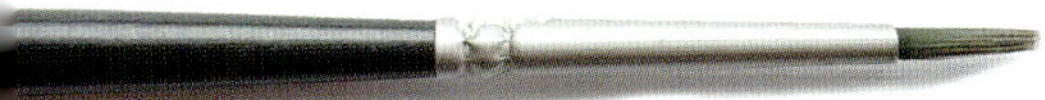

Arteza Brush Size 1

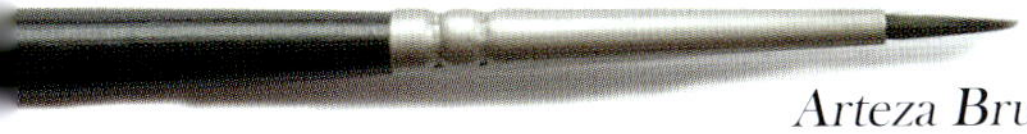

Arteza Brush Size 0

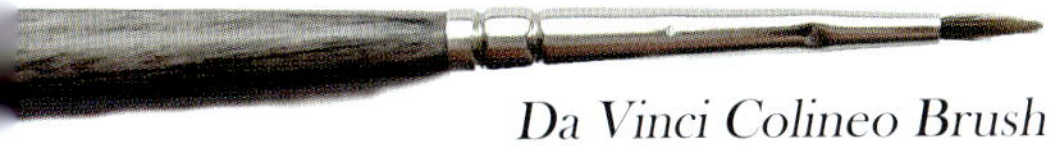

Da Vinci Colineo Brush Size 3/0

The World of Watercolor Paper

From my years of painting, it's become clear to me that the quality of your paper can dramatically shape the outcome of a watercolor piece. There's a broad range of watercolor papers available, differing in weight, texture, and overall performance.

Watercolor paper is sold as individual sheets, but I prefer watercolor blocks. These are stacks of paper gummed along all four edges, keeping the sheet flat while you work. Once a painting is dry, you can release the top sheet by sliding a palette knife around the edges.

The texture of the paper on the surface is known as its grain, or tooth. There are three types of textured surfaces, known as hot press, cold press, and rough (also known as cold press, but with a much more pronounced texture). Hot-press paper is smooth with very little tooth, ideal for precise, detailed line work. Cold-press paper has a lightly textured surface that absorbs washes well, giving the artist more control as they build up layers.

Watercolor paper also comes in a wide variety of weights, also known as thickness or grammage. The weight is usually described as the weight of a ream of Imperial-size sheets in pounds (lb) or grams per square meter (gsm). The lightest weight of paper starts at about 90 pounds (190 gsm) and the heaviest weight at about 400 pounds (850 gsm).

For the majority of my work and the projects in this book, I use a cold-press paper at 140 pounds (300 gsm). An excellent brand I often use and always recommend is ARCHES®.

Additional Equipment

These are some useful pieces of additional equipment that can be explored as you build your own style and skills in watercolor.

Palette: Palettes come in various shapes and sizes, and usually are composed of either plastic or ceramic. Plastic palettes are convenient when perhaps painting outdoors or for easy transportation, but ceramic palettes are much better quality.

Pencil: For sketching outlines and preparing drafts, I always reach for a sharp, high-quality HB pencil. Keeping the point crisp makes it much easier to achieve clean, precise lines.

Sponge: A small, natural sponge can be useful in a watercolor kit. It can be used to wash off paint when a mistake has been made, or for softening edges. You can also apply paint with it to build up interesting textures.

Paper Towel: A paper towel is a surprisingly versatile tool. I keep a piece beside me to blot excess water from my brush, and it's also invaluable for "lifting out" techniques, where gently removing paint helps create bright, luminous highlights.

Water Pot: The bigger, the better. Water containers are pieces of equipment that you do not need to buy. I like to use old recycled jam jars, and other artists use containers like yogurt pots! Water for diluting colors will quickly become dirty, so do make sure that you are regularly changing the water and also cleaning the containers, as sediment can build and dry at the bottom.

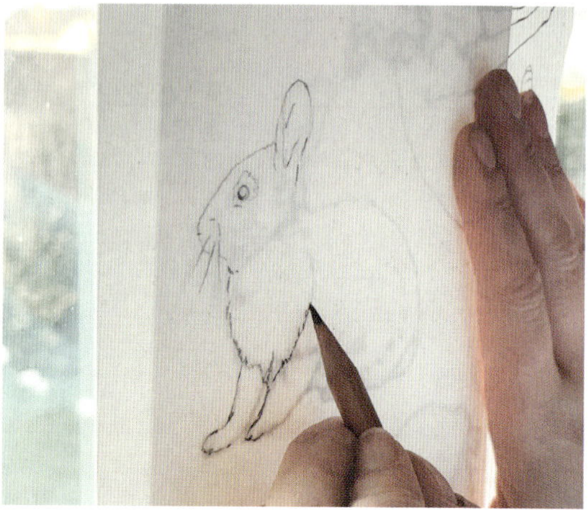

Drawing: How to Use Templates

At the back of this book, you will find a series of templates that will match the tutorials in each chapter. There are various methods that you can use to transfer the picture to your piece of watercolor paper.

Tracing: Place your template under a sheet of drawing paper and trace its outlines lightly with a sharp HB pencil, using a light box or holding the template and paper together against a natural light source, such as a window.

Graphite Transfer: Shade the back of your template with a soft graphite pencil, place it graphite side down on your drawing paper, and trace the front lines on the template using a sharp HB pencil. The pressure transfers the graphite onto your drawing paper. Erase any smudges using a putty eraser.

Freehand: Keep the template nearby and use it as a visual guide while drawing freehand. This method is great for developing hand-eye coordination and practicing and forming personal style while maintaining proportions and reference accuracy.

Brushwork

While it's possible to build a painting entirely with flat washes, the texture and direction of your brushstrokes play a crucial role in bringing watercolor to life. Thoughtful brush marks and techniques can transform a painting from flat and static into lively and dynamic. This is very useful when it comes to painting fur and other details like dimpling and folding of petals and foliage.

Line Work

Holding the brush near the top of the handle allows a looser, freer approach with more expressive strokes.

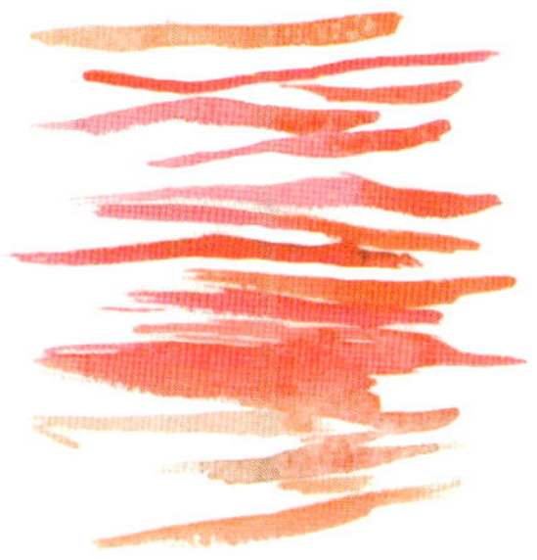

Holding the brush tightly close to or at the ferrule allows maximum control and can result in the tidiest brushstroke. Light pressure with the point of the bristles will give precise, delicate lines, also called brush drawing.

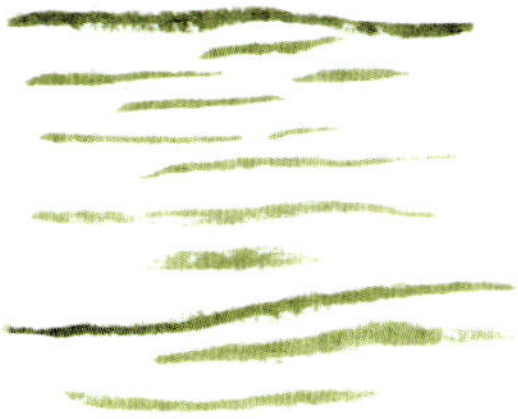

In my work, as with many watercolor artists, great importance is placed on the quality of brushstrokes, the weight of each line, and the precise control over the brush to achieve clean, detailed results. It's helpful to spend time familiarizing yourself with your brushes and experimenting with the different marks the bristles can make on a spare sheet of paper before starting a painting. A round brush allows you to make highly descriptive shapes by varying the pressure. You can begin at just the tip of the brush and then eventually press more firmly to see a variation of the stroke effects.

Splatter Effects

Splattering is another excellent method of suggesting dotted texture. Splattering is achieved by loading the bristles of the brush with a fluid mixture of paint and flicking or spraying droplets of paint onto the dry surface of paper. I will often use this method when painting the surface of a bird's egg. My favorite way to create the splatter effect is to dip a large brush in paint and run the bristles through my finger to release the paint in minuscule, delicate droplets.

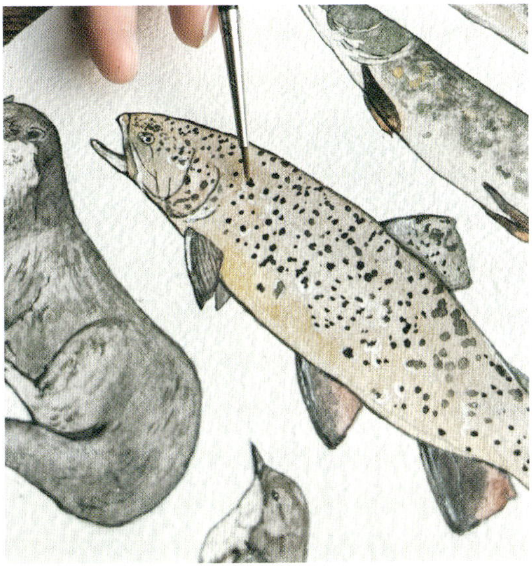

Dry Brushing

Dry brushing is painting with the bare minimum of paint on the dry bristles of a brush so that the color only partially covers the paper, giving a bushy, coarse effect. This is a very effective method in creating texture on fur—for example, the tail of a squirrel or a fox. Several layers of dry brushwork can be laid over one another, either in the same or contrasting colors. The direction of the brushstroke can also be varied to build up a structure of fine lines. Like all watercolor techniques, dry brushing requires practice. If the paint is too wet, it will go on as a solid wash; if too dry, it will not apply at all. The technique involves a small amount of paint being picked up on the end of a brush with the bristles slightly splayed to produce a series of fine lines, rather like hatching or crosshatching in drawing.

Blending

Blending means achieving a soft, gradual transition from one color or layer to another. There is a series of techniques that you can use in order to create smooth transitions, soft shadows, and natural-looking gradients.

Wet-on-Wet: The wet-on-wet method involves applying each new layer of color while the layer underneath is still damp. To achieve this, apply clean water or a wet wash to your paper first, and while it is still damp, apply a layer of color on top. When you drop a new color into the still wet wash, the weight of the water forces the first color outward so that the colors on the page bleed into one another without actually mixing, causing a natural gradient. This will create soft, flowing transitions and ethereal backgrounds.

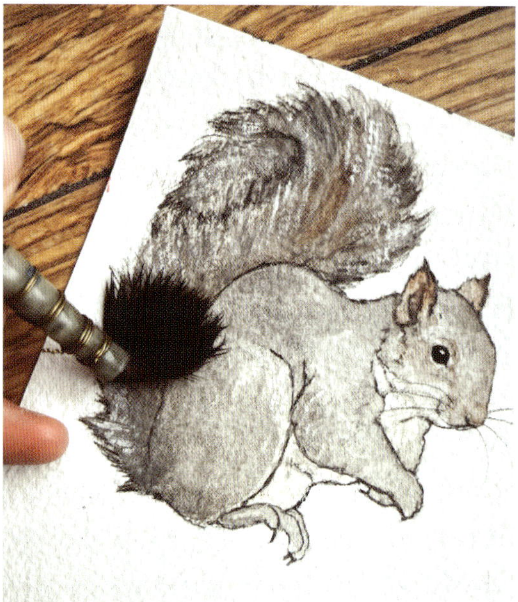

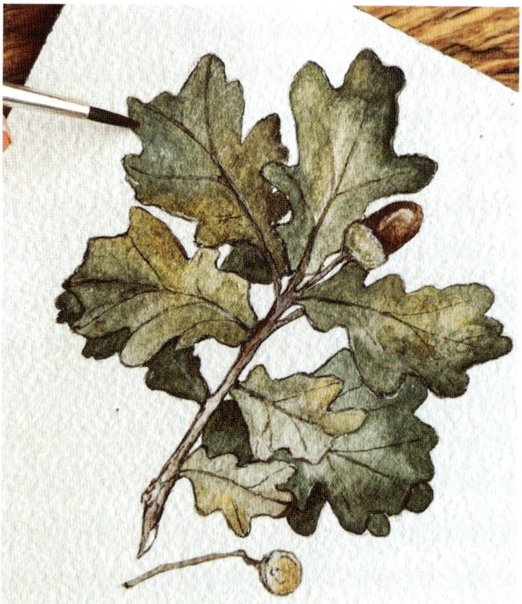

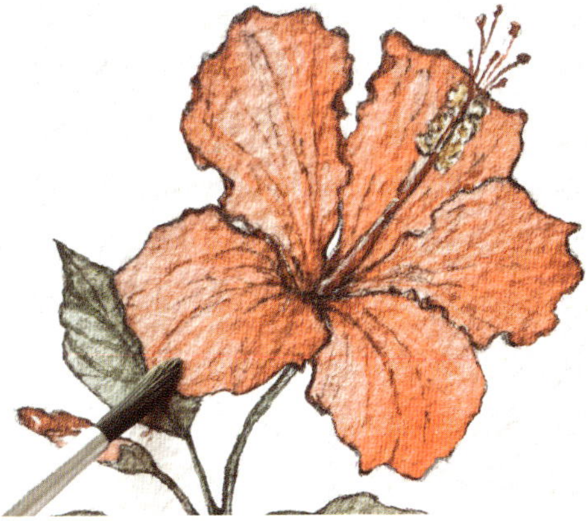

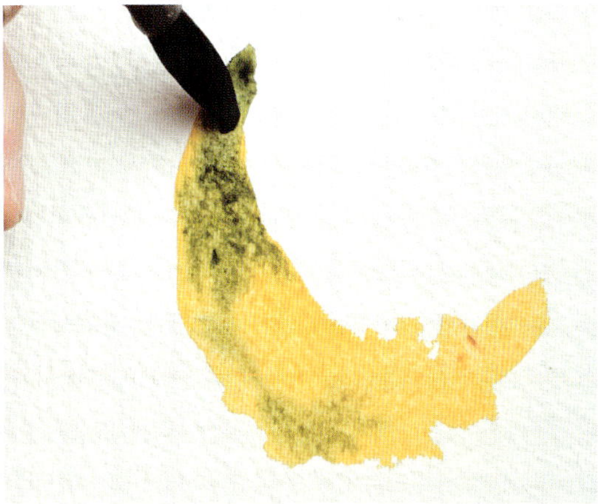

Wet-on-Dry: The wet-on-dry method is a classic technique of layering new wet washes over earlier ones that have been allowed to dry. Wet-on-dry work often leaves crisp, hard edges that form as each layer of color dries—it is more predictable and allows for easier control of paint flow. This method is very effective in creating gentle gradients without losing detailing.

Softened Edges: This method can be used to create smooth, natural-looking edges, perfect for shadows and rounded forms. While the paint is still wet, gently drag a damp, clean brush along the edges of a shape to blur or soften it.

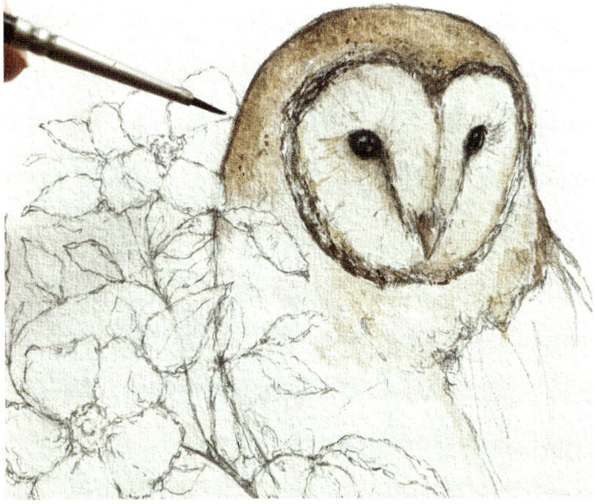

Dropped-In Color: Dropping in color involves adding a concentrated pigment to a damp wash and allowing it to spread, blend, and create organic effects. To achieve this, prepare a wet wash of color on the page, load your brush with a more concentrated color, and gently touch it onto the wet area. The pigment will spread and blend with the wet wash, creating soft gradients, color variations, or textures.

Highlights

Highlights indicate the areas where light strikes a subject most intensely. Watercolor has a natural luminosity, which is ideal for capturing this sense of sparkle and bringing realism to your work through layered washes. There are also simple techniques to emphasize light and give your paintings a strong sense of having a three-dimensional effect. In my practice, highlights are typically created by preserving the paper's natural white color, lifting off color with a damp brush or tissue, or adding highlights with another medium such as gouache or acrylic.

Lifting Out

One effective method for creating highlights is to do so during the wet-on-wet technique. Begin by laying down a wash of color on your paper. While the surface is still damp, take a clean, dry brush and gently press it onto the areas of the paper where you want to lift some of the pigment. The moisture in the paper allows the pigment to be absorbed into the brush, leaving behind a lighter, softer area that reads as a highlight. This technique works particularly well for small details or precise shapes, such as foliage, particularly leaves and petals. By controlling the amount of pressure and the size of your brush, you can achieve subtle variations in tone and create a sense of depth and dimension.

Another method I rely on frequently involves the use of a paper towel to lift color. Start by applying a glaze of color to your desired area and allow it to dry completely. Then, dip a clean brush in water and gently wiggle or move the bristles over the section where you want to remove some pigment. This agitation loosens the dried paint and allows it to be lifted from the paper. Immediately press a piece of paper towel onto the dampened area. The towel absorbs the pigment, producing soft-edged, luminous highlights that feel natural and vibrant. This technique is particularly useful for larger areas where a gentle gradient of light is needed.

Using Gouache and Acrylic Paint

Gouache is essentially the opaque counterpart to watercolor. It is made by mixing pigments with gum arabic and white chalk, giving it a thick consistency that dries to a matte, slightly chalky finish, which is quite different from the delicate transparency of traditional watercolors.

Acrylic paint is a versatile, fast-drying, water-based paint that consists of three main components: the pigment (color), a binder (the acrylic polymer that holds the color in place), and water (the vehicle that makes it a liquid you can paint with).

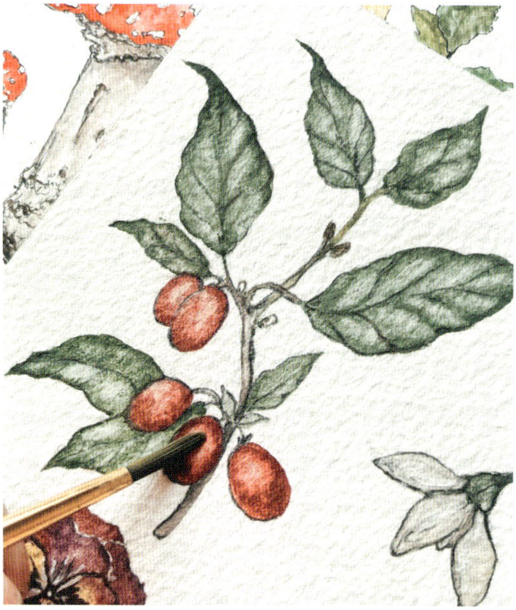

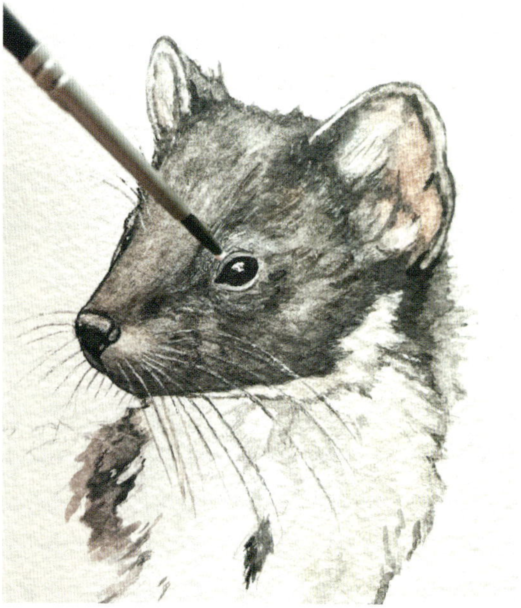

In my work, I often squeeze a small amount of gouache or acrylic onto my palette and use the tip of my finest brush to add tiny highlights. This technique is particularly effective for capturing the reflective shine in an animal's eye or the glint on an insect's wings. I personally prefer acrylic for these details as it dries with a subtle sheen, whereas gouache, with its matte finish, can sometimes appear dull next to the luminous washes of watercolor.

Adding Salt into Color

Adding salt is a classic and fun technique in watercolor for creating interesting textures and subtle highlights. When sprinkled onto wet watercolor, salt absorbs the water and pigment around it. This creates small, irregular lighter areas as the pigment is pushed away from the salt crystals. Once dry, you can brush off the salt, leaving behind starburst-like or speckled highlights.

Mistakes: How to Alter & Erase

Watercolor painting is an unpredictable medium that can be equal parts rewarding and frustrating. Its translucency and luminosity can also lend itself to being difficult to control. There are ways of making corrections if you are unhappy with a certain effect.

Erasing: A watercolor or kneaded eraser can lift dry pigment from the paper's surface. You can use this eraser by lightly dabbing or rolling it over the area to remove or soften color. Kneaded erasers are best for subtle adjustments, while standard erasers may lift more pigment. Erasers are good for refining small details, lightening edges, or correcting pencil lines under washes, but do be careful not to put too much pressure on the paper, as this may cause some damage to the delicate texture of the paper fibers.

Scratching Out: This technique, also known as sgraffito, is used to create small, sharp highlights. The most common method involves scraping away at a layer of paint using a sharp tool like a scalpel or craft knife to reveal the bare paper underneath. This must be done with care, though, as the blade could tear holes in the paper.

Overpainting with White: Untidy edges or obvious errors can be cleaned up by painting over them with white acrylic or gouache paint.

Blotting: If a light wash of color has created an unwanted effect and is still damp, the excess pigment can be absorbed by a piece of paper towel or a small sponge.

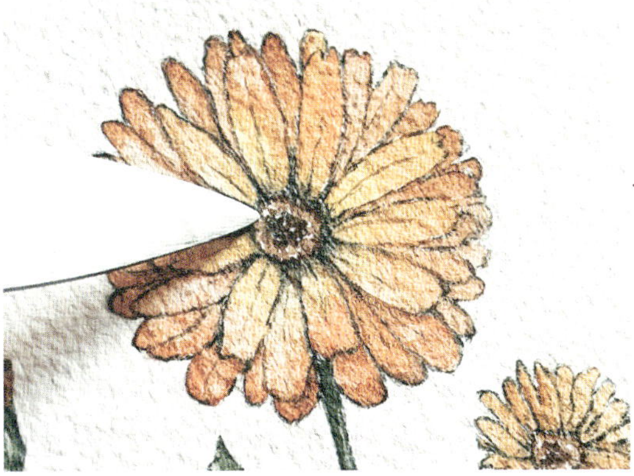

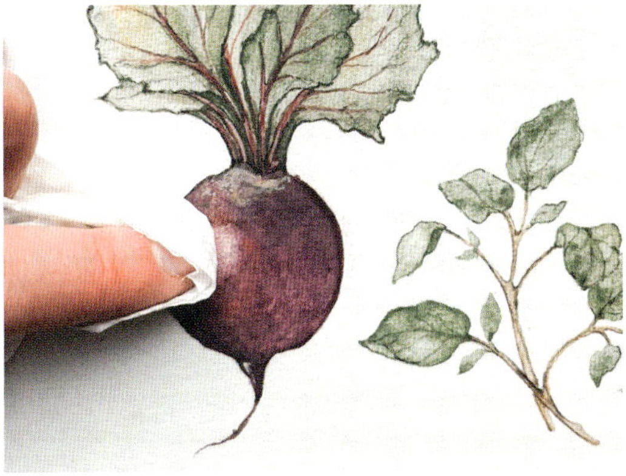

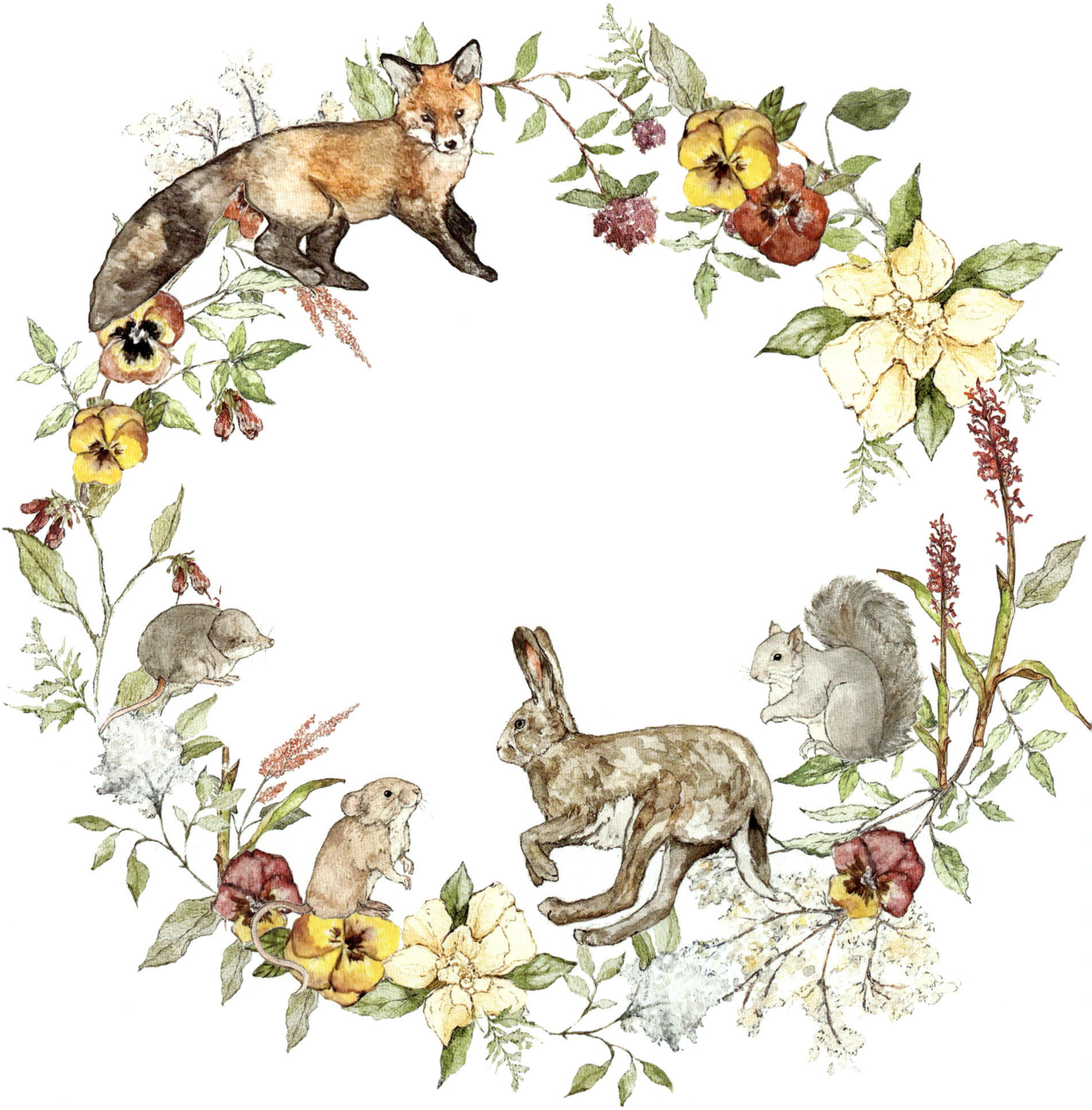

Garden Wildlife

We have wandered into the quiet world of the garden, where small creatures move between petals, branches, and patches of warm sunlight. From the quick, alert movements of the gray squirrel to the gentle charm of the fawn, each visitor brings its own distinct character to the backyard.

In this chapter, you will learn how to capture the qualities that make garden wildlife so captivating. We'll explore the sleek shape and bright expression of a fox cub as it passes along the garden's edges, and study the soft, earthy tones of the wild hare when it pauses in the grass.

I have even included one of my favorites, the humble and shy shrew. Some may think that painting will keep them deskbound, but these projects invite you to be led outside into the serenity of the garden and let these creatures emerge gently from your brush step by step.
Let's get started!

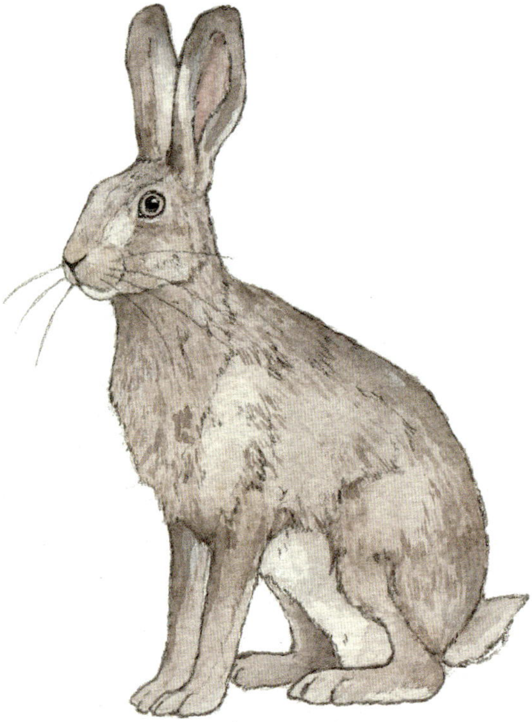

Hare

There's a quiet sort of magic in the Irish countryside on a frosty spring morning; mist rising from the fields, the air thick with the scent of rain and earth, and then, just at the edge of vision, a hare appears. Not a timid creature like the rabbit, but a wilder, older spirit. The hare seems to belong to another world entirely; their elongated, lithe proportions and glint of alertness in their eyes make them feel almost supernatural! In this tutorial, we will bring this magical spirit to life, creating a sense of balance between minute details and almost translucent washes of paint.

Materials Needed

1 sheet of cold-press 140-pound (300-gsm) aquarelle/watercolor paper

HB pencil

Brushes

- > Size 4
- > Size 1
- > Size 3/0
- > Size 0

Watercolor paints

- > Sepia
- > Vandyke brown
- > Ivory black
- > Indian red
- > Burnt umber

Acrylic white

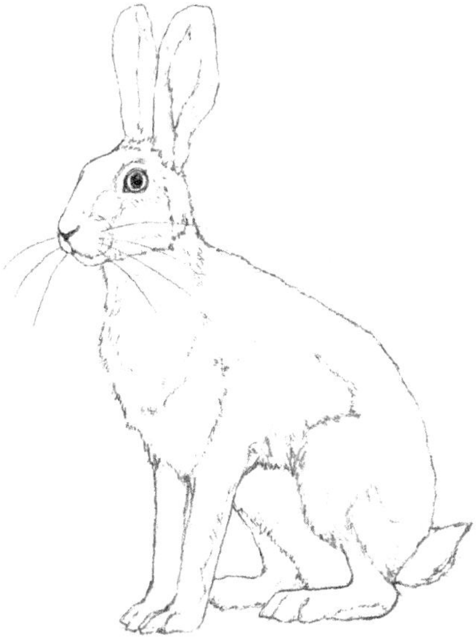

Step 1: Draw the Outline

Starting on a sheet of cold-press watercolor paper, draw the hare's outline with a sharp HB pencil using the template provided on page 183. Fill in the eye (we will deepen this with black paint later), making sure to leave two dots on the upper right-hand side of the pupil uncolored for a highlight.

Take note that the hare has varying textures; it has a fluffy chest and smooth ears, so play with your use of the pencil, keeping confident, flowing lines for where its fur is smooth, and softer, more organic lines where the fur is more textured and fluffier.

(continued)

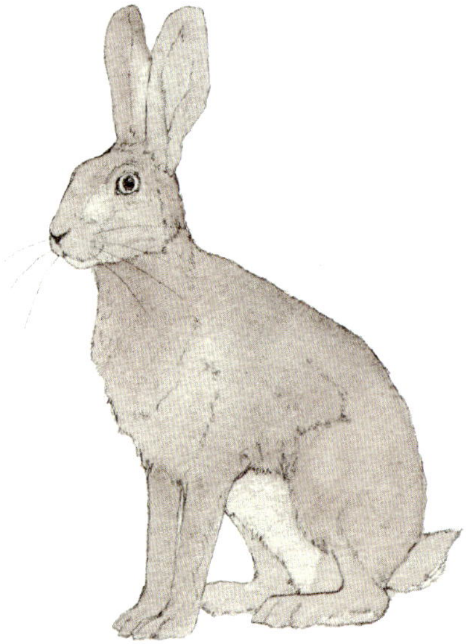

Step 2: Paint the Base Layer

To paint the base layer for the hare, use a size 4 brush to create a light-toned mix of sepia and water. We want this to be a very light, cool-toned brown. Load this watery brown onto the bristles and glaze the mixture over the entire face and body of the hare, avoiding the pupil of the eye. Allow this mixture to dry, then paint another layer of this light-toned sepia onto the hare again, this time avoiding the underbelly, as we want to keep this a lighter tone of sepia. Allow the paint to fully dry.

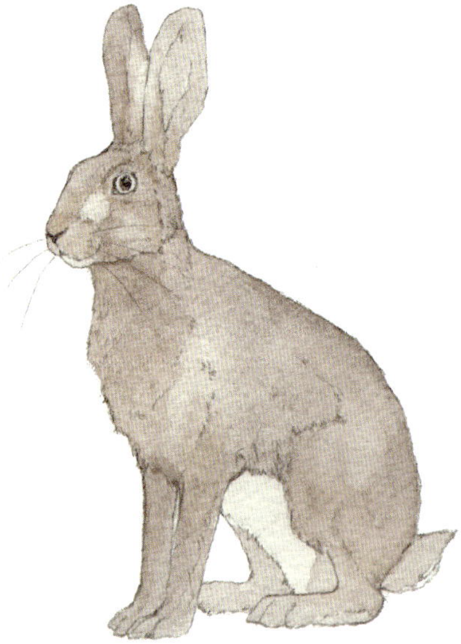

Step 3: Create Texture and Color

To give the face and front of the hare's body some texture and dimension, use a size 1 brush to mix a light-toned glaze of sepia with a small touch of Vandyke brown. We want this color to be a slightly warmer variation of the light-toned sepia we mixed in step 2 where we created the base layer of the hare, so only a small amount of Vandyke brown is needed.

Load this warm brown onto your brush and apply it along the left-hand side of the left ear, moving the paint downward, glazing the forehead down to the tip of the nose and the entirety of the cheek fur, avoiding a small section just between the eye and nose. Apply more of this glaze along the front of the chest fur, traveling downward to the left-hand side of both of the legs and paws.

Finally, glaze the upper back all along the spine, then downward to the lower fur of the back right leg. Soften the edges of the glaze layers by gently pushing the paint outward until the harsh lines of paint disappear. Clean the brush.

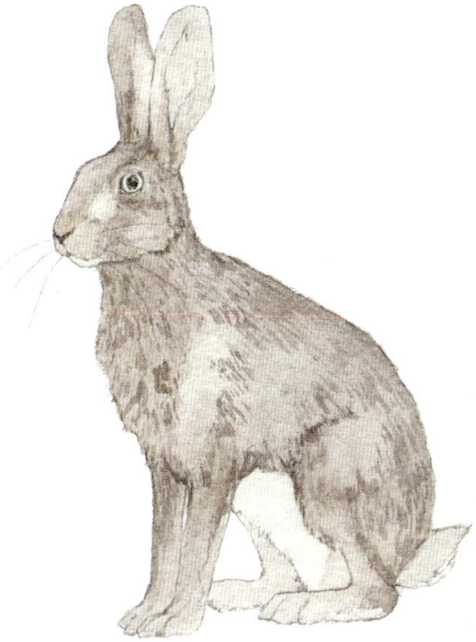

Step 4: Add Texture to the Fur

To create the textured fur, use a size 3/0 brush to mix a mid-toned solution of sepia and water, and load the color onto the bristles. Hold the brush at the ferrule so you can have the most control over the brushstrokes. Beginning at the lower left ear, paint short, delicate brushstrokes following the natural growth pattern of the fur on the face, flowing downward, around the eye, and eventually growing sparser and looser at the cheek.

Follow this natural growth pattern of downward flow from the neck, down along the spine, and filling along the back leg, lower belly, and midway along the front legs. The fur will be slightly denser along the backside and front chest of the hare, so paint slightly more and thicker lines along these areas to give a sense of fullness. Clean the brush.

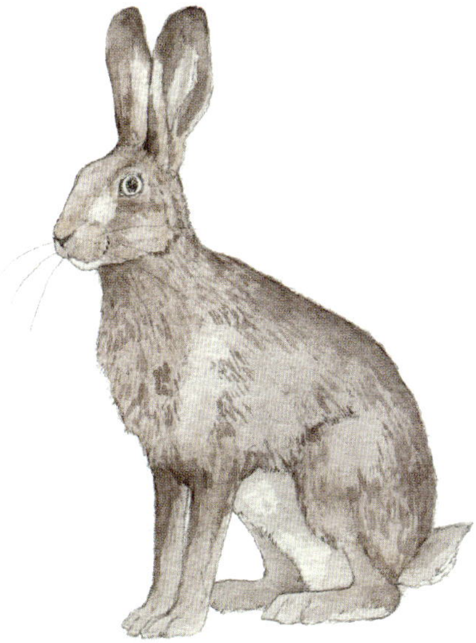

Step 5: Add Depth and Shadow

To create the color that we will use for the shadow, use a clean size 1 brush to mix a mid-toned solution of sepia with a very slight touch of ivory black. As black is naturally very heavily pigmented, we do not want it to completely overtake the warmer tones of the sepia brown, so only a slight dab of this black is needed to create a deeper shade of the original sepia base layer that we painted the entire body of the hare with in step 2.

Load this deep brown mixture onto your brush and glaze it along the upper ears of the hare, working downward along the left-hand side of the left ear, and along the entire edges of the right ear. Glaze this dark brown mixture softly along the spine of the hare, the upper chest right below the chin, and the upper to left-hand side of both frontal feet.

(continued)

Next, we want to create an even lighter glaze of this color to paint the lower belly fur. To do this, swirl your size 1 brush into water and add the wet bristles back into the dark brown paint mixture; this will dilute the paint slightly. Gently glaze this watery dark brown along both of the back feet and the right-hand side of the fur on the lower belly. Glaze some on the tail and finally along the left-hand side of the nose and full cheeks of the hare.

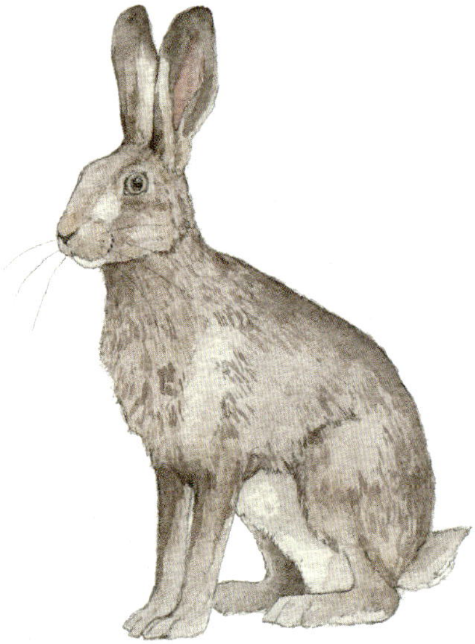

Step 6: Add Color and Further Shadows

Using a size 0 brush, mix a light-toned solution of sepia with a slight touch of ivory black. We want this solution to be slightly more cool toned and black than the dark brown in step 5, so add a slightly heavier dab of black to create a watery pale gray. Glaze this solution on the right-hand side of the left back foot and lower left-hand side of the right ear where it meets the upper forehead. This will create a deeper sense of shadow.

Clean the bristles of the size 0 brush. Next, we will create the warm pink that will fill the hare's inner ear. Using the clean size 0 brush, mix a mid-toned solution of Indian red and water. Glaze this gently along the center of the hare's ear. While this layer is still drying, add a tiny dab of sepia to the mid-toned Indian red solution to create a slightly darker red mixture, and gently drop a small amount to the very bottom of the inner ear. Allow the paint to dry.

Finally, to create the color needed for the pupil of the eye, use a clean size 3/0 brush to mix a light-toned solution of burnt umber and water, and gently paint a layer on the pupil of the eye. Clean the brush.

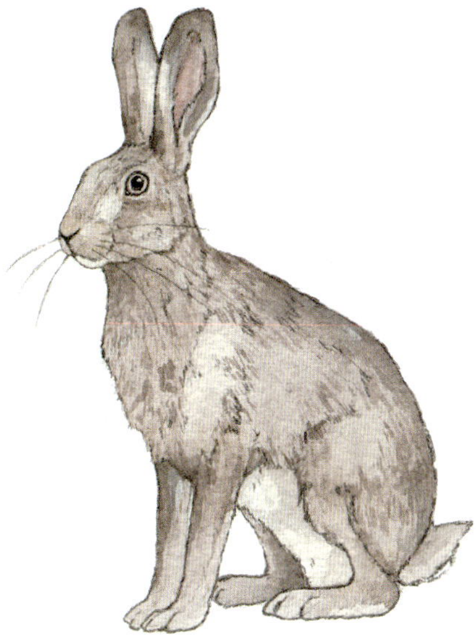

Step 7: Add Finishing Details

Using the clean size 3/0 brush, mix a dark-toned solution of ivory black and water, and load it onto the brush. We do not want this solution to be dry, so ensure that it is mixed with enough water so it is slick yet syrupy. Use the tip of the brush to fill in the pupil with this pure, thick black color, avoiding the dots that will be used for highlights. Use the tip of the brush to trace the lines of the whiskers.

Clean the bristles of the size 3/0 brush. Then, mix a mid-toned solution of sepia and water, load the bristles, and gently outline the fur on the entire body of the hare. Softly paint with the bristles to create fluffy lines, especially along the chest and lower belly fur. Paint the fur on the right cheek using this mid-toned brown solution.

Clean the bristles of the brush again. Finally, squeeze a small amount of acrylic white onto your palette, and using the same size 3/0 brush, paint in the two tiny dots on the eye for a subtle, luminous highlight. Paint a small amount of white on the upper left paw, along the left-hand side of the center of the right ear, and on the lower fur on the tail. The hare is now complete. Well done!

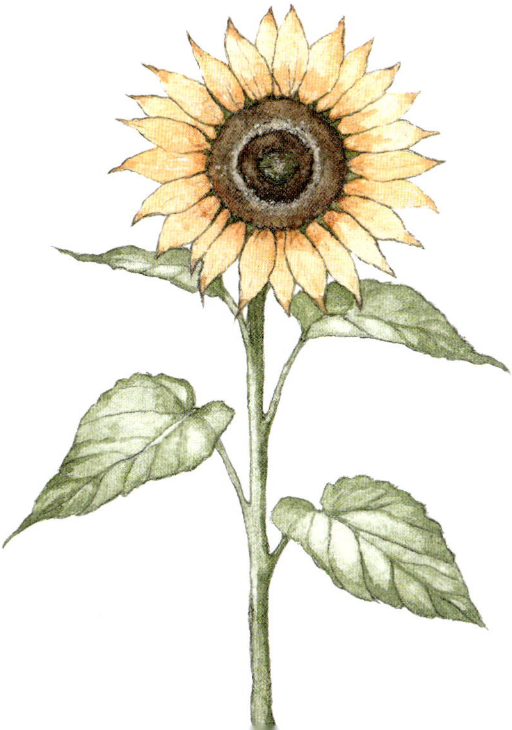

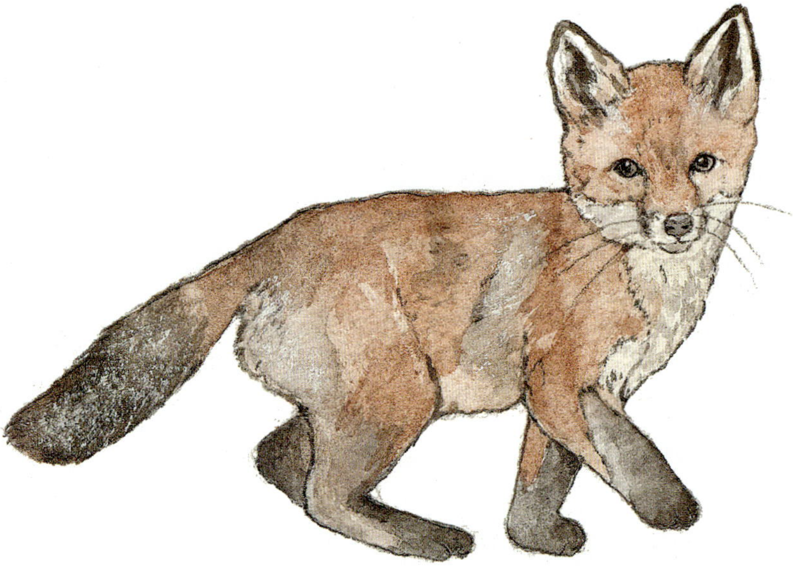

Fox Cub

To get a rare sighting of a fox cub in the garden is a reassuring sign that wild animals can adapt and coexist with us humans. Even if the sight of their fiery red faces is fleeting, it is hard not to feel deep affection for them as they are just so adorable! The focus of this tutorial will be on experimenting and building the skill of the dry brushing technique, a wonderful way to suggest the bushy texture found on the tail and body of a fox cub.

Materials Needed

1 sheet of cold-press 140-pound (300-gsm) aquarelle/watercolor paper

HB pencil

A piece of paper towel

Brushes

- Size 4
- Size 1
- Size 3/0
- Size 2/0 Isabey

Watercolor paints

- Burnt sienna
- Chinese white
- Raw umber
- Lamp black
- Sepia
- Ivory black
- Burnt umber

Acrylic white

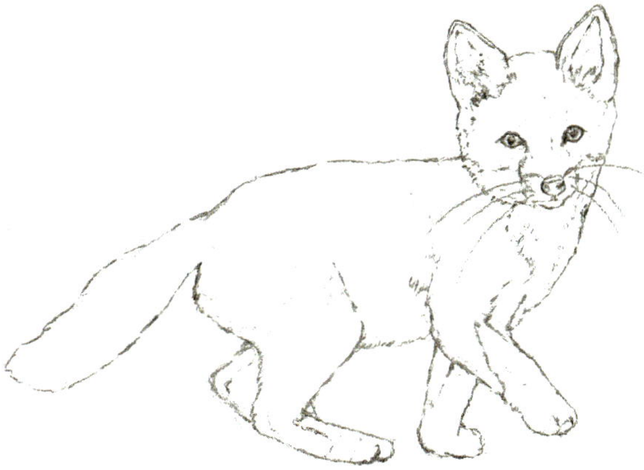

Step 1: Draw the Outline

Starting on a sheet of cold-press watercolor paper, draw the fox cub's outline with a sharp HB pencil using the template provided on page 183.

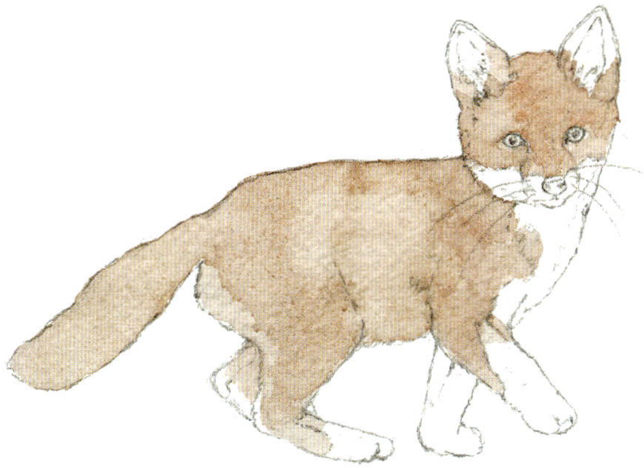

Step 2: Paint the Base Layer of Orange Fur

To prepare the base layer of color that will fill the head and fur on the cub's body, use a size 4 brush to mix together a mid-toned solution of burnt sienna and water. Load the paint onto the bristles of the brush and glaze the upper head, body, lower to middle sections of the outer ears, upper legs, and tail with a wash of this warm, rusty mixture. Allow the paint to fully dry and clean the brush.

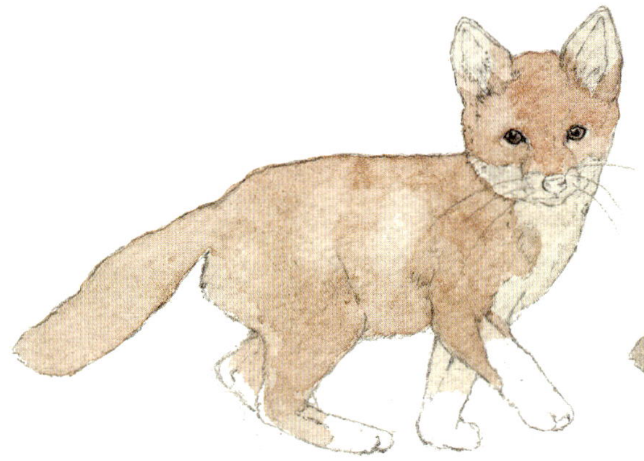

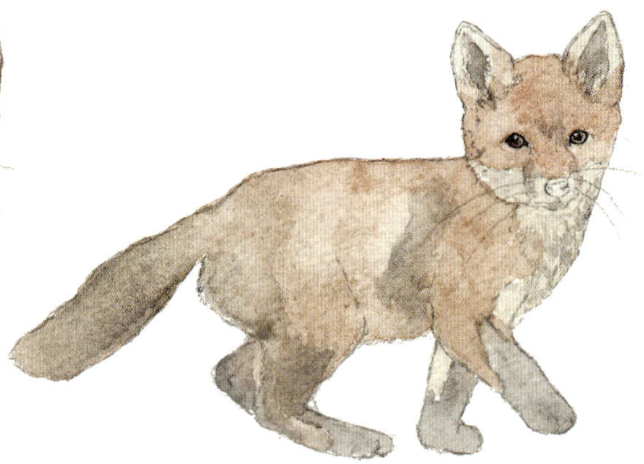

Step 3: Paint the Rest of the Base Layer

Using a size 1 brush, mix a mid-toned solution of Chinese white with a swirl of raw umber to create a warm, creamy mixture. Load this color onto the bristles and paint a glaze on the fur on the cheeks, around the nose and chin, front chest, and top of the inner front paw. Glaze a thin layer of cream on the upper sections of the ears. Allow this paint to dry and clean the brush.

Switch to a size 3/0 brush and mix a lightly saturated solution of raw umber and water. Fill in the irises of both eyes. Allow the paint to dry and clean the brush.

Finally, swirl the clean size 3/0 brush into lamp black until the brush is loaded with color. Carefully use the tip to outline the eyes, and fill in the pupils with the dark, inky black, leaving a tiny dot in the center unpainted; it will be filled in later with acrylic white for a highlight.

Step 4: Create Shadows and Depth

To create the color that will be the base layer of darker fur that is on the fox cub, use a size 1 brush to mix a light-toned solution of sepia with a dab of ivory black. We want this color to be a pale, earthy gray color. Load this color onto the bristles and fill in the inner sections of the ear with a thin glaze of watery gray, then the lower edges of the mouth, lower sections of each of the paws, and the entire tail. Allow this paint layer to dry.

Next, we want to create shadow and depth, but with a fur-like texture. Using the same size 1 brush and the watery gray mixture, paint short, loose brushstrokes that follow the natural fur growth pattern of the fox cub on the right-hand side of the torso, moving down and across where the fur meets the front paws. Paint short, sparse brushstrokes down the front of the chest and along the curve of the back leg and the very back of the body on the left-hand side

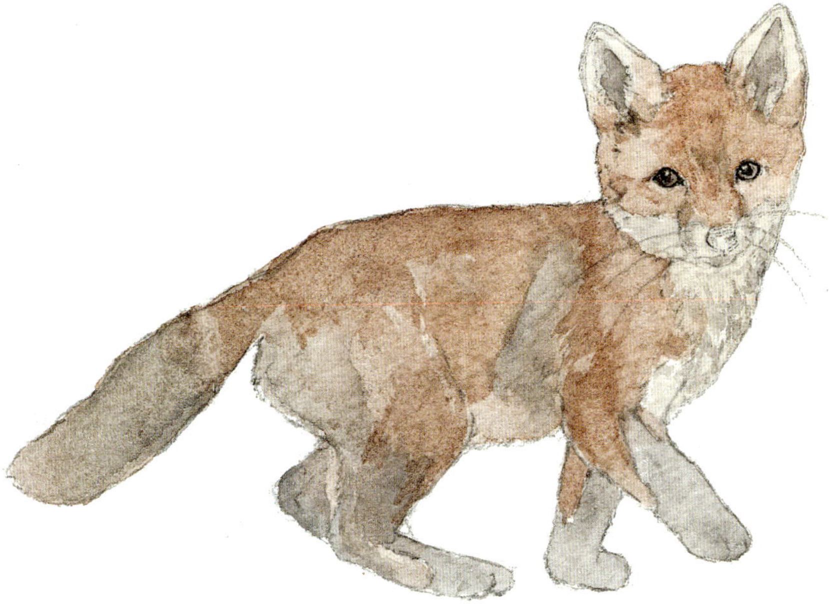

where the fur meets the beginning of the tail. The fur is denser and more compact at the lower sections of the back legs, so keep the brushstrokes tight here rather than loose. Paint a few small sparse brushstrokes between the eyes. Clean the brush.

Step 5: Add Copper Reds

To prepare the color that will be used for the shadows on the upper body fur of the fox cub, use a clean size 4 brush to mix a lightly saturated solution of burnt sienna with a dab of burnt umber. This color will be a warm, deep rust color.

Glaze a wash of this hue over the entire curve of the spine, extending into the left-hand side of the belly, the upper section of the tail, and the orange fur on the upper contours on the right-hand side of the back leg. Add a layer of this color to the very top of the front legs, extending downward to meet the gray sections of the lower paws.

For the face, use the same brush and rusty copper color to paint short, sparse brushstrokes beginning at the forehead and flowing downward to the center of the head and to the bridge of the nose. Use the tip of the brush to paint loose brushstrokes at the edges of the cheeks.

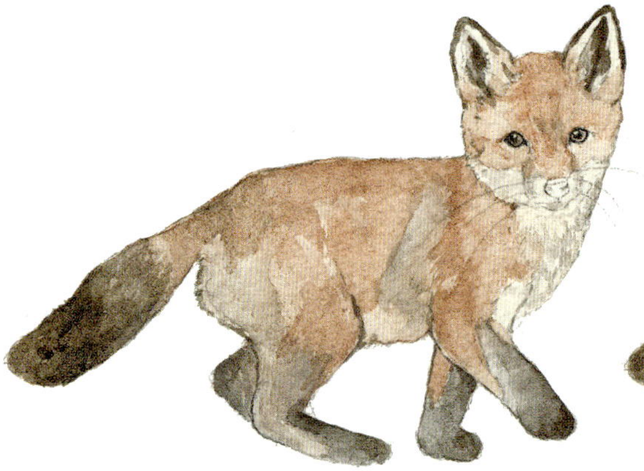

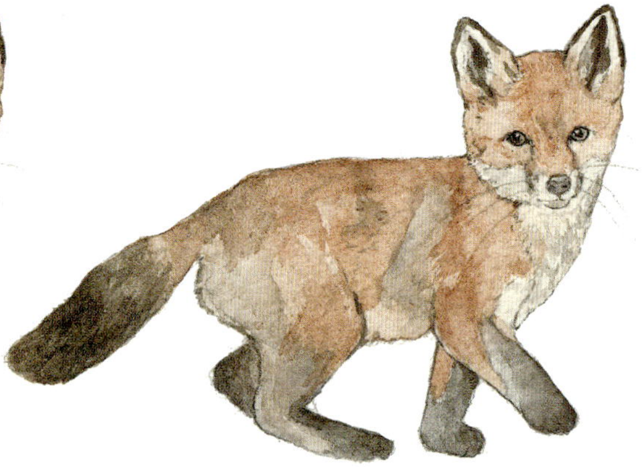

Step 6: Create Darker Layers of Fur

Using a clean size 1 brush, mix a mid-toned solution of sepia with ivory black. We want this color to be a deep, earthy brown that has a very rich chocolate hue. Load the bristles with this mixture and trace a thin layer of earthy brown on the inner outlines of the ears. Glaze the inner sections of the ears and entire tail, stopping just at the orange fur transition where it joins to meet the body. Glaze a thin layer of earthy brown along the lower sections of the four paws.

While these layers are drying, swirl the brush back into this earthy brown and drop the pigment at the very tip of each of the paws and at the very tip of the tail. As this extra layer is drying, gently soften any harsh edges between the layer underneath by gently pushing the paint upward to blend seamlessly into the first layer of paint underneath it, creating a seamless transition of shades. Allow these paint layers to dry fully.

Step 7: Add Subtle Details

Using a clean size 3/0 brush, mix a simple light-toned solution of ivory black and water to create a gray dilute. Load this color onto the bristles and fill in the entire nose of the fox cub. Trace down both sides of the bridge of the nose, extending the black fur outward onto the edges of the mouth. Trace along the outlines of the outer ears, and follow the contours of the outlines of the orange fur on the face to create greater outline definition. Paint sparse, short brushstrokes of fur along the midsection of the fox cub's torso, focusing at the top toward the spine and flowing downward halfway. Trace the outline of the body, head, ears, legs, and fur along the chest.

Using the same brush and light-toned mixture, swirl a small amount of ivory black onto the bristles and mix this into the solution, making it slightly thicker and a darker gray. Load this color onto the bristles and paint long, soft lines on the tail of the fox cub to portray the bushy fur. Keep the brushstrokes sparse and flowing to create a sense of texture. Clean the brush.

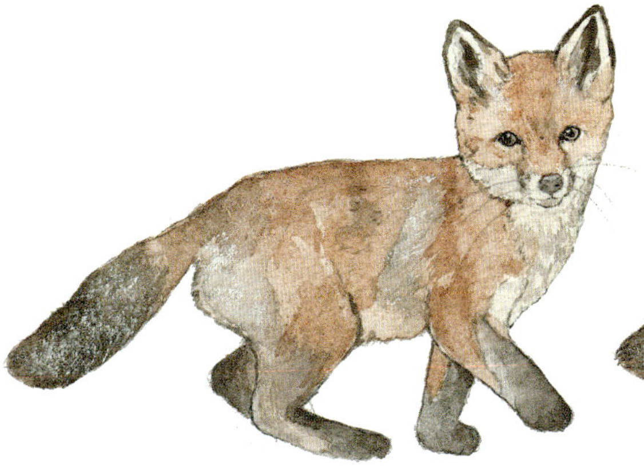

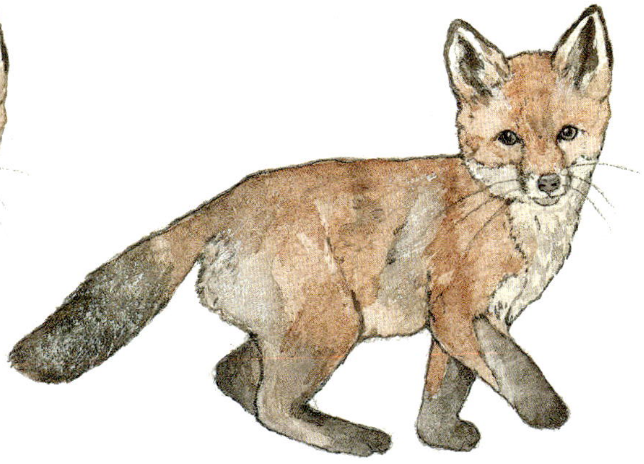

Step 8: Paint Bushy Fur

For the bushy coarse hair on the fox cub, squeeze a small blob of acrylic white onto your palette. Then, take a dry Isabey size 2/0 brush and swirl the bristles on a piece of dry paper towel. This will separate the bristles to splay outward. Dip the tip of the dry brush into the acrylic white and very lightly brush the tips of the bristles along the shape of the tail. As the solution is going to be quite dry, you will need to dip and brush repeatedly to build up texture and color on the paper, but this will give a very dry and coarse "bushy" effect.

Repeat this to build a layer along the upper contours of the back leg on the left-hand side and on the right-hand side of the torso where it meets the upper front legs. Paint a thin layer of bushy fur on the upper left and right side of the head where the fur joins to meet the lower ears.

Clean the brush with water, and switch to a clean size 3/0 brush. Dip the tip into the acrylic white and paint a small dot on the center of each eye to create a luminous highlight. Clean the brush.

Step 9: Add Finishing Touches

Using a clean size 3/0 brush, mix a mid-toned solution of sepia and water. Load the bristles with this warm, earthy brown and carefully trace the outline of each whisker. Use the tip of the brush to paint short, quick, sparse brushstrokes traveling downward along the curves of the cream fur on the front chest and along the contours of the upper hind leg and tuft of fur at the very back left-hand side where it meets the beginning of the tail.

Fill in tiny brushstrokes of fur along the bending joints of the legs and front paws. Use the same brush and dark brown color to outline the inner cheeks and bottom of the ear, again using short, quick brushstrokes to create a furry texture. The fox cub is now complete. You did a great job!

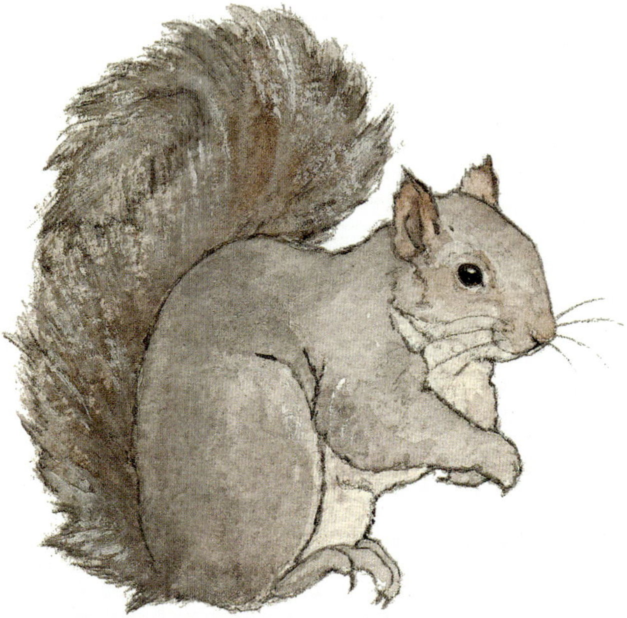

Gray Squirrel

Agile, cunning, and skilled climbers, gray squirrels are frequent visitors to gardens with bird tables and feeders. It can be a joy to watch them be so sprightly as they forage for nuts, seeds, buds, and flowers of the trees and plants growing in the backyard. Some people may see them as pests, but they play a very vital role in seed dispersal in quite a comical way! They are known to carry their food and bury it in several locations, but they sometimes forget exactly where. This helps these buried seeds and nuts sprout and grow the following spring. For painting, squirrels make a great subject when it comes to learning how to build up coarse fur texture. Their bushy tails give a wonderful opportunity to practice some dry-brush painting techniques.

Materials Needed

1 sheet of cold-press 140-pound (300-gsm) aquarelle/watercolor paper

HB pencil

A piece of paper towel

Brushes

- Size 4
- Size 3/0
- Size 1
- Size 2/0 Isabey

Watercolor paints

- Chinese white
- Raw umber
- Ivory black
- Sepia
- Burnt sienna
- Burnt umber
- Vandyke brown

Acrylic white

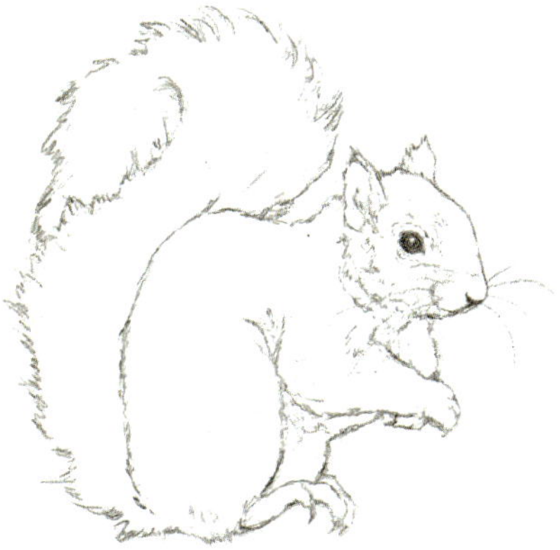

Step 1: Draw the Outline

Starting on a sheet of cold-press watercolor paper, draw the gray squirrel's outline with a sharp HB pencil using the template provided on page 183. Do not worry about the fine bushy details of the tail, as this will be painted on later. Fill in the eye, but make sure to leave a dot inside uncolored.

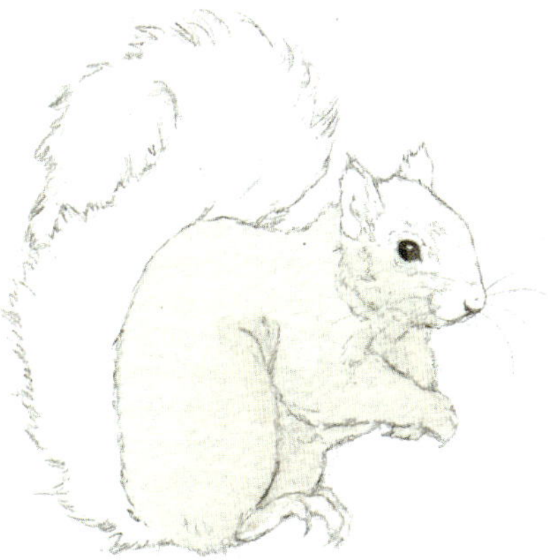

Step 2: Paint the Base Layer

Using a size 4 brush, mix a mid-toned solution of Chinese white with a small dab of raw umber to create a warm cream color mixture. Load this color onto the bristles and glaze a layer of cream onto the entire body, arms, paws, and lower cheek, extending the paint to where the fur meets the eye on the face. Allow this paint layer to dry and clean the bristles of the brush. Use a size 3/0 brush to mix a dark-toned solution of ivory black and water, and fill in the eye, leaving the highlight unpainted. Clean the brush.

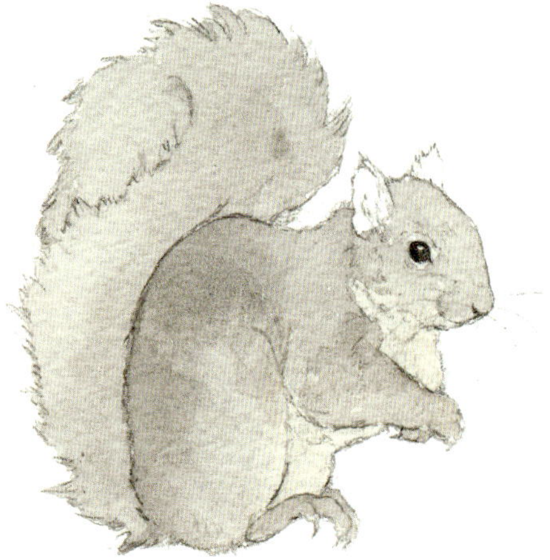

Step 3: Add Gray Fur

To create the base gray color for the majority of the fur on the gray squirrel's body, use a clean size 4 brush to mix a light-toned solution of ivory black with a tiny touch of sepia to create a warm gray dilute. Load this color onto the bristles and paint a layer of this solution onto the tail, face, neck, arms, body, and paws of the squirrel. Leave the chest fur, lower belly, and inner sections of the arms and paws cream, not filled in by gray.

While the first warm gray layer is still damp, swirl the brush back into this solution and glaze the curve of the spine, gently pushing the paint along the body to the right, and glazing the left arm and upper and lower paws. Gently drop some warm gray solution at the very base of the tail. Allow these layers of paint to dry and clean the brush.

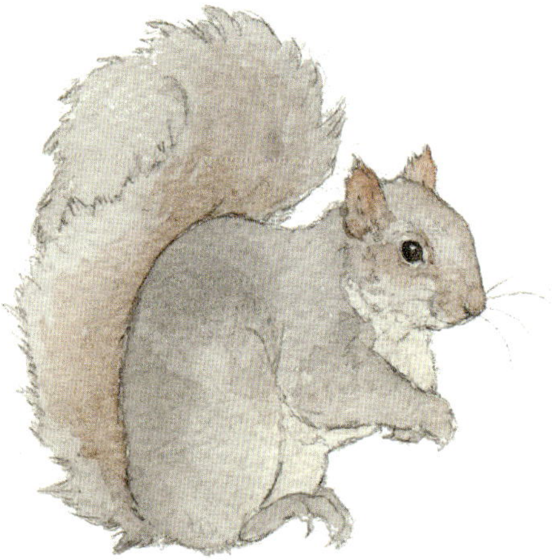

Step 4: Create Pops of Color

For the rusty copper fur that appears as little pops of color along the tail and body of the gray squirrel, use a size 1 brush to mix a light-toned wash of burnt sienna with a swirl of burnt umber. We want this color to be copper and rusty, belonging to the same family of burnt-looking tones. Load the bristles and gently glaze the ears and around the eye, flowing softly to the cheeks and nose, and very gently tracing the curve at the top of the head.

While this layer is still damp, swirl the bristles back into this copper solution and drop some color into the tips of the ears. As this layer is drying, it will disperse naturally down the ear, creating a natural gradient where the saturation is slightly more concentrated at the tip and gradually blends into the lighter copper layer below it.

Clean the bristles of the brush and swap to a clean size 4 brush. Swirl the bristles into the light-toned solution and paint a light wash of copper along the right-hand side of the tail where it meets the body, from the base flowing upward and gradually dispersing into sparse, flicking brushstrokes toward the top of the tail where it is bushier. Allow these layers to dry and clean the brush.

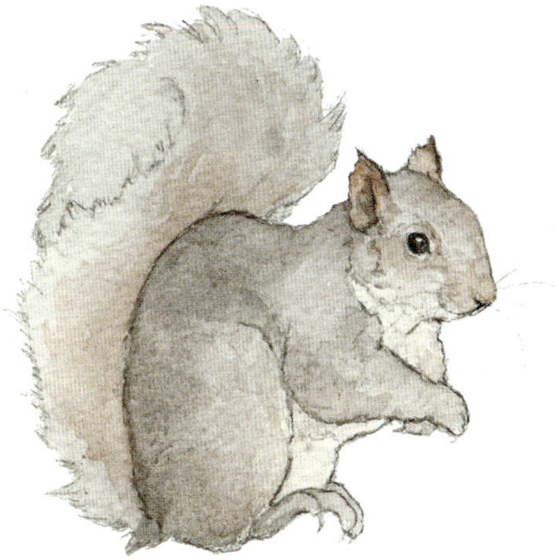

Step 5: Add Darker Tones

Using a clean size 4 brush, mix a mid-toned solution of sepia with a tiny dab of ivory black and water. Load the bristles with this color and glaze a thin wash of deep, earthy brown on the outlines and inner sections of the ears, along the curve of the top of the forehead, down the back of the head, and along the contour of the spine, filling in where the arm and leg are bent and meet at the belly, and flowing down the left-hand side of the body to the foot and along the lower back, running into the fur at the bottom of the body where it meets the tail and into the heel. Paint a thin layer of warm brown on the outer edges of each of the arms. Allow these layers to dry and clean the brush.

Switch to a clean size 3/0 brush and swirl it into the mid-toned earthy brown. Use the tip of the brush to carefully outline the body, the fur on the outline of the arms, and the ears and face. Hold the brush at the ferrule to have the most control over the lines. The fur should be soft and fluffy on the face and ears, so rather than keeping the lines flowing, make them very short, quick strokes to create texture. Clean the brush.

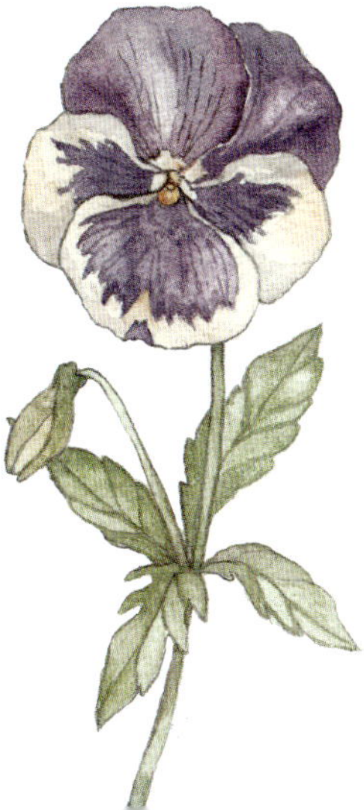

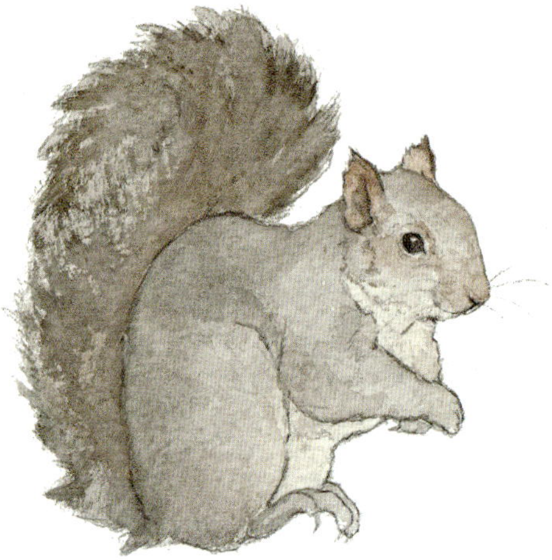

Step 6: Paint the Base Layer for the Tail

Use a clean size 4 brush to mix a dark-toned solution of sepia with a dab of ivory black. We want this to be a deeper and thicker solution in comparison to the previous solutions we mixed. Take a dry Isabey size 2/0 brush, and swirl the bristles on a piece of dry paper towel. This will separate the bristles outward. Dip the tip of the dry brush into the brown solution, and very lightly brush the tips of the bristles along the shape of the tail. As the solution is going to be quite dry, you will need to dip and brush repeatedly to build up texture and color on the paper, but this will give a very dry and coarse "bushy" effect.

Build up layers of dry color at the tips of the fur around the edges, and the fur that is dense and compact toward the base of the tail where it meets the body. Clean and dry the bristles of both brushes.

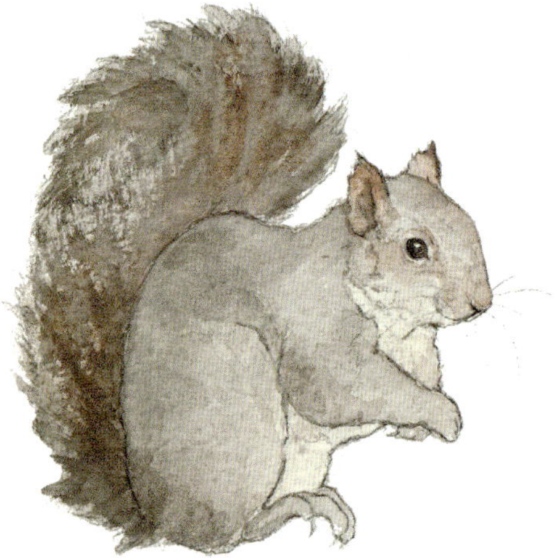

Step 7: Add Dimension

Using a clean size 4 brush, mix a concentrated swirl of Vandyke brown and a hint of burnt sienna into the dark-toned brown that we mixed in step 6. This will give the solution a warmer, more autumnal and copper burnt hue. Using the same dry brushing method with a clean and dry Isabey size 2/0 brush, dip the tip of the dry brush into the warm, rusty brown solution and very lightly brush the tips of the bristles along the dense, compact fur along the base of the tail where it meets the body.

Paint some bushy fur along the right-hand side of the tail at the top where it is beginning to curl to the left. Paint some bushy copper highlights on the tips of the bushy fur around the edges of the tail. Clean the brush.

Switch to a clean size 1 brush and mix a mid-toned solution of ivory black with a hint of sepia to create a warm gray. Load this color onto the bristles and glaze the base of the squirrel's body, the very base of the tail, the curve of the spine, and the left-hand side of the arm where the elbow is bent. Allow these paint layers to dry, and repeat by adding another layer of warm gray to the base of the body and base of the tail where it meets the back, deepening the shadows on these areas.

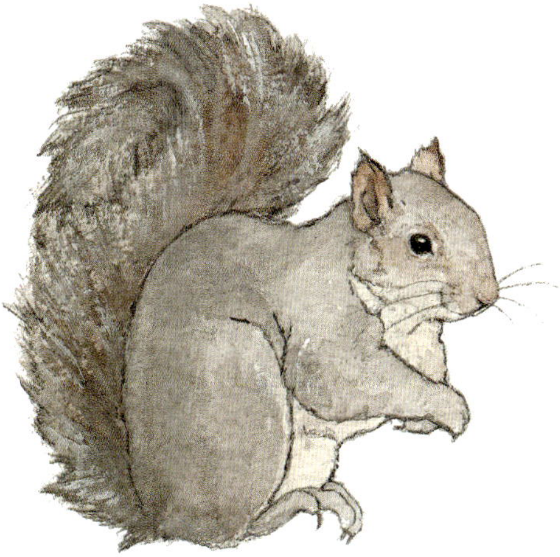

Step 8: Add Finishing Touches

To add definition on the bushy, coarse hair on the squirrel's tail, first squeeze a small blob of acrylic white onto your palette. Then, take a clean, dry Isabey size 2/0 brush and swirl the bristles on a piece of dry paper towel. This will separate the bristles outward. Dip the tip of the dry brush into the acrylic white and very lightly brush the tips of the bristles along the shape of the tail, focusing on the hair at the edges. Swap to a clean size 3/0 brush and paint short, quick brushstrokes of fur along the bend of the elbow, curve of the knee, and very edge of the cheek. Add a tiny dot of white on the eye using the very tip of the brush. Clean the brush.

Next, using the clean size 3/0 brush, mix a mid-toned solution of sepia and water. Load the bristles with this warm, earthy brown and carefully trace the outline of each whisker.

Use the tip of the brush to paint in short, quick, sparse brushstrokes to outline a furry texture on the outline of the head, arms, belly, legs, and ears. The gray squirrel is now complete! You did a great job!

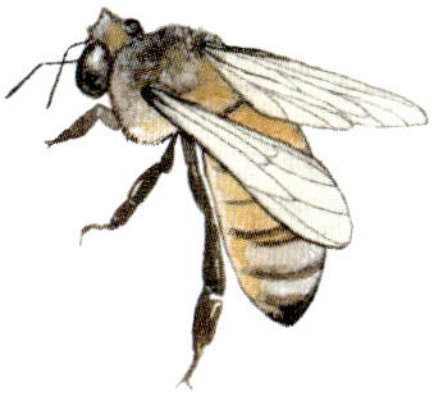

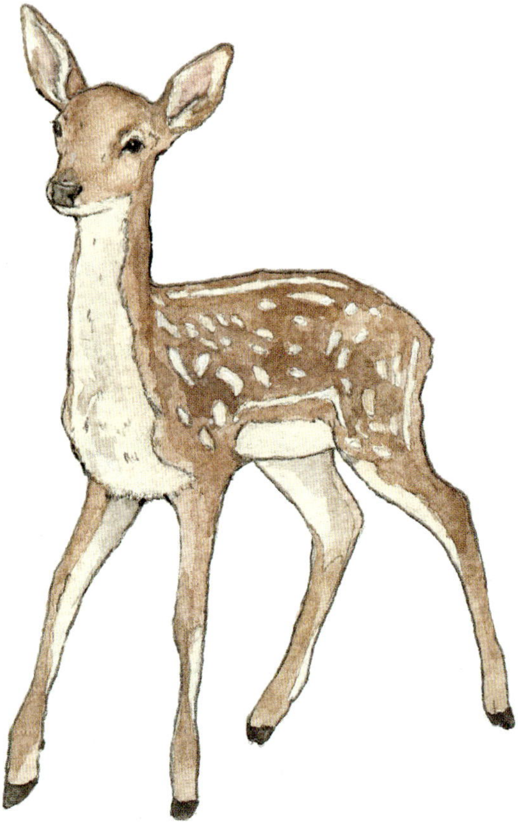

Fawn

A fawn carries an embodiment of softness paired with clumsy new life. You might glimpse one in the countryside, half hidden among tall grasses, its wide eyes watchful and obedient to its mother, making sure not to make a sound in its protective nest!

In this tutorial, you will learn how to capture the tender, soft texture of its fur and the delicate white markings that pattern its coat. We'll explore layering fine details with small brushes, navigating how to build realistic features with control and without being too heavy-handed.

Materials Needed

1 sheet of cold-press 140-pound (300-gsm) aquarelle/watercolor paper

HB pencil

Brushes

- Size 4
- Size 1
- Size 3/0

Watercolor paints

- Chinese white
- Raw umber
- Vandyke brown
- Sepia
- Ivory black
- Indian red

Acrylic white

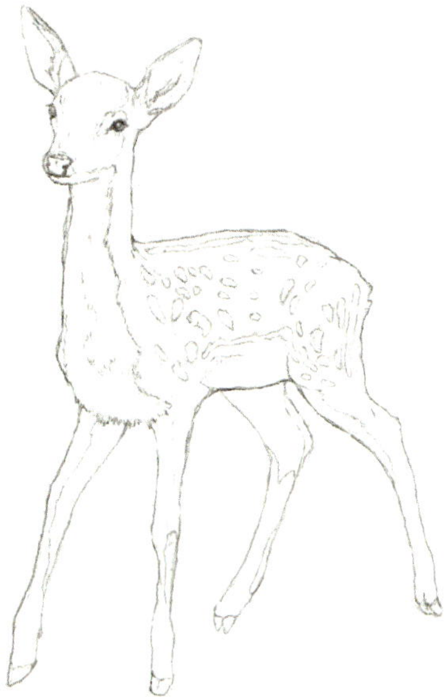

Step 1: Draw the Outline

Starting on a sheet of cold-press watercolor paper, draw the fawn's outline with a sharp HB pencil using the template provided on page 183. Take note that the hair varies in textures; it has a fluffy chest and a smoother body with long, elegant legs. Play with your use of the pencil, keeping confident, flowing lines for where its fur is smooth, and softer, more organic lines where the fur is more textured and fluffier.

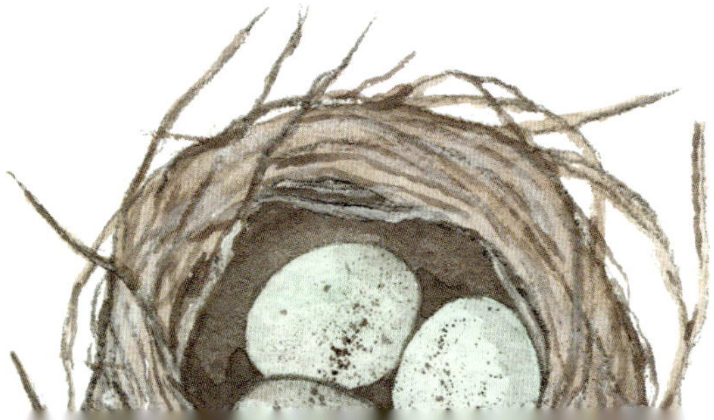

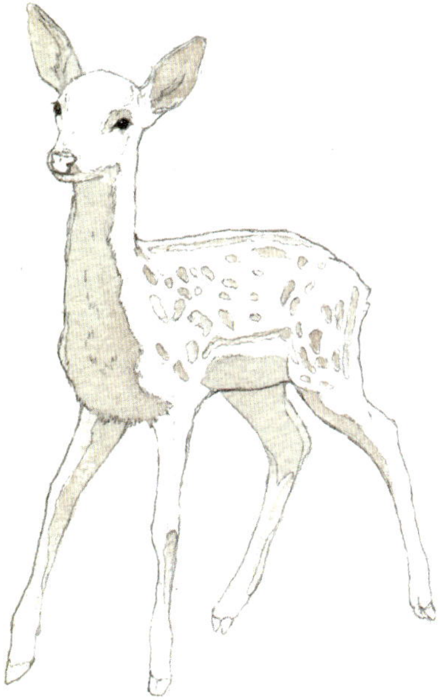

Step 2: Paint the Cream Base

For the cream color that will fill different sections on the coat of the fawn, use a size 4 brush to mix a mid-toned solution of Chinese white with a small dab of raw umber. We want this color to be a warm-toned cream rather than a cool-toned pure white. Load this solution onto the bristles and glaze the fur on the front chest, neck, and lower mouth of the fawn, flowing downward onto the right-hand inner section of the left and right legs, the inner sections of the back legs, the lower belly, the markings on the back and above the eyes, and finally the fur in the inner ears. Allow this paint to dry.

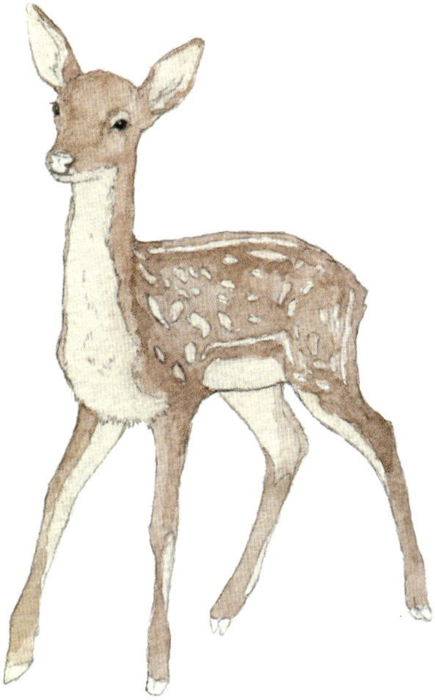

Step 3: Add Color

To create the color that will fill the main body of the fawn, use a size 1 brush to mix a mid-toned solution of raw umber with a dab of Vandyke brown. We want this color to be a warm, earthy caramel color that is not too yellow. Load this color onto the bristles and glaze the face of the fawn, extending downward onto the outer sections of the neck and legs and the torso. If you find that the sections of the torso that surround the markings on its back are very delicate to navigate, switch to the size 3/0 brush to fill in these areas.

While this first layer of warm caramel is drying, load the size 1 brush once again with another coating of this mid-toned solution and paint another thin coating on the forehead, extending up to the outer layers of the ear, around the left-hand side of the right eye, on the outer edges of the legs, and along the line of the spine. This extra layer on these sections will create subtle depth and dimension. Clean the brush.

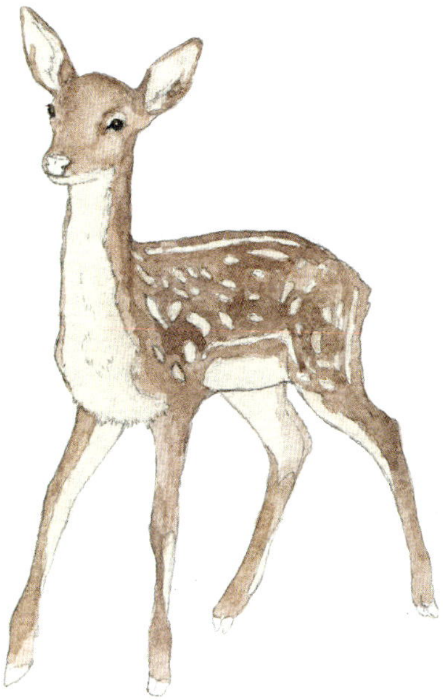

Step 4: Create Shadow

Using a clean size 1 brush, mix a small swirl of sepia into the mid-toned earthy caramel color you mixed in step 3. This will deepen and enrich the color, creating a slightly browner hue, which will act as the shadow on the coat of the fawn.

Load the bristles with this mixture and paint a thin coat on the top of the forehead, on the outer edges of the ears, around the left side of the right eye, extending downward along the outer edges of the neck, along the spine, and delicately around the markings on the torso. Gently direct the paint down along the tops of the legs, extending and softening the paint until it reaches the hooves, concentrating the dark brown paint at the outer edges and center of the shins. Clean the brush.

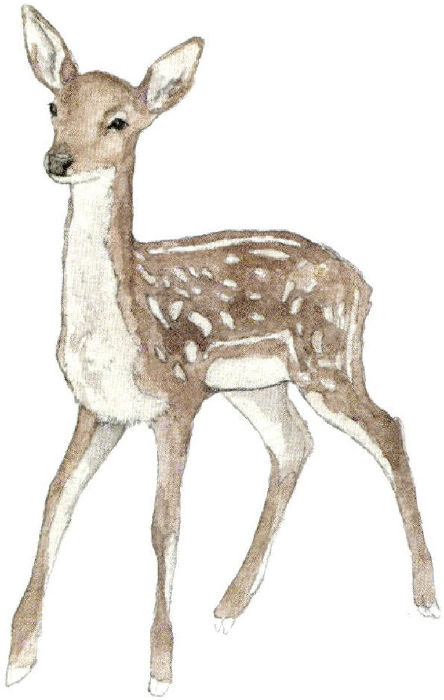

Step 5: Add Fine Details

To create more realistic depth and shadow, use a clean size 1 brush to mix a simple light-toned solution of ivory black and water to create a light, watery gray. Load the bristles and paint a thin layer of watery gray on the underside of the chin, extending down the center of the neck to the bottom of the chest where the layer tapers off into a few delicate, short brushstrokes, which will be the shadows on the lower chest of the fawn.

Glaze a thin layer of gray on the inner section of the fawn's left leg where it meets the body, and the inner right section of the back left leg. Use the tip of the bristles to fill in the nose and inner section of the ear, concentrating the gray at the bottom center of the inner ear and splaying up to the left- and right-hand sides of the cream sections.

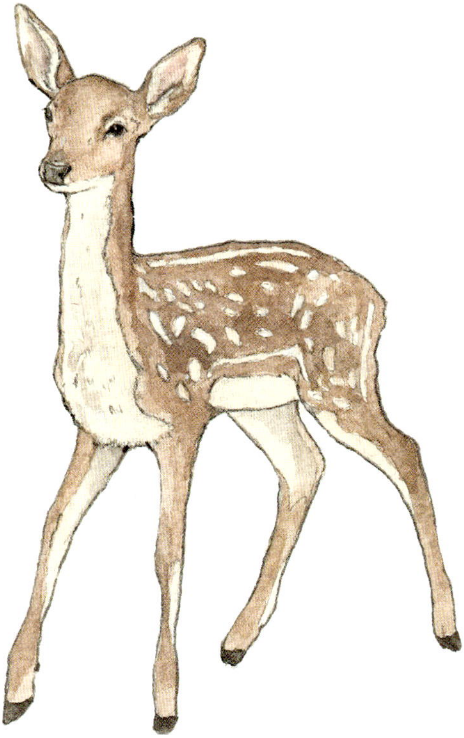

Step 6: Add Finishing Touches

Next, we will create the warm pink that will fill the fawn's inner ear. Using a clean size 3/0 brush, mix a light-toned solution of Indian red and water. Glaze this gently along the center of the cream section in the fawn's ear. Allow this layer to dry and clean the brush.

Using the clean size 3/0 brush, mix a mid-toned solution of ivory black and water. Load the bristles, and holding the brush at the ferrule to ensure the most control over the lines, outline the body, delicate markings, ears, nose, legs, and tiny tufts of fur along the chest. Use the same warm black mixture to fill in the nostrils and hooves. Fill in the eye and eyelashes, leaving two tiny dots left of center in the eye unpainted; they will be filled with acrylic white for a highlight. Clean the bristles.

Finally, squeeze a small amount of acrylic white onto your palette. Using the same size 3/0 brush, paint in the two tiny dots in the eye for a subtle, luminous highlight. Add a small dab of this acrylic white onto the left-hand side of each of the markings on the back of the fawn. The fawn is now complete. You did a great job!

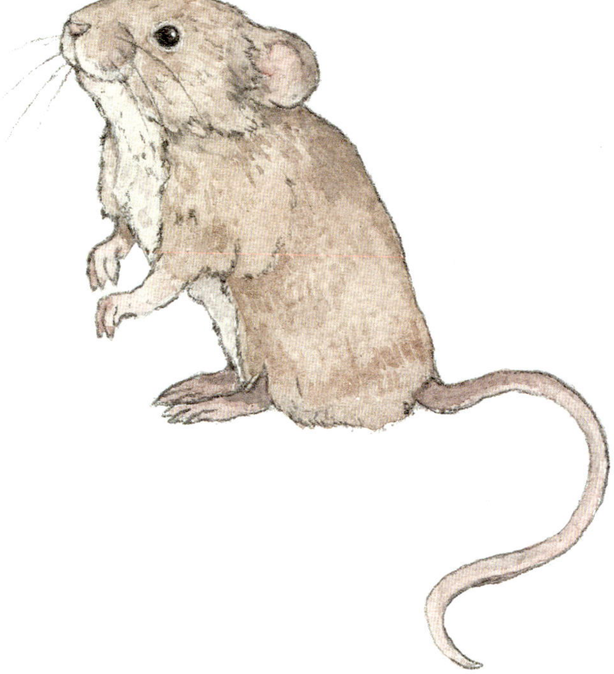

Hazel Dormouse

Hazel dormice can be difficult to spot in the garden; not only do they come out solely at night, but they spend a lot of their time hibernating and are known to snore! They sometimes have been found asleep in old bird nests, but they also weave their own nests, often in garden brambles or other shrubs, surrounded by a layer of green leaves. If you ever do spot one, sleeping or awake, you will certainly know them from their golden-brown fur and adorable large black eyes!

In this tutorial, you'll discover how to suggest softness and texture through careful layering and fine brushwork rather than individual hairs, which can be very effective when creating realism.

Materials Needed

1 sheet of cold-press 140-pound (300-gsm) aquarelle/watercolor paper

HB pencil

Brushes

- Size 1
- Size 4
- Size 3/0

Watercolor paints

- Chinese white
- Raw umber
- Vandyke brown
- Indian red
- Sepia
- Ivory black

Acrylic white

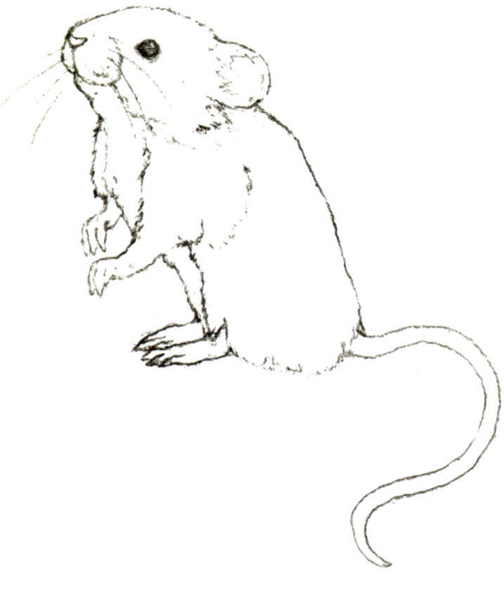

Step 1: Draw the Outline

Starting on a sheet of cold-press watercolor paper, draw the hazel dormouse's outline with a sharp HB pencil using the template provided on page 185. Fill in the eye (we will deepen this with black paint later), making sure to leave a dot on the upper right-hand side uncolored for a highlight. The mouse has delicate, fluffy fur at the front of its body with a smoother back and tail, so vary the textures of your lines to ensure greater realism.

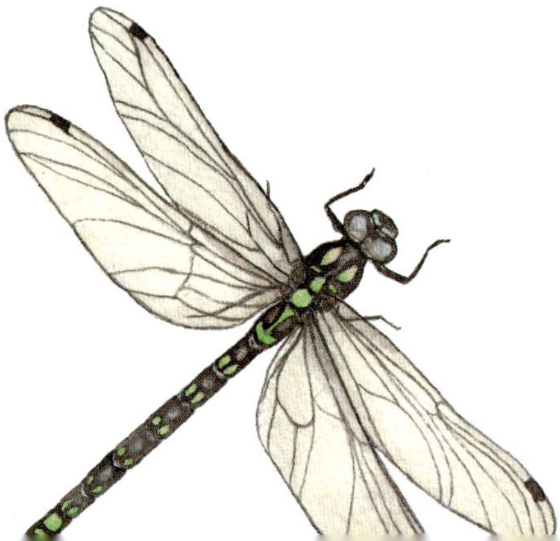

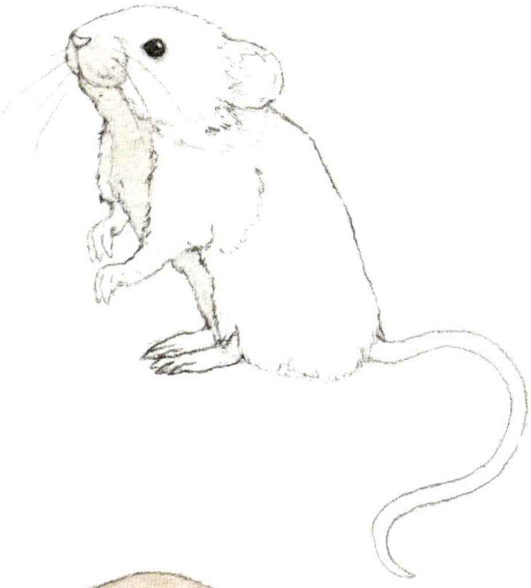

Step 2: Paint the Chest

Using a size 1 brush, mix a mid-toned solution of Chinese white with a small dab of raw umber to create a warm cream color. Load the bristles of the brush and gently glaze the cheeks, chin, and front belly of the mouse. Leave this layer to dry and clean the brush.

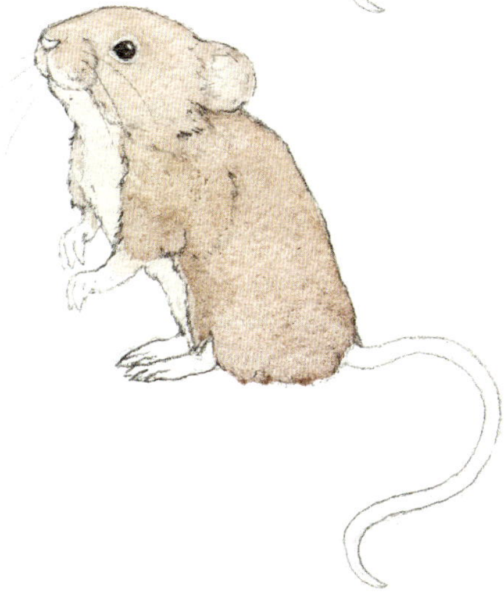

Step 3: Add Color to the Fur

Using a size 4 brush, mix a mid-toned solution of raw umber with a tiny swirl of Vandyke brown to create a warm, rusty caramel color that is not too saturated with sunny yellow tones. Begin at the center of the ear, then cover the entire face around the eye, three-quarters of the way down the cheeks, and along the arms and main body of the mouse. Allow this layer to dry.

Then, repeat this step and add another layer of warm caramel to the same areas, this time avoiding the center of the ear to leave a lighter tone underneath. While this second layer is drying, dip the brush back into Vandyke brown and swirl this into the caramel mid-toned mixture, deepening its shade to a light rust brown. Glaze this color along the bottom of the body of the mouse where it meets the tail. Gently push the paint upward along the body to the midsection, along where the fur meets the chest and the bottom of the right arm, making sure to soften the edges and allowing the deeper brown layer to blend seamlessly into the warm caramel underneath. Allow these layers to dry.

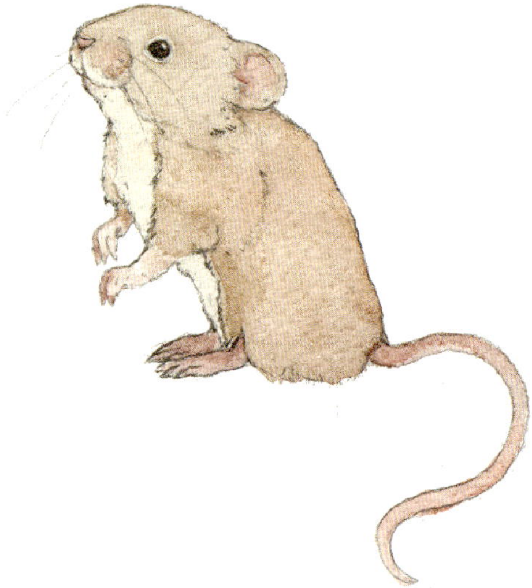

Step 4: Create Pops of Color

Using a clean size 1 brush, mix a light-toned solution of Indian red and water. We want this mixture to be a pale blush pink. Using the tip of the brush, glaze this color over the feet, tail, nose, three-quarters of the cheek, and inner ear. While the paint is still damp, add another layer of this blush pink to the section of the tail where it meets the fur of the lower body, the tip of the tail, the top sections of the feet, and the tips of the paws. Be sure to soften the edges of these shadow layers to allow them to blend seamlessly into the base layer of pale pink underneath.

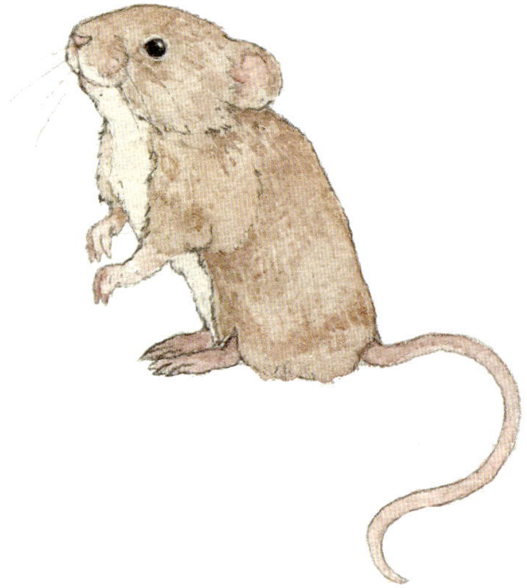

Step 5: Paint Fur

Now we'll paint the soft fur of a mouse through gentle layering and fine brushwork. The goal is not to paint every individual hair but to suggest the softness and direction of the fur with subtle strokes. With a size 3/0 brush, mix a simple light-toned solution of Vandyke brown and water. Use short, directional strokes to build up the fur. Follow the natural contours of the mouse's body; strokes on the back and sides should curve gently, while those on the face and belly should be straighter and more compact around the cheek and forehead.

Build up a layer of dense strokes around the bottom of the body where the fur meets the foot, with flowing, short strokes coming from the crease of the arm and where the head meets the neck. Allow the paint to dry and clean the brush.

Step 6: Add Definition and Shadow

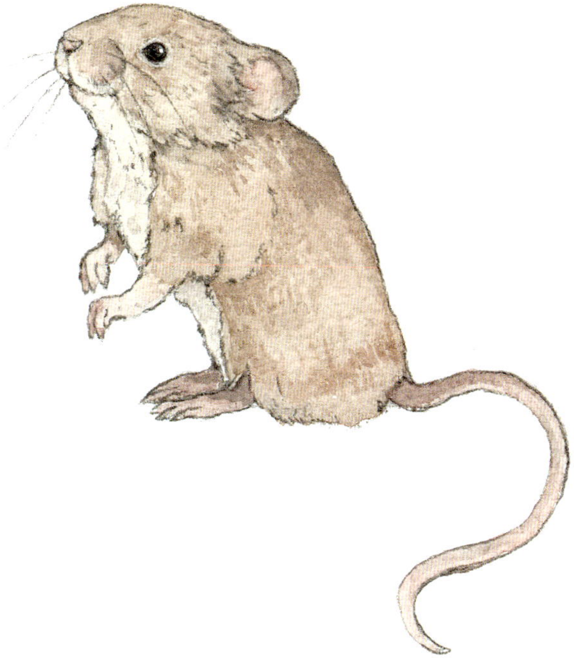

Next, we will add more texture and density to the patches of fur where there should be shadow and darker tones of color. Using a clean size 3/0 brush, mix a mid-toned solution of sepia and water, and load the paint onto the bristles. Paint a thin layer of short strokes following the growth pattern of the fur along the curve of the upper cheek, along the right-hand side of the face, on the underside of the lower face where the fur meets the body, down along the cream chest, underneath the right arm, and along the curve of the ear.

Add a small amount of water to the mid-toned solution to desaturate the color and create a more diluted mixture. Using the same brush, glaze a thin layer of this light brown along the curve of the spine, around the ear at the tops of the feet, and along the upper side of the tail, concentrating especially where it meets the body. Allow these paint layers to dry and dip the brush back into this light brown solution. Trace along the outline of the mouse, feet, and ear to create crisper definition. Clean the brush.

Using the clean size 3/0 brush, mix a dark-toned solution of ivory black and water, and load it onto the brush. Use the tip of the brush to fill in the pupil of the eye with this pure, thick black color, leaving the dot highlight unpainted. Use the tip of the brush to trace the lines of the whiskers. Clean the brush.

Finally, squeeze a small amount of acrylic white onto your palette, and using a clean size 3/0 brush, paint in a tiny dot on the upper right-hand side in the eye for a subtle, luminous highlight. Well done; the dormouse is now complete!

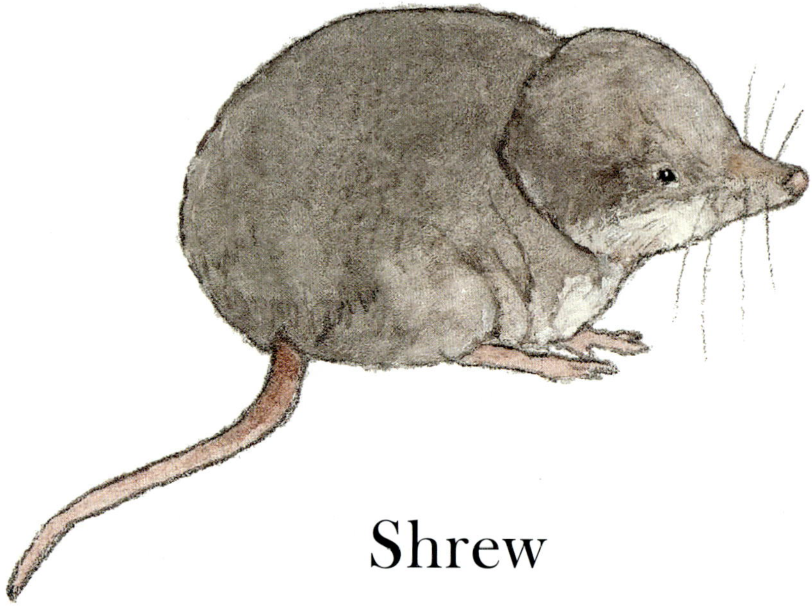

Shrew

There's something irresistibly charming about a shrew! Something about their instantly recognizable long snout and bright eyes seems to completely capture my heart. Growing up in the countryside, I once found one tucked into a head of cabbage that came from the garden. I can still remember its soft, trembling body in my hands before I set it free among the grass.

In this project, I wanted to capture both their curiosity and their delicacy. You'll learn how to use light washes and gentle shading to bring to life its rounded form, velvety fur, and tiny pink nose. The aim is to create softness and warmth rather than precision.

Materials Needed

1 sheet of cold-press 140-pound (300-gsm) aquarelle/watercolor paper

HB pencil

A piece of paper towel

Brushes

- Size 4
- Size 1
- Size 3/0

Watercolor paints

- Sepia
- Ivory black
- Burnt umber
- Indian red
- Chinese white

Acrylic white

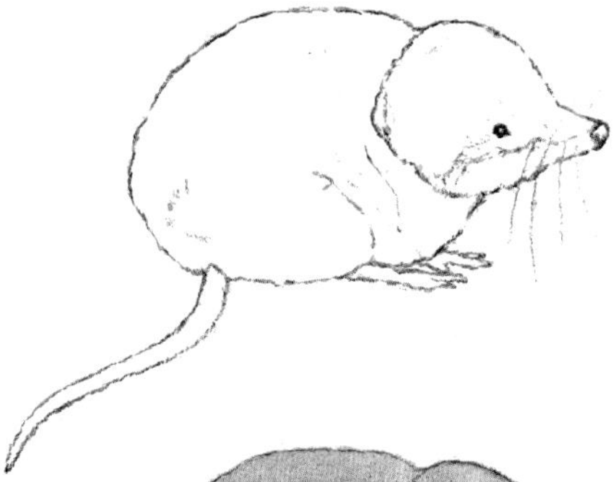

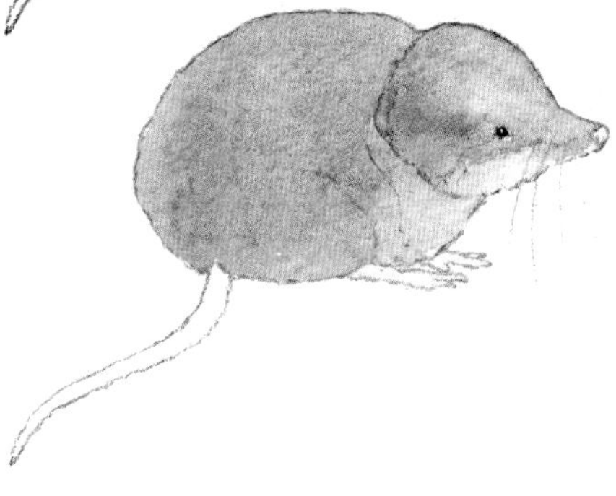

Step 1: Draw the Outline

Starting on a sheet of cold-press watercolor paper, draw the shrew's outline with a sharp HB pencil using the template provided on page 185. The shrew is naturally quite smooth haired yet soft in appearance, so try to keep your lines delicate.

Step 2: Paint the Base Layer

To create the color that we will use to paint the body of the shrew, use a size 4 brush to mix a light-toned solution of sepia with a small dab of ivory black. We want this color to be a light, watery, cool-toned brown that has a gray hue. Load this mixture onto the bristles and glaze the head, snout (be sure to avoid the very tip!), and body of the shrew, avoiding the tail and feet. When this mixture is almost dry, glaze another coat of this color that we mixed onto the body of the shrew and three-quarters of the head, avoiding the front chest and lower part of the cheeks. Allow this mixture to fully dry.

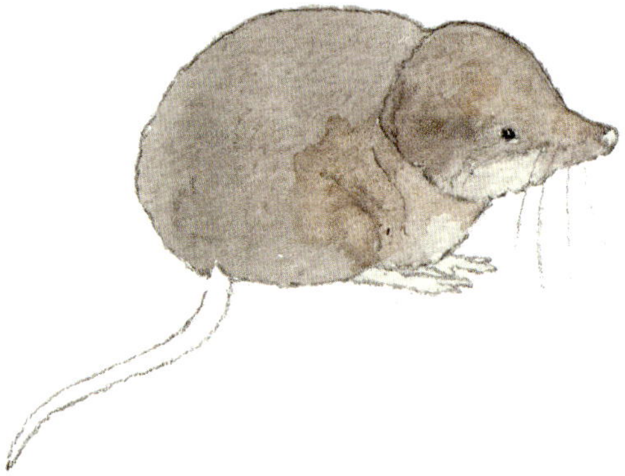 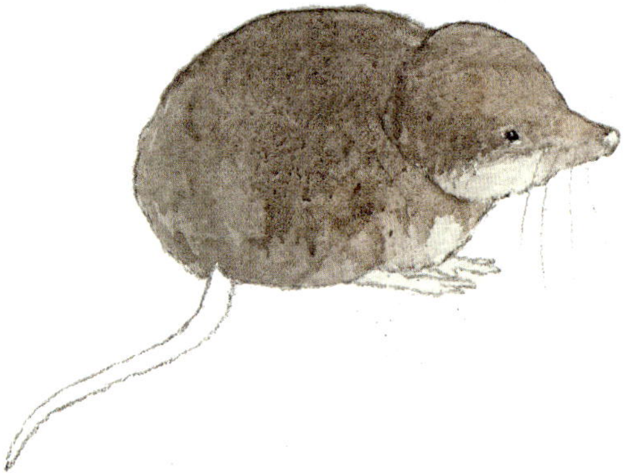

Step 3: Add Color

Using a size 1 brush, mix a light-toned solution of burnt umber with a small dab of sepia to create a watery warm rust mixture. Apply a gentle coating of this along the snout, along the eye and left-hand side of the head, following downward to the chest, and along the right-hand side of the back leg. Allow this layer to dry and clean the brush.

Step 4: Add Shadow and Dimension

To create shadows on the fur of the shrew, use a clean size 1 brush to mix a mid-toned solution of sepia with a tiny dab of ivory black. We want this color to be a dark brown without too much of a black hue, so only a tiny amount of black is needed. Gently dab a layer of this color along the left-hand side of the head, following along the curve of the spine and downward to the feet, and along the underside of the neck to midway down the chest, gently softening the edges of the paint layer until it blends into the paper underneath. Allow this layer to dry and clean the brush.

Step 5: Add Highlights

To add highlights to the shrew, swirl a clean size 1 brush in water and agitate the paint on the right-hand side of the face, flowing down toward the snout, and do the same on the paint on the curve of the back leg. Once the paint and pigment have been lifted onto the bristles of the brush, press a piece of paper towel firmly onto these dampened agitated areas and then lift to reveal a highlight underneath.

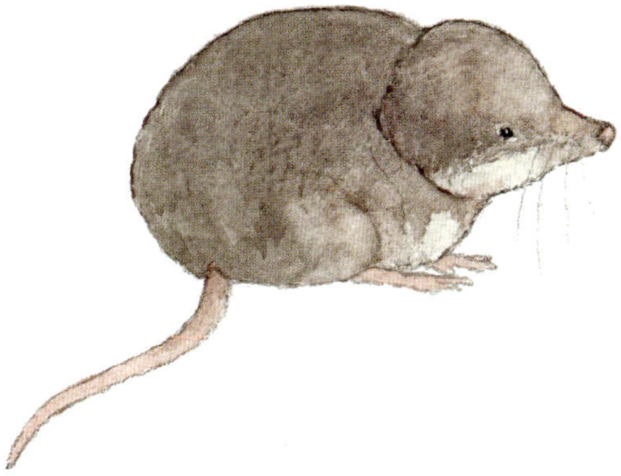 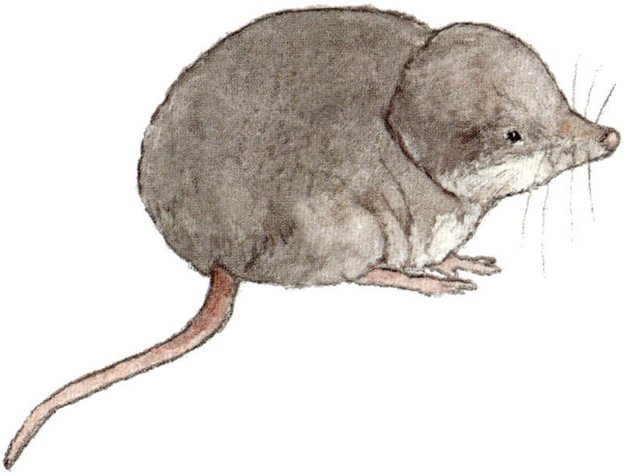

For the pink, which we will apply to the paws and tip of the snout, use a size 3/0 brush to mix a light-toned solution of Indian red with a tiny swirl of Chinese white to create a pale powdery pink. Gently glaze this pale pink along the tail, feet, and tip of the snout. Clean the brush, then mix a light-toned solution of sepia and water, and gently paint a thin layer of this at the top of the tail where it meets the body to create shadow, softening the edges of the paint by dragging the layer downward to blend any hard lines. Allow these layers to dry.

Step 6: Add Finishing Touches

For the finishing touches of the tail, using the same size 3/0 brush, apply another thin layer of the light-toned solution of sepia and water that we mixed at the end of step 5 to the top of the tail where it meets the body, deepening its shadow and again softening any harsh lines gently into the paper.

Return back to this light-toned solution of sepia but create it into a mid-toned solution by swirling in some more sepia until the tone deepens slightly and the consistency is less watery. Load the bristles of the size 3/0 brush, and holding it close to the ferrule, softly outline the entire body, feet, head, and whiskers of the shrew, making sure to also gently outline the creases of the body at the midsection. Add some definition to the smooth fur by creating short, loose lines flowing outwardly from the snout on the face and flowing down by the top of the tail where it meets the body.

Clean the bristles of the brush, then swirl the wet brush into ivory black. Carefully fill in the eye, omitting the dot for a highlight. Clean the bristles of the size 3/0 brush.

Finally, squeeze a pea-size amount of acrylic white onto your palette, and dip the clean size 3/0 brush into it. Paint a tiny dot in the center of the eye to create a luminous highlight. Use the same bristles and acrylic white to create tiny white hairs of fur along the left-hand side of the lower cheek, along the curve of the back leg, and along the front of the chest. The shrew is now complete. Good job!

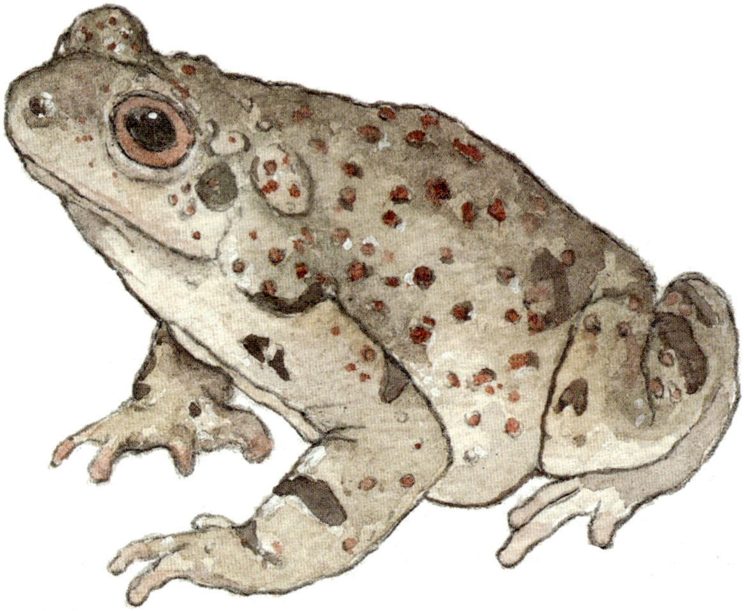

Toad

Toads are such exciting little creatures to spot in the garden, and they make patient, still muses for painting. They have a love for nocturnal hours, damp log piles, and deep leaf litter, feeding on worms, slugs, and insects found crawling through the garden soil. Their knobbly skin, soft, earthy colors, and spotted markings may seem like a daunting prospect when aiming for a realistic result in watercolor, but through gentle layering and subtle dots and movements, you will learn how to build that bumpy texture perfectly.

Materials Needed

1 sheet of cold-press 140-pound (300-gsm) aquarelle/watercolor paper

HB pencil

Brushes

- Size 4
- Size 1
- Size 3/0
- Size 0

Watercolor paints

- Raw umber
- Hooker's green light
- Raw sienna
- Sepia
- Vandyke brown
- Light red
- Ivory black
- Burnt sienna

Acrylic white

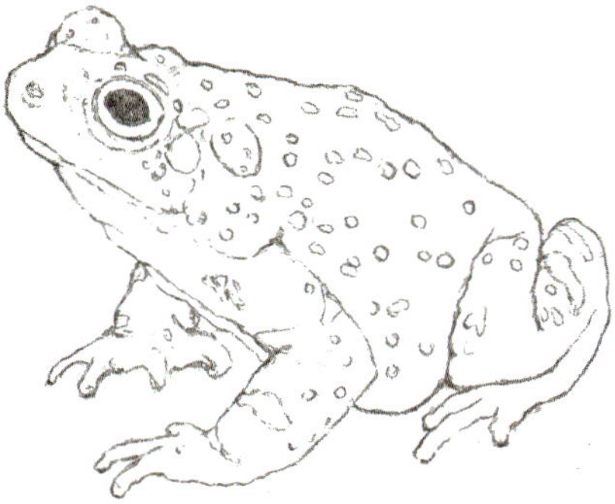

Step 1: Draw the Outline

Starting on a sheet of cold-press watercolor paper, draw the toad's outline with a sharp HB pencil using the template provided on page 185.

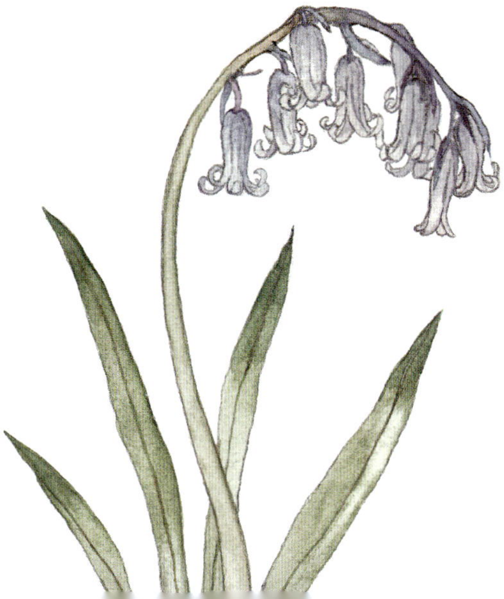

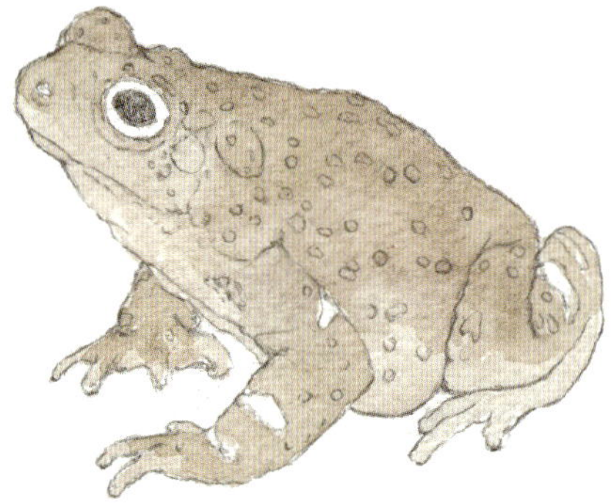

Step 2: Paint the Base Layer

Use a size 4 brush to mix a light-toned solution of raw umber with a small dab of Hooker's green light and a tiny dab of raw sienna. We want this color to be a watery sandy color with a slight green undertone that is very subtle.

Load this color onto the bristles and glaze the body and head of the toad, making sure not to fill the eye and some small oval-shaped markings on the upper and lower legs. While this layer is still drying, swirl the brush back into the warm sandy color and paint another layer of color along the upper face, following down along the curve of the back to the midsection of the belly and upper back and front legs. Allow these layers to dry.

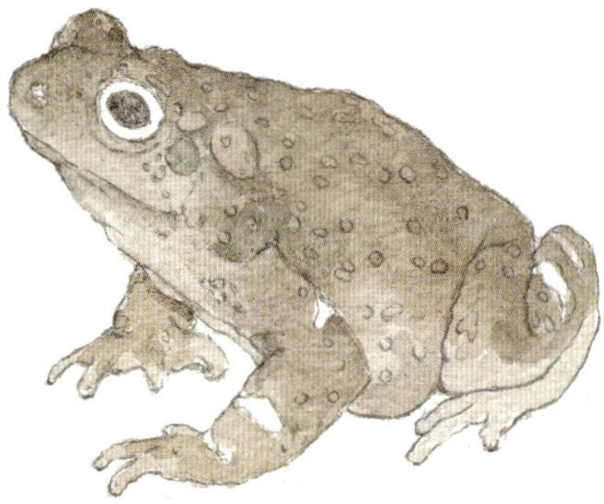

Step 3: Add Deeper Greens

Using the same size 4 brush and light-toned solution that we mixed in step 2, swirl in some more Hooker's green light and a tiny dab of sepia. We want this color to be a muddy, earthy green that has a slightly thicker texture.

Load this color onto the bristles and glaze a layer of green around the nose and upper face of the toad and along the upper and middle sections of the body, and a thin layer on the right-hand side of the back leg, flowing along the front legs, and stopping at the undersides of the feet.

While this layer is still drying, add another layer of deep muddy green on the upper face around the eyes and nose and along the curve of the spine, pulling the paint gently downward to soften the edges and letting it blend seamlessly into the previous layers beneath it. Add another layer of green on the spotted markings on the lower right-hand side of the eye and at the crease at the top of the arm where it meets the body.

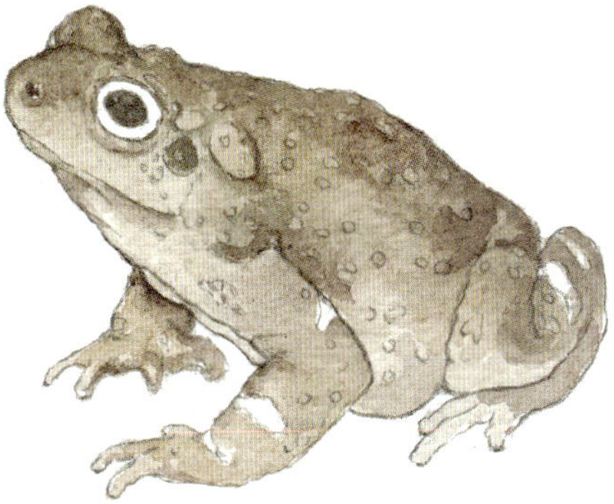

Step 4: Add Further Definition

Using a size 1 brush, mix a mid-toned solution of Vandyke brown with a small dab of sepia to create a warm, earthy brown. Load this color onto the bristles and glaze a thin layer of warm brown on the upper face, on the eyelids, and down along the curve of the spine, spreading the paint to cover more of the body once it reaches the back right-hand side toward the back leg.

Paint a layer of brown on the underside of the mouth, then down along the left-hand side of the neck and the crease of the right arm where it meets the body and upper stomach. Paint a layer along the inner outline of the left arm, running down along the right-hand side, and outlining the spread feet.

Paint a layer of brown along the left-hand side of the right arm, then finally along the right-hand side of the back right leg. Swap to a size 3/0 brush and fill in the nostril, and paint a layer on the marking on the lower right-hand side of the eye. Paint a thin layer of this warm brown into the center of the eye. Allow these layers to dry and clean the brushes.

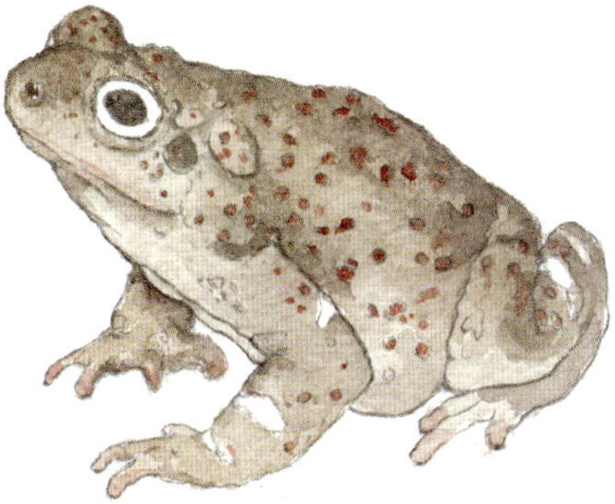

Step 5: Paint the Markings

Use a clean size 3/0 brush to mix a dark-toned solution of light red and water. We want this mixture to be highly pigmented and thick. Load the solution onto the bristles and fill in each of the dotted markings on the body, legs, and cheeks of the toad. Fill in some small dots on the eyelids and around the nose and mouth. Allow these layers to dry.

Next, add water to this dark red mixture to dilute it to a light-toned watery pale pink. Load this color onto the size 3/0 brush and paint a thin line of pink along the outline of the upper lip and the toes on each of the front and back feet. Allow these layers to dry and clean the brush.

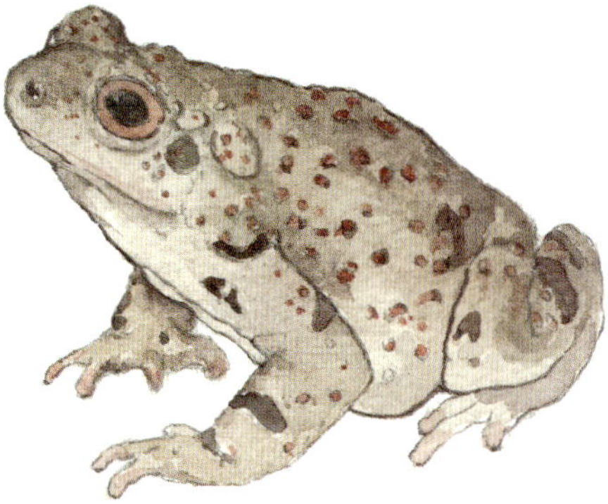

Step 6: Fill In the Eye and More Markings

Using a size 0 brush, mix a simple mid-toned solution of sepia and water, and load the bristles with this earthy brown color. Carefully fill in the rest of the larger markings on the right- and left-hand sides of the legs. Use the tip of the brush to then carefully outline the curves of the body and legs.

Clean the bristles, and then use the same brush to mix a mid-toned solution of ivory black and water. Load this color onto the bristles and carefully paint a thin layer of black on top of the top three brown markings on the front right leg. Paint a thin layer of black into the middle of the eye. Allow these layers to dry and clean the brush.

Next, swap to a clean size 3/0 brush and mix a mid-toned solution of burnt sienna and water. Fill in the outer section of the eye. Allow these layers to dry and clean the brush.

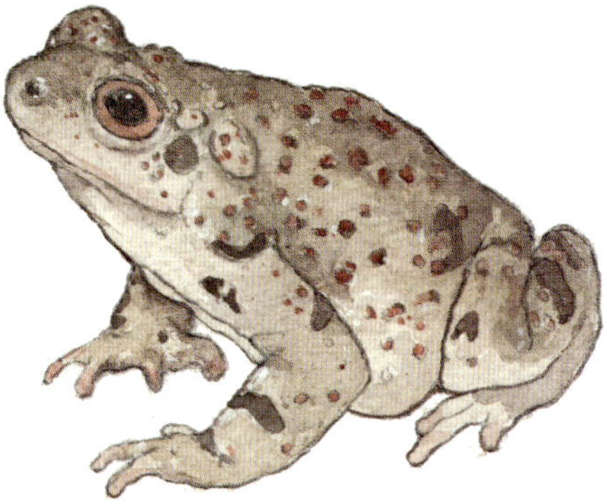

Step 7: Add Definition

Using a clean size 3/0 brush, mix a mid-toned simple solution of sepia and water to create a warm, earthy brown. Load this color onto the bristles and carefully outline the lines of the body, eye, face, and mouth, and add small outlines around the red-spotted markings on the body of the toad.

Clean the bristles and squeeze a pea-size amount of acrylic white paint onto the palette. Dip in the clean size 3/0 brush to get some acrylic paint onto the bristles, and dab a tiny white dot onto the upper center of the eye to create a subtle, luminous highlight. Dab a highlight around the right-hand side of the nostril, plus some small highlights on the upper eyelid and along the underside of the eye.

Paint some small, sparse dotted highlights at the top of the right arm where it meets the body and along the center and lower belly. Allow these layers to dry.

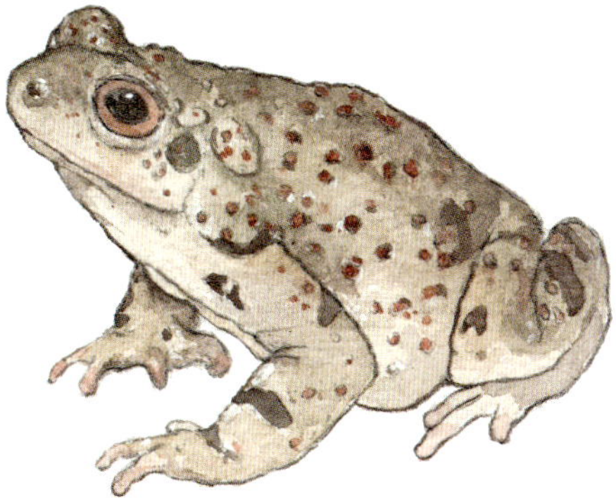

Step 8: Add Finishing Touches

Use a clean size 0 brush to mix a light-toned solution of burnt sienna and water to create a pale rusty orange that isn't too highly pigmented. Load this color onto the bristles and glaze a thin wash of color on the underside of the eye and flowing down to the upper lip, along the right-hand side of the upper right arm, and along the left-hand side of the back leg.

Next, mix a dark-toned solution of light red with a swirl of burnt sienna to create a deep rusty red, and dot each of the spotted markings along the back and body of the toad. The toad is now complete. Well done!

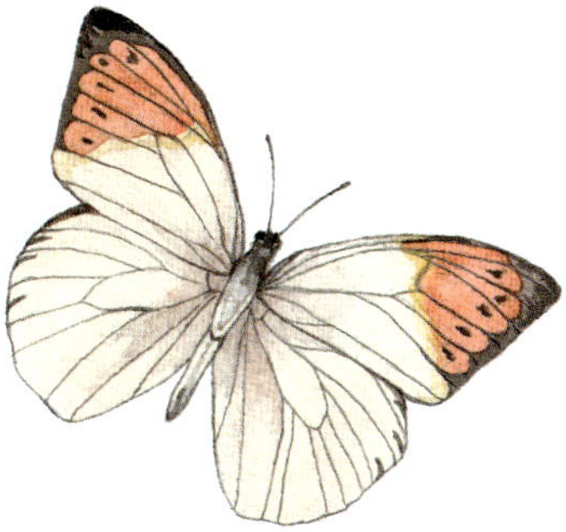

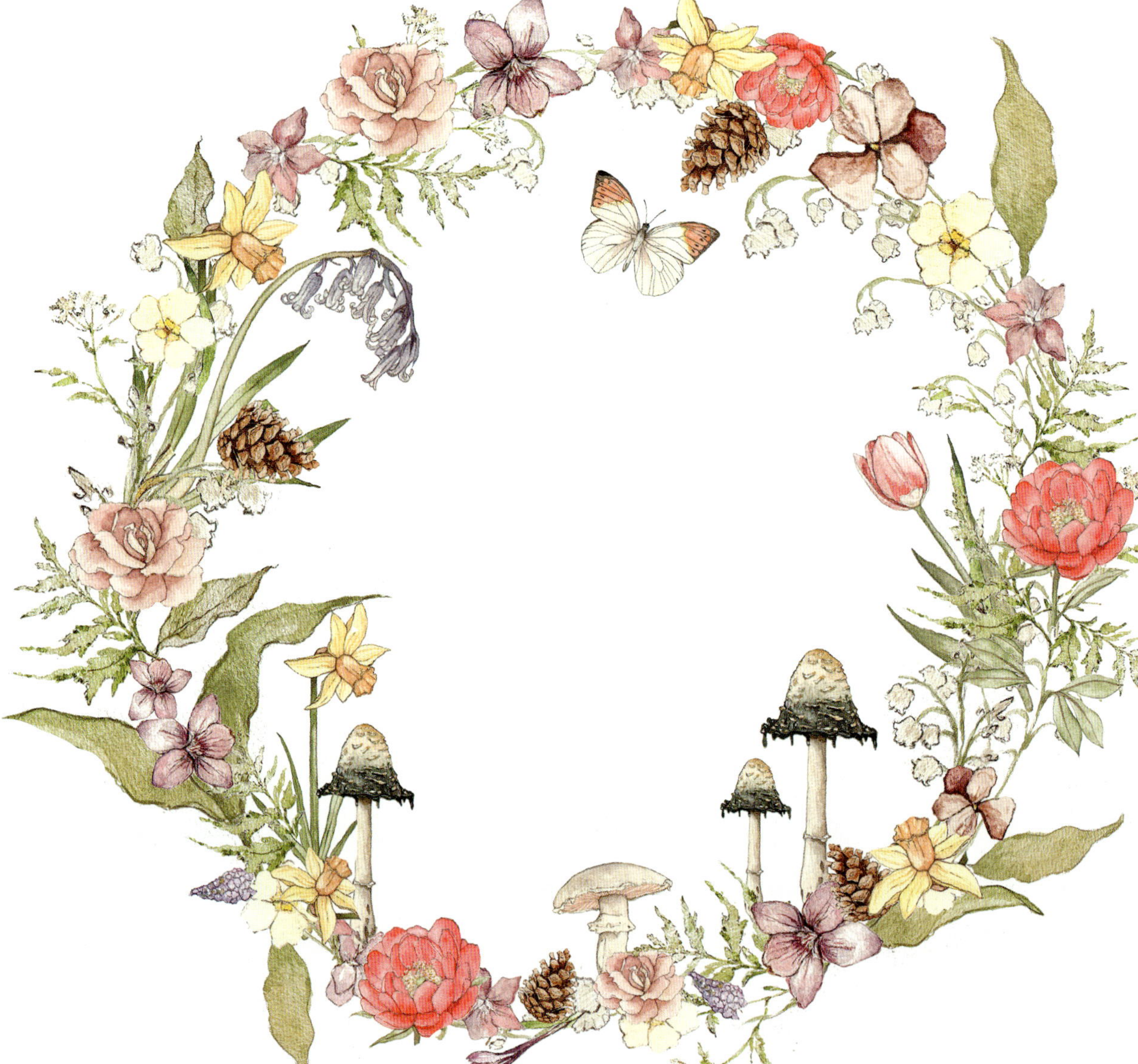

Fantastic Flora & Fungi

This chapter is devoted to the vivid personality of a favorite subject of many artists around the world: flowers. Though, I could not ignore and omit one of my personal favorites too: fungi! So I thought, why not combine them in these tutorials, allowing you to explore color, form, and texture through your brush of not just blossoms but the magic of the mycelium underworld in the garden too.

The field mushroom and shaggy inkcap toadstool, with soft curves and earthy tones, offer calm, grounding studies. You'll learn to build subtle shadows beneath the caps, suggest the delicate structure of their gills, and create the sense of quiet stillness yet whimsical quality that mushrooms carry in the garden when you spot them.

We will also celebrate a bouquet of garden flowers for their vibrancy: the peony inviting you to explore rich layers of petals, the garden rose helping you practice building depth with pale washes of color, and the daffodil, with bright centers and elegant trumpets, teaching you to balance crisp edges with glowing layers of yellow.

With so many beautiful things to paint, let's grab our brushes and make a start!

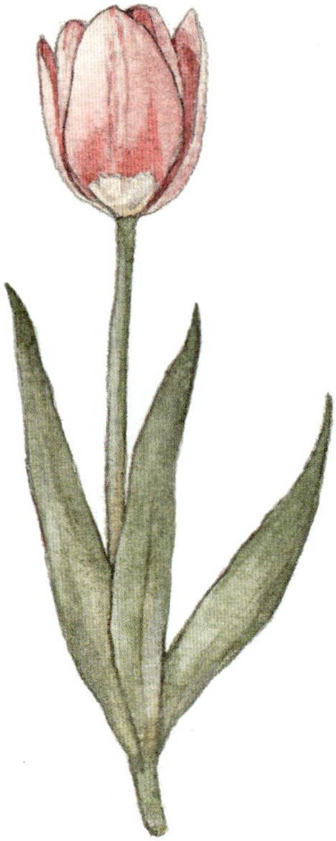

Tulip

One of the simplest and, for me, most beautiful of all garden flowers, tulips are the perfect spring flowers. Not only do they grow in a vast array of colors, which makes them very versatile subjects to explore when you are expanding your watercolor palette, but also their crisp shapes with papery leaves give a great opportunity to explore clean lines and subtle washes of color to portray the almost translucent texture found on the petals of the blossom.

Materials Needed

1 sheet of cold-press 140-pound (300-gsm) aquarelle/watercolor paper

HB pencil

Brushes

- Size 1
- Size 4
- Size 3/0
- Size 0
- Size 4/0

Watercolor paints

- Chinese white
- Raw umber
- Rose madder
- Alizarin crimson
- Hooker's green light
- Yellow ochre
- Sepia

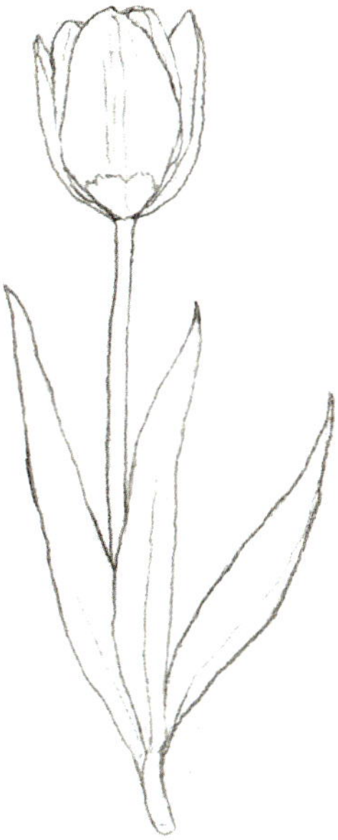

Step 1: Draw the Outline

Starting on a sheet of cold-press watercolor paper, draw the tulip's outline with a sharp HB pencil using the template provided on page 185.

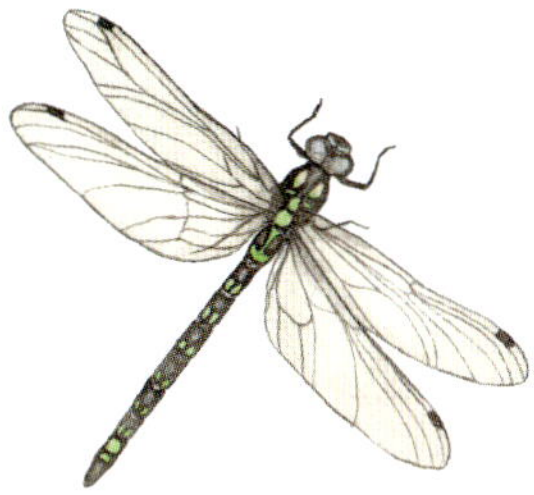

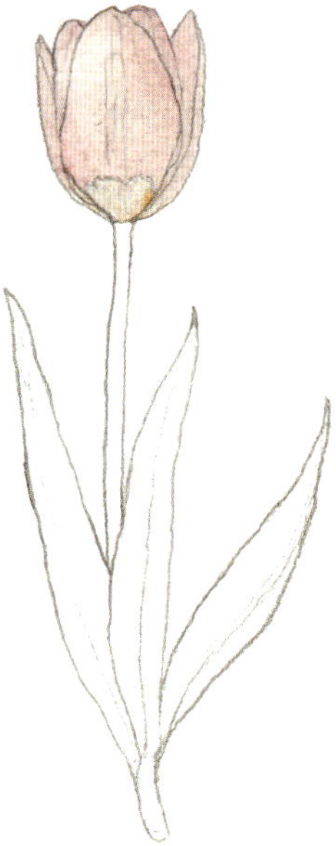

Step 2: Paint the Base

To prepare the cream color that will sit at the base section of the petals where the head of the bloom meets the stem, use a size 1 brush to mix a mid-toned solution of Chinese white with a small dab of raw umber to create a warm cream mixture rather than a cool-toned white. Glaze a layer of this creamy mixture onto the base section of the petals.

While this section is still damp, swirl the tip of the brush into raw umber, and drop the pigment on the right-hand side of this bottom section of the tulip, using the tip of the brush to spread the paint downward along the outline to the base where it meets the stem. As this pigment dries, it will create a subtle caramel accent on the base outline of the blossom. Clean the brush.

Next, we will mix the pale pink color that will fill the upper petals. Use a size 4 brush to mix a simple light-toned solution of rose madder and water to create a watery pale pink dilute. Load this color onto the bristles and glaze a layer of this solution onto the entire upper section of the petals. Allow the paint to dry.

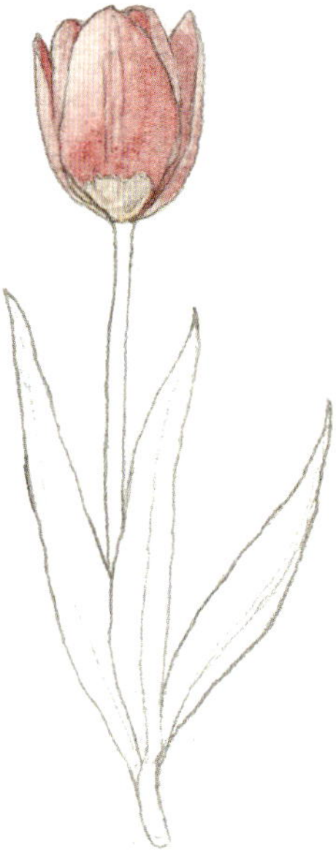

Step 3: Create Definition

Using the same size 4 brush and light-toned pink that we used in step 2, swirl the bristles into Alizarin crimson in the pink to deepen the texture and enrich the color to a warmer and darker tone of pink. This color will be used to define the veins and shadows on the petals on the head of the tulip.

Load the bristles with this deep pink color and paint a layer on the inner side of each petal as they fold inward, concentrating another layer of pigment at the base of the inner petal, where they are growing from the stem and more densely placed together. Glaze a thin layer of deep pink along the base of the upper pink section of the front petal where it meets the cream, gently dragging the paint upward and along the right-hand side, softening the edges as the paint flows upward to the tip on the right. This will create a seamless blend of the deeper pink shadow on top with the lighter layer of pink below it.

Switch to a size 3/0 brush and load this deep pink shade onto the bristles. Gently trace the central lines on the middle front-facing petal to create a subtle dimpling and folding appearance. Allow these paint layers to dry and clean the brushes.

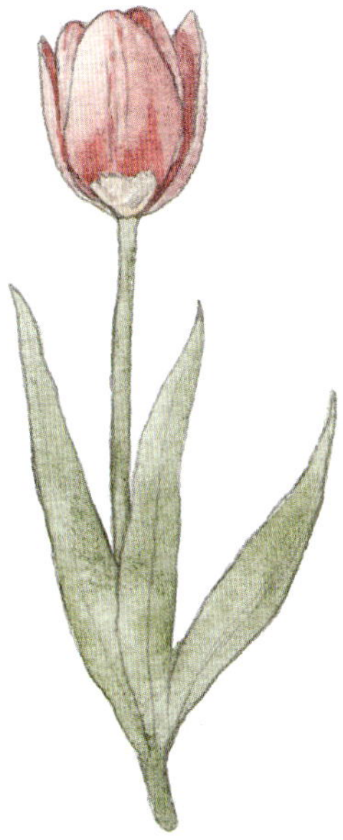

Step 4: Paint the Stem and Petals

Next, we want to deepen the layers of pink shadow that we applied in step 3. Use a size 0 brush to swirl back into the mid-toned rose madder and Alizarin crimson deep pink mixture, and apply another layer of this solution along the inside of each of the petals as they fold inward. Paint a thin layer along the base of the pink section of the front central petal, where it meets the cream section at the bottom. After you have applied this initial layer of paint, clean and dry the brush, and then gently stroke the bristles up toward the middle of the petal. This will soften the edges while still giving a shadow effect. Clean the brush.

Swap to a size 4/0 brush, and load the bristles with the same deep pink color. Trace along the central veins of the middle petal. Allow these layers to dry.

For the stem and leaves of the tulip, use a clean size 4 brush to mix a mid-toned solution of Hooker's green light and water. Load this color onto the bristles and glaze a wash of green onto the entire stem, leaves, and base. Clean the brush.

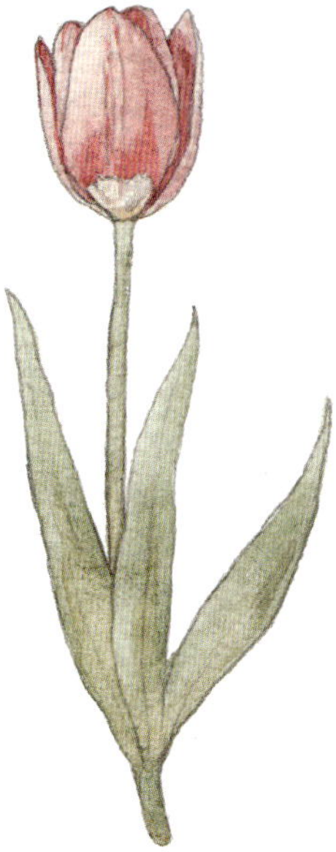

Step 5: Add a Subtle Color Gradient

While the layers of Hooker's green light that we applied in step 4 to the leaves and stem are still drying, use a clean size 1 brush to mix a mid-toned solution of yellow ochre with a small dab of raw umber. Gently drop this color to the base of the stem where it meets the overlapping leaves and also along the central rib of each leaf to create a subtle caramel pop of highlight. Allow these layers to dry and clean the bristles.

Swap to a clean size 3/0 brush and mix a mid-toned solution of Alizarin crimson and water. Load this color onto the bristles of the brush, and paint in the top inner section of each petal. Allow these layers to dry and clean the brush.

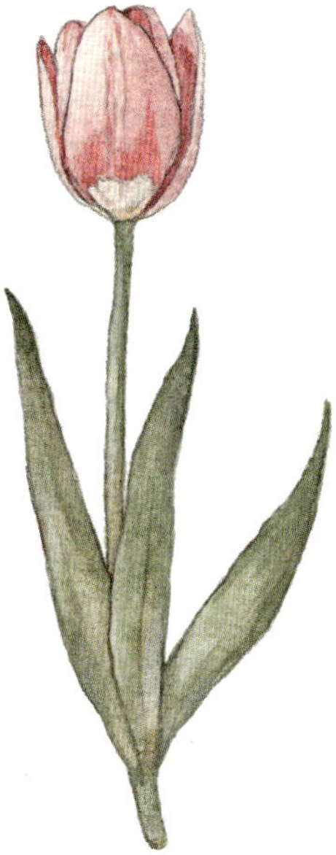

Step 6: Add Depth

Using a clean size 0 brush, mix a mid-toned solution of Hooker's green light with a dab of sepia to create a deeper earthy green. Gently dab along the top of the stem where it joins the head of the flower and the very tips and base of the leaves where they meet the stem, allowing the darker pigment to softly disperse and create a natural layered shadow. Dip back into the green and use the tip of the brush to trace along the very bottom of the stem upward to the center.

Finally, using a clean size 3/0 brush, mix a mid-toned solution of rose madder with a dab of sepia. Glaze the bottom crevices of the inner petals where they grow from the base. Use the tip of the brush to outline each of the petals. The tulip is now complete. Well done!

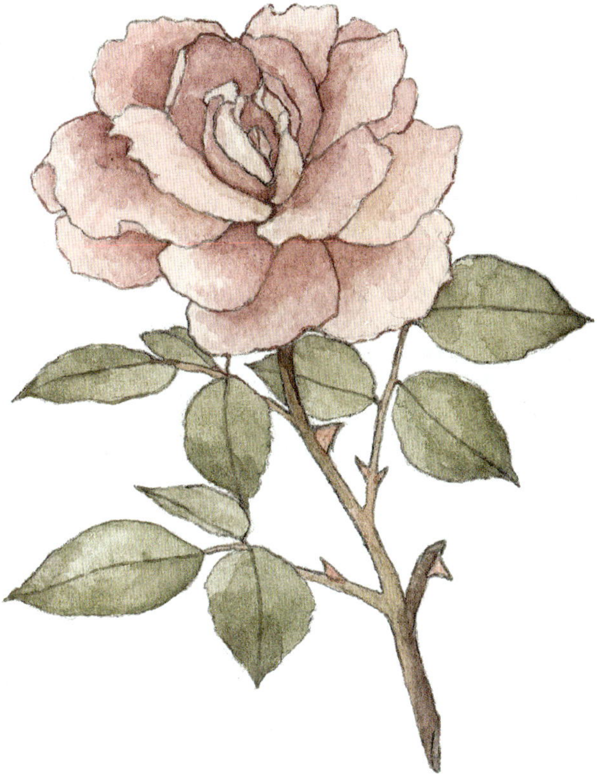

Garden Rose

Garden roses, or the "Queen of Flowers," add a magical finishing touch to any flower bed. While they're heavily laden with symbolism after centuries of cultivation, varying from love to wisdom to the fleeting nature of life, it is hard not to become completely enchanted by their layered velvety flowers and intoxicating yet innocent scent. Their petals make for a wonderful subject to paint. For this project, we will learn to emphasize sheer delicacy and how to build the soft, velvety body of the bloom through control of the brushstroke.

Materials Needed

1 sheet of cold-press 140-pound (300-gsm) aquarelle/watercolor paper

HB pencil

Brushes

- > Size 1
- > Size 4
- > Size 0
- > Size 3/0

Watercolor paints

- > Chinese white
- > Raw umber
- > Alizarin crimson
- > Rose madder
- > Indian red
- > Vandyke brown
- > Hooker's green light
- > Sepia
- > Burnt sienna

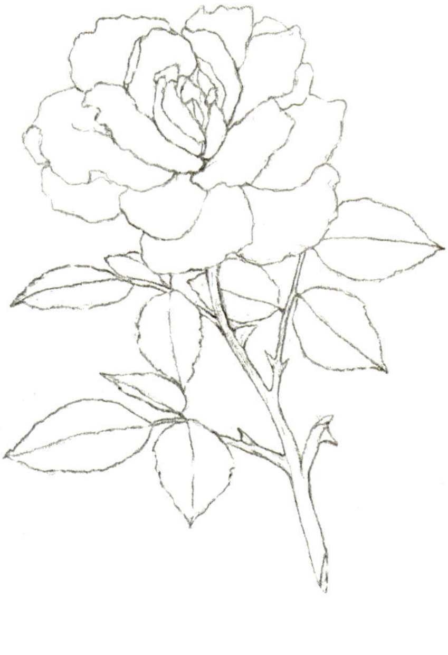

Step 1: Draw the Outline

Starting on a sheet of cold-press watercolor paper, draw the garden rose's outline with a sharp HB pencil using the template provided on page 187.

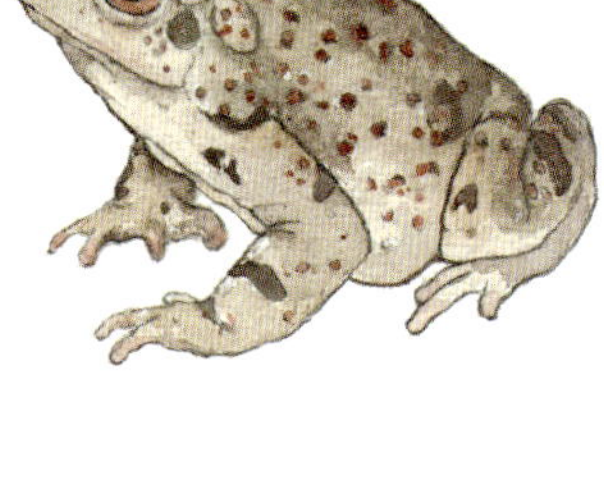

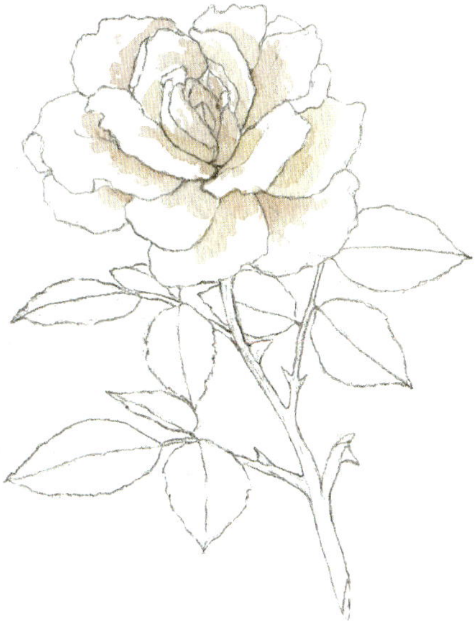

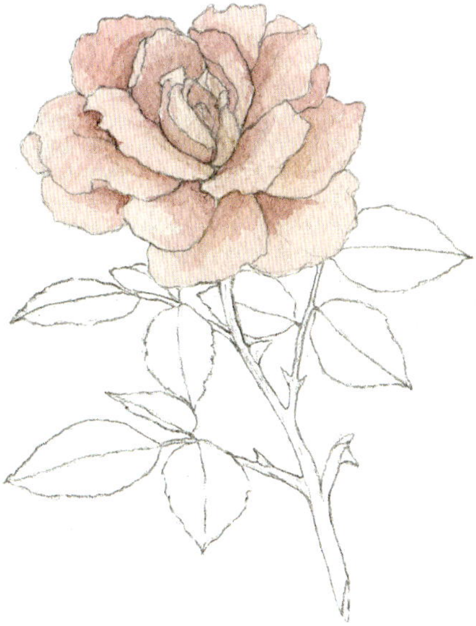

Step 2: Paint the Inner Layers

Use a size 1 brush to mix a mid-toned solution of Chinese white with a swirl of raw umber to create a warm, caramel-toned cream color.

Load this color onto the bristles and glaze a wash of this creamy mixture on the very central bud of the flower. As the petals flow outward, paint the very inner crevices of where they are growing from the center of the blossom. Gently pull the paint upward to the midway point of the petals. Leave these layers to dry and clean the brush.

Step 3: Fill In the Petals

For the pink that will fill the base color of the petals on the head of the flower, use a size 4 brush to mix a light- to mid-toned solution of Alizarin crimson and water, using enough pigment to tint the water but still keeping the solution translucent. Load this light, powdery pink onto the bristles and glaze each of the petals on the head of the rose. Allow this layer of pink to dry.

Next, using a size 0 brush, mix a mid-toned solution of rose madder and water, and glaze this mixture over the inner crevices of each individual petal, focusing on where they naturally grow from the center, where not as much light would reach. This will deepen the edges and folds of the petals, as using a deeper tone of pink that we used for the base of the rose gives a more natural and realistic effect.

Clean and dry the brush, and gently stroke the bristles over the edges of the shadow tones upward toward the outer edges to soften them and have them blend seamlessly into the base layer. Let these deeper pink layers dry.

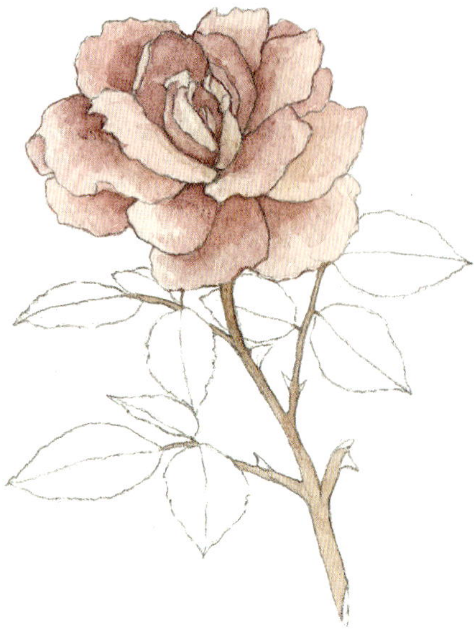

Step 4: Add Depth and Color

Using the same size 0 brush and mid-toned rose madder wash, swirl in a dab of Indian red to give the rosy pink solution a slightly deeper wine hue. Repeat the same painting steps that we did in step 3 in creating the base shadow layers, glazing this deep pink mixture over the inner crevices of each individual petal, focusing on where they naturally grow from and overlapping at the center where not as much light would reach. Paint the entire inner section of the petals that fold and grow above the inner bud.

Clean and dry the brush, then gently stroke the bristles over the edges of the shadow tones upward toward the outer edges to soften them and have them blend seamlessly into the layers beneath them. Clean the brush. Swap to a clean size 1 brush to mix the mid-toned solution of Vandyke brown and water. Load this solution onto the bristles and gently glaze the entire stem.

While this layer is still drying, swirl the brush back into the Vandyke brown mixture and drop the pigment at the points of the stem where it meets the petals. Softly drag the paint downward on the stem to soften the hard edges. Allow this layer to dry and clean the brush.

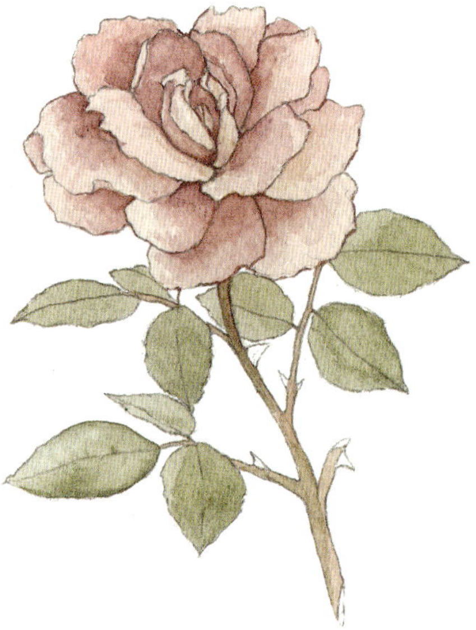

Step 5: Paint the Leaves

Using a clean size 0 brush, create a mid-toned glaze of Hooker's green light and water, and paint all the leaves growing from the stem with a thin glaze. While these layers are drying, using the same size 0 brush, swirl some water into the Hooker's green light solution to make a very watery green dilute. Gently glaze this color along the center of the stem and along the branches growing from the left-hand side. Clean the brush.

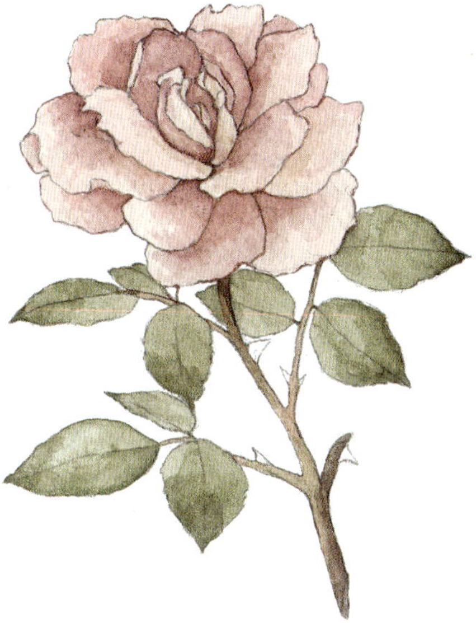

Step 6: Define Leaf Details

Using a clean size 0 brush, mix a mid-toned solution of Hooker's green light with a dab of sepia to create a deeper earthy green. Gently dab along the very tips of the leaves, allowing the darker pigment to softly disperse inward, creating a natural, layered shadow. Dip back into the green and use the tip of the brush to trace along the very bottom of the stem upward and to the center. Allow these layers to dry and clean the bristles of the brush.

Next, to deepen the shadows on the stem, use the clean size 0 brush to mix a simple mid-toned solution of sepia and water. Paint a thin layer of the pigment at the points of the stem where it meets the petals, as shadow would naturally fall here. Softly drag the paint downward on the stem to soften the hard edges. Allow this paint layer to dry and clean the bristles.

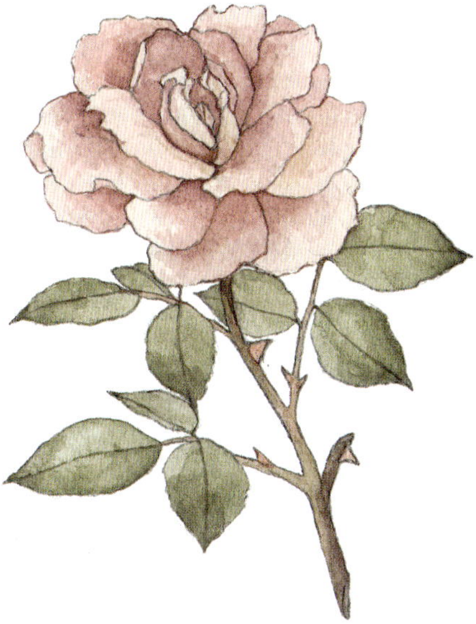

Step 7: Add Finishing Touches

Prepare the color for the thorns by using a clean size 0 brush to mix a simple mid-toned solution of burnt sienna and water. Using the tip of the brush, fill in the thorns running up the stem and branches that grow on either side.

Next, swap to a size 3/0 brush and mix a simple mid-toned solution of Vandyke brown and water. Load the color onto the bristles, and holding the brush at the ferrule, gently trace the central rib flowing along the middle of each leaf and also the outlines of the individual petals, leaves, thorns, and stem. Allow these paint layers to dry. The garden rose is now complete. You did a wonderful job!

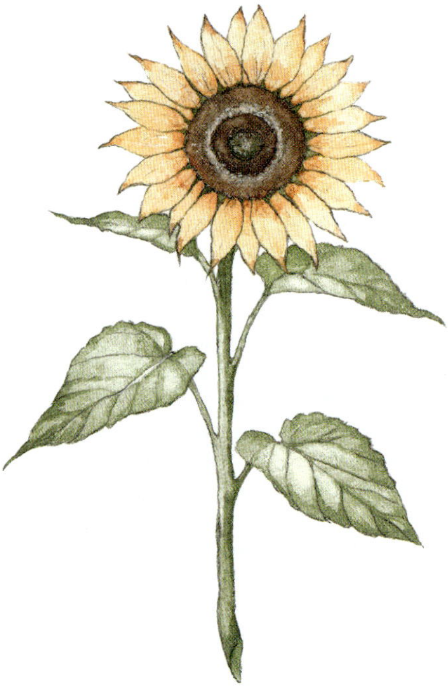

Sunflower

To me, sunflowers are the ultimate symbolic flower of summertime. Their petals and faces just seem to radiate cheer and warmth, almost like there is a patch of miniature orbs of sunshine popping up from the soil right outside the door!

I find it difficult to find shades of color that I could deem perfection, but the warmth of their yellow petals has just the most amazing intersection of vibrancy and grounding earthiness, which speaks to what I adore in a color palette as an artist. I have a very vivid memory from childhood of buying an entire sunflower head to eat from the farmer's market and being completely mesmerized by not only the taste and nutty flavor but also the pattern of the spiral of seeds tucked inside, waiting to be cracked open! This project is an homage to not only the gorgeous color of the sunflower but also how it is such an interesting and challenging flower to observe in both how perfectly uniform yet organic it is in its shape.

Materials Needed

1 sheet of cold-press 140-pound (300-gsm) aquarelle/watercolor paper

HB pencil

A piece of paper towel

Brushes

- Size 4
- Size 1
- Size 0
- Size 3/0

Watercolor paints

- Cadmium yellow
- Yellow ochre
- Burnt sienna
- Sepia
- Vandyke brown
- Hooker's green light
- Raw umber

Acrylic white

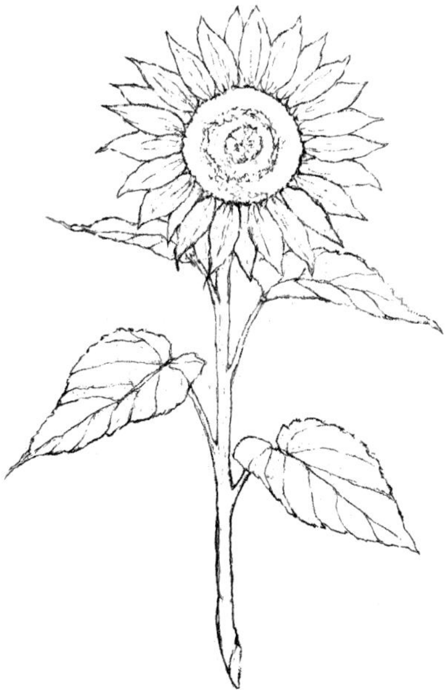

Step 1: Draw the Outline

Starting on a sheet of cold-press watercolor paper, draw the sunflower's outline with a sharp HB pencil using the template provided on page 187. Take note of the forms and shapes of a sunflower; its petals are quite uniform and smooth, and its center is rounded yet has a softer and more organic outline. Make sure that your line is strong and confident as you draw each petal, but it can be looser and gentler to convey the center of the head where all the petals grow from.

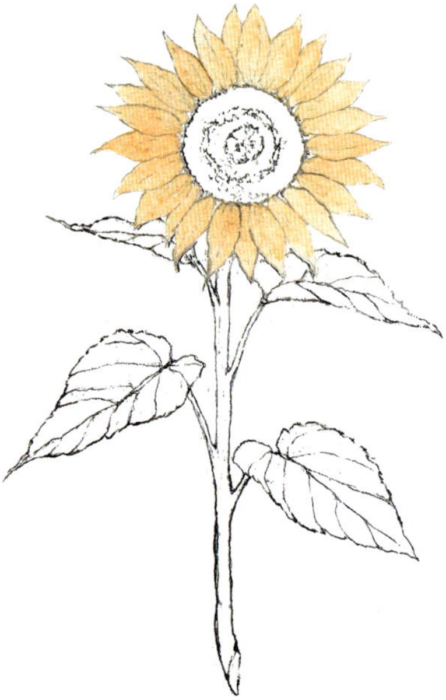

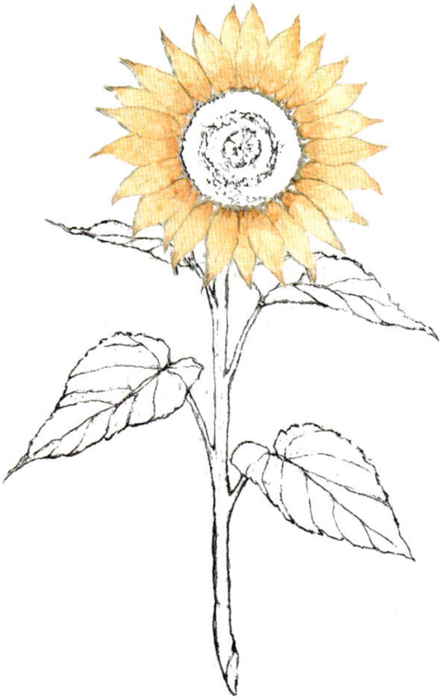

Step 2: Paint the Petals

Prepare the base color for the petals by using a size 4 brush to mix a mid-toned wash of cadmium yellow with the tiniest dab of yellow ochre. We want this to appear as a warm sunshine yellow that has an autumnal burnt hue. Cadmium yellow by nature is a bright, vibrant color, but for the sunflower petals we want to give the color some warmth while still keeping its vibrancy, so the addition of a tiny amount of yellow ochre will bring a sense of warmth and sunshine. Glaze the warm yellow mixture over the petals of the sunflower head. Clean the brush.

Step 3: Add Shadows

Next, we will prepare the color that will add depth and dimension to the petals. While your paper is still damp, use a size 1 brush to mix a light-toned solution of burnt sienna and water, and mix a dab of this into the warm sunshine yellow you mixed in step 2. This will create a darker, earthy yellow, which will pair alongside the base color that you mixed for the sunflower petals.

Using the same size 1 brush, gently dab this earthy mixture onto the inner part of the damp petals where they meet the center of the head. Use the bristles of the brush to concentrate the color at the bottom of each petal where the shadow is at its most intense, then gently extend the light wash upward toward the outside of the petals to create a shadow, which gradually becomes softer as it fans upward.

Dip the very tip of the bristles into the earthy yellow and gently fill in the very tip of each petal, repeating the action of gently extending it inward, softening the shadow. Allow the paper to dry and clean the brush.

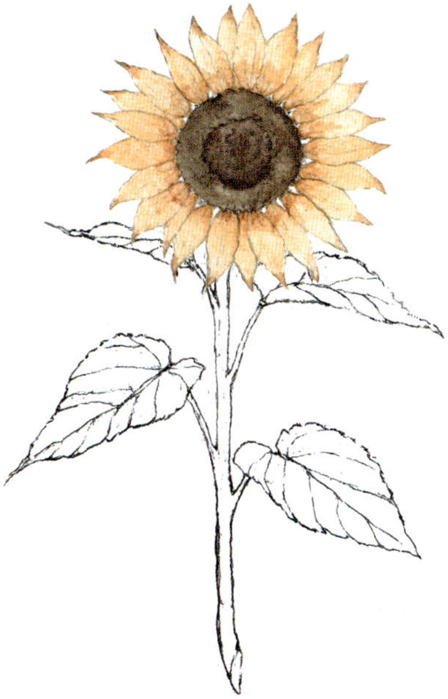

Step 4: Paint the Center

Using a clean size 4 brush, we will now create the base color that will be used as the glaze for the center of the sunflower. Mix a simple mid-toned solution of sepia with water and gently fill in the entire head. While the center is still damp but not wet, use a clean size 1 brush to add a dab of Vandyke brown to the mid-toned sepia solution. This will give the base brown a warm and burnt tone.

Using the clean size 1 brush with this warm brown, gently fill in the central circle on the head of the sunflower, concentrating on the outer edges and extending the color inward. Allow the paint to dry and clean the brush.

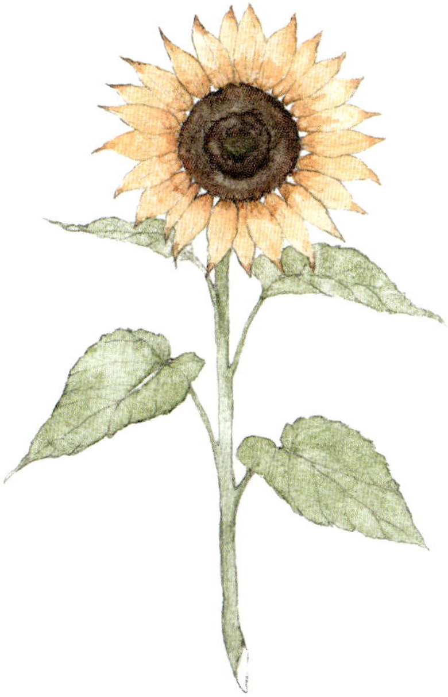

Step 5: Add the Stem and Green Leaves

Using a clean size 1 brush, create a simple mid-toned glaze of Hooker's green light and water and paint the entire stem and leaves. Allow the paint to dry and clean the brush.

Pick up a size 0 brush and load the bristles with this mid-toned simple green solution. Focusing on the very center of the head of the sunflower, paint a very thin, organic, loose circle at the middle of the head, giving the illusion now of three concentric circles sitting in the head of the sunflower. Allow the paint to dry and clean the brush.

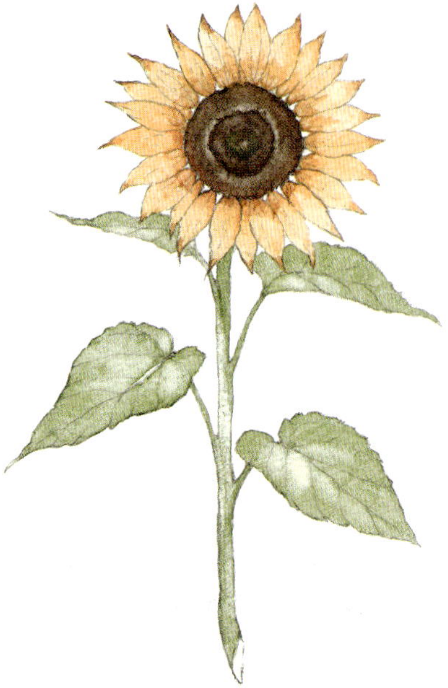

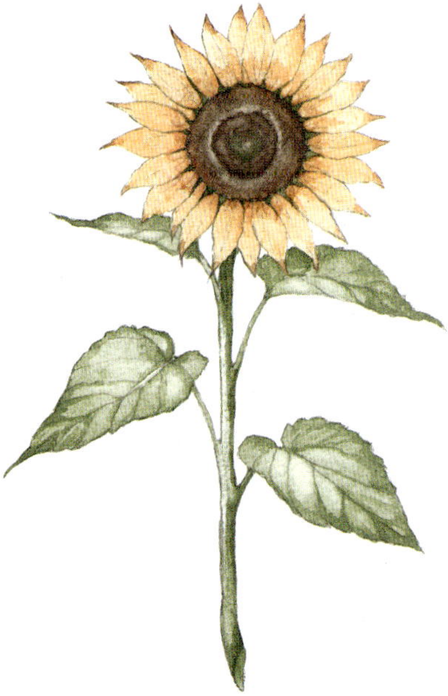

Step 6: Create Luminosity

To create highlights, dip a clean size 0 brush into water and wiggle it on the very center section between each vein on the individual leaves to cause the paint to lift up and sit on top of the paper. Taking a clean, dry paper towel, press the paper towel firmly to absorb the paint and leave behind a delicate highlight.

Repeat this exact step on the very outside edge on the middle circle and the center of the more inner circle on the head of the sunflower. This will give an excellent three-dimensional effect and luminosity to the sunflower. Clean the brush.

Step 7: Create Depth and Shadow

Using a clean size 0 brush, dab a small amount of raw umber onto the tip. Mix this warm brown into the simple mid-toned solution of Hooker's green light that we mixed in step 5, creating a deeper, earthy-toned hue. Using the tips of the bristles, delicately fill in the segments on the head of the sunflower that sit in between the petals, close to the head of the stem.

Next, we will use a clean size 1 brush and the same warm, earthy green to create shadows on the leaves and stem. Dip back into this solution and trace along the very bottom of the stem upward to the center along the right-hand side. Where the stem meets the head of the sunflower, the shadow will have more natural coverage and depth, so concentrate more color here and also right at the bottom of the stem. Using the very tips of the bristles of the brush, gently glaze the tips of each leaf, softly pulling the paint inward and up along the veins of each leaf to give them a smooth outline.

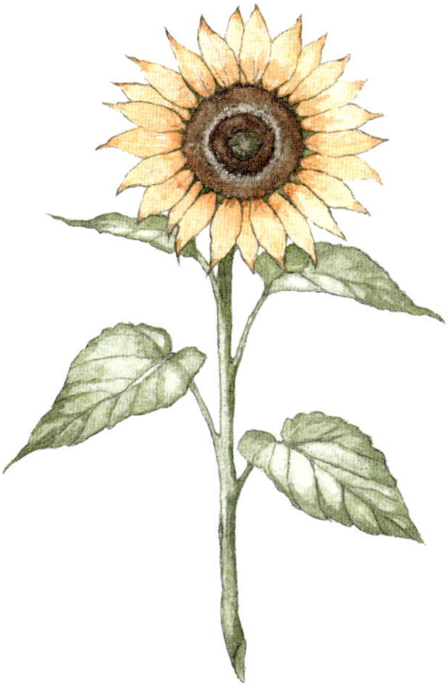

Step 8: Add Finishing Touches

Using a size 3/0 brush, mix a mid-toned solution of raw umber and water. Load the bristles with this simple glaze, and using the very tip of the bristles, delicately outline each petal, holding the brush close to the ferrule so you have the most control over the stroke of the line. Load the brush again with this mid-toned earthy brown and delicately trace the outline of the stem and leaves, following upward along the lines of the veins.

Clean the bristles from this brown mixture and dry the brush. Squeeze less than a pea-size amount of acrylic white onto your palette. Dip the tip of the clean size 3/0 brush into this mixture and very delicately paint tiny feathery dots along the edge of the middle circle on the head of the sunflower, concentrating on painting more soft feathery dots along the line of the outside of the middle circle and having them gently disperse and soften as they extend upward into the largest circle in the head.

Dip back into the acrylic white and paint a small cluster of tiny feathery dots in the middle of the central, smallest circle of the head. Allow the painting to dry. The sunflower is now complete. Well done!

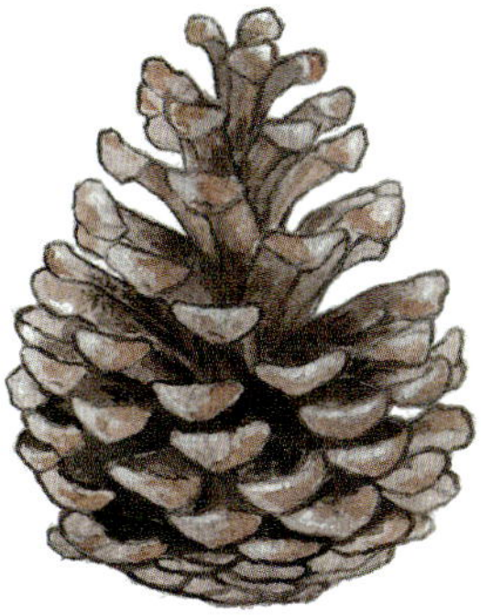

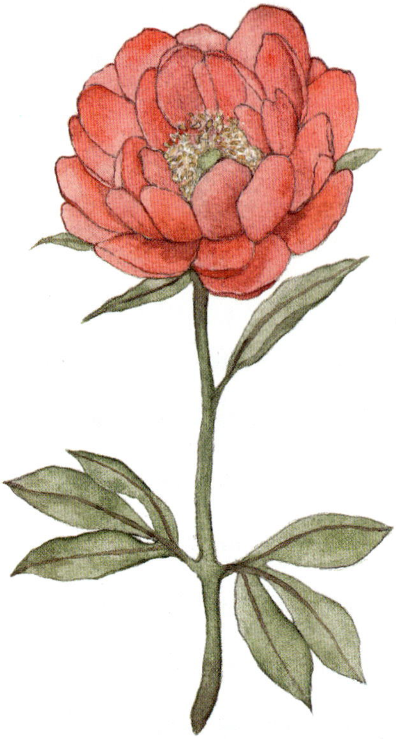

Peony

A star addition to any garden, peonies are a favorite among flower lovers for their lush, fluffy blooms and delicate fragrance, and are widely regarded as a symbol of love, prosperity, and good fortune. Although their layered, almost geometric structure may make them appear intimidating at first, their petals reward watercolor techniques as they are so delicate and almost translucent, like folded tissue paper. Simple techniques can be very satisfying when creating realistic flowers!

Materials Needed

1 sheet of cold-press 140-pound (300-gsm) aquarelle/watercolor paper

HB pencil

Brushes

- Size 3/0
- Size 4
- Size 1

Watercolor paints

- Hooker's green light
- Yellow ochre
- Burnt umber
- Rose madder
- Alizarin crimson
- Sepia
- Vandyke brown

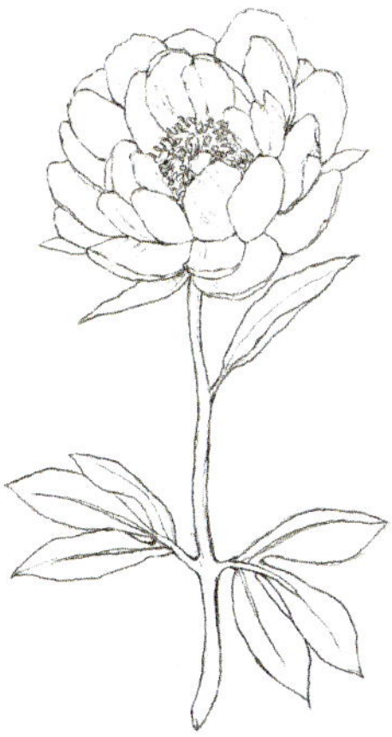

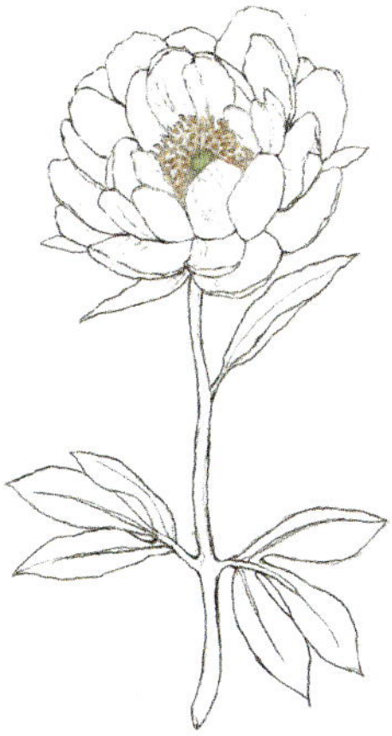

Step 1: Draw the Outline

Starting on a sheet of cold-press watercolor paper, draw the peony's outline with a sharp HB pencil using the template provided on page 187. The inner blossom on the head of the flower has many intricate and delicate tendrils, so take your time and trace slowly and carefully to ensure that your lines remain organic and flowing.

Step 2: Paint the Inner Blossom

Using a size 3/0 brush, mix a simple mid-toned solution of Hooker's green light and water. Load this color onto the bristles and gently glaze the very center of the inner blossom on the head of the peony. Allow this paint layer to dry and clean the bristles.

(continued)

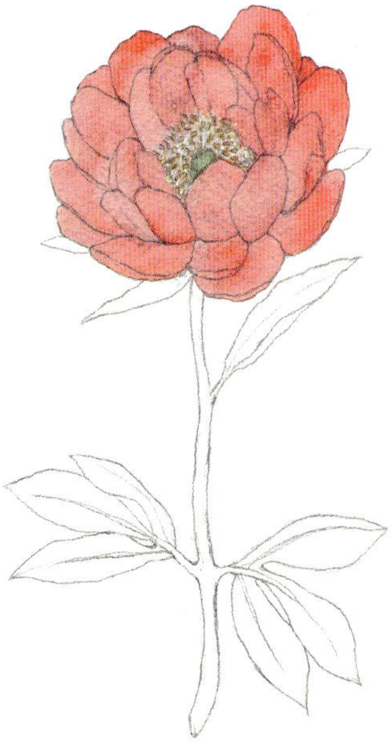

Next, using the same brush, mix a light-toned solution of yellow ochre and water, and carefully fill each tendril that surrounds this central bud. While these tendril layers are still damp, swirl the size 3/0 brush into burnt umber and drop the pigment onto the upper outline of each of the tendrils, allowing the paint to naturally disperse and dry, blending seamlessly into the lighter yellow ochre layer beneath it. Allow these layers to dry and clean the bristles of the brush.

Step 3: Fill In the Petals

Using a size 4 brush, mix a simple mid-toned solution of rose madder and water. Load this color onto the bristles and coat each of the petals on the head of the peony with this warm cerise-pink color. While the paint is still damp, swirl the brush back into the mid-toned pink and drop the pigment at the tips of the petals of the outer layers on the top edge of the flower.

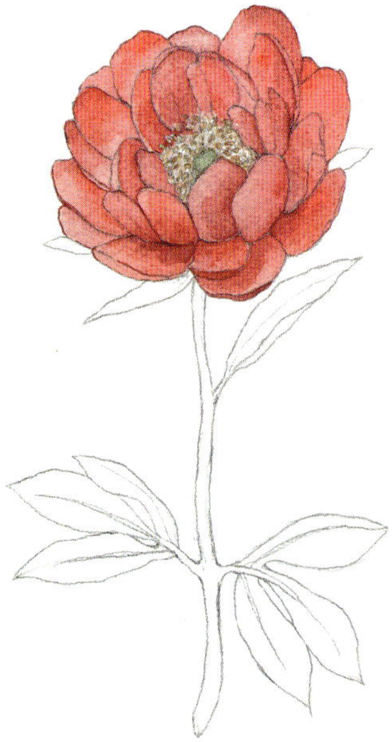

Step 4: Create Shadows and Layers

To prepare the color that will be the shadow on the petals of the peony, load a size 1 brush with a mid-toned mix of rose madder, then swirl a little Alizarin crimson into it so the color is slightly deeper.

Work on one petal at a time. On the petals on the upper half of the head of the peony, glaze the outline of upper curvature of each petal, then gently drag the brush downward so the wash becomes lighter as it spreads. Keep the strokes soft and quick so the edges stay smooth without any harsh lines. For the lower half of the petals on the head of the peony, glaze the bottom outline of the petals, dragging the wash upward so it becomes lighter and softer toward the tips of the petals. Allow these paint layers to dry.

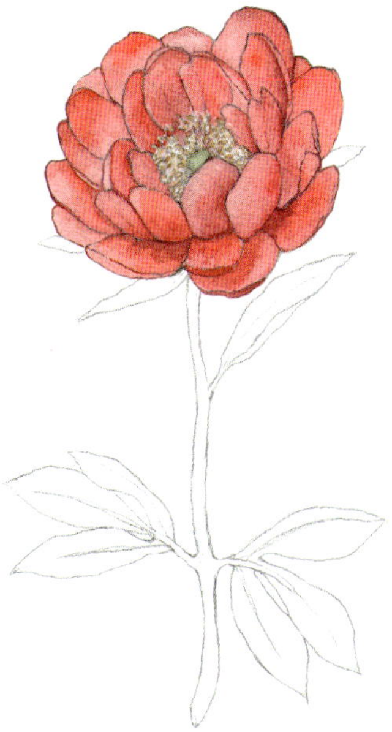

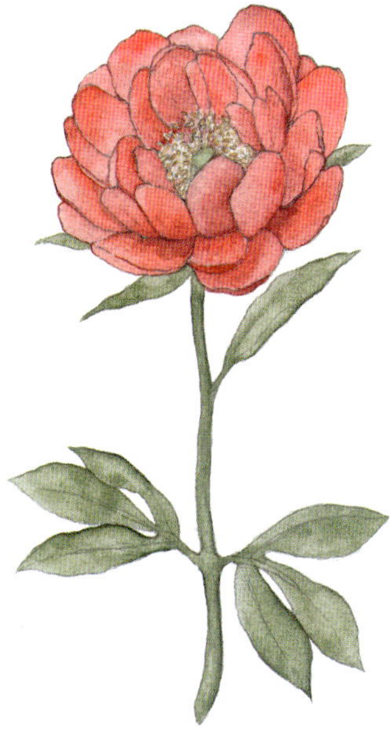

Swirl your brush back into the deep pink mixture and repeat the steps of the wash at the base of each lower petal, focusing on the part tucked closest to the center. Let the wash naturally lighten as the brush travels upward toward the tip. The fading color creates the sense that the petal is catching more light at the tip and is darker with shadow as it has layers of petals overlapping above it.

Step 5: Create Definition

Next, swap to a clean size 3/0 brush and mix a simple mid-toned solution of sepia and water. Holding the brush at the ferrule to ensure the most control over the lines, carefully trace along the outlines of each of the petals. Notice that some of the petals have central veins, which create a folding and dimpling effect. Clean the brush.

Using the same mid-toned deep pink solution that we mixed in step 4, swirl the size 1 brush back into this solution and paint another layer of shadow along the outer petals on the bottom half of the flower, focusing on the parts of the petal tucked closest to the center. Let the wash naturally lighten as the brush travels upward toward the tip to emphasize a gradient of shadow to light. Clean the bristles of the brush.

Step 6: Paint the Stem and Leaves

For the stem and leaves of the peony, use a clean size 1 brush to mix a mid-toned solution of Hooker's green light and water. Load the bristles and fill the stem and leaves with this color.

(continued)

While this layer is still damp, drop in another coating of this mixture to the tips of the leaves, gently dragging the paint along the outer sides of the leaves, and also where the leaves join to meet at the center of the stem and where the upper leaves meet the head of the flower. As these layers of green dry, swirl the brush back into the green mixture and glaze a thin layer of color on either side of the stem.

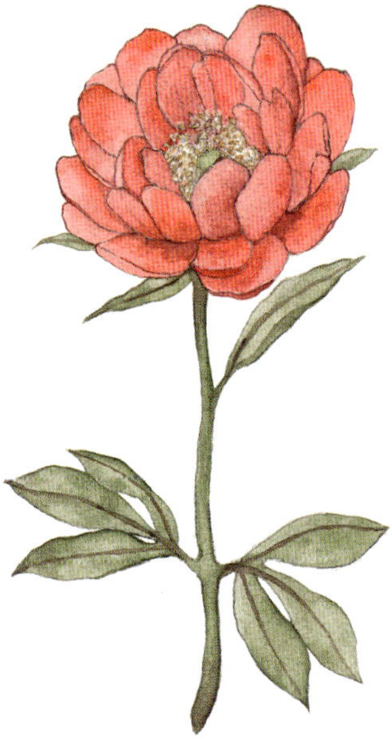

Step 7: Add Finishing Touches

Now we want to mix the color that will define the central veins and other details on the leaves and stem. Using a clean size 3/0 brush, mix a simple mid-toned solution of Vandyke brown with a swirl of sepia to create a warm, earthy brown. Load this color onto the bristles and trace along the central vein of each leaf, letting the bristles glide along to where they meet the stem. Allow these layers to dry.

Next, we want to create a soft, subtle shadow on the stem by diluting the mid-toned earthy brown to a light toned solution. Swirl the bristles of the size 3/0 brush into water and mix into the earthy brown to create a paler solution. Glaze this mixture on the bottom and very top of the stem, gently dragging the paint toward the center of the stem to soften the outlines. The peony is now complete. Great job!

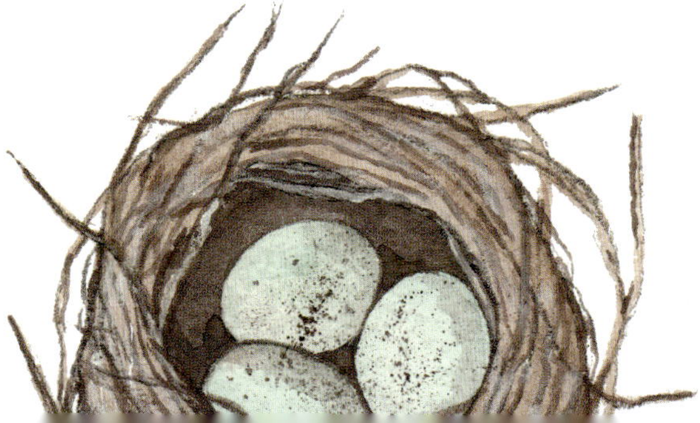

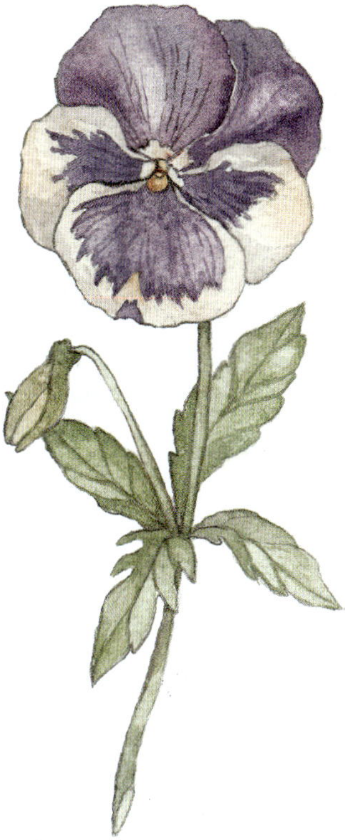

Pansy

Pansies are like little faces scattered throughout the garden. They are hardy little flowers, yet equally bright and just full of personality. They can range from summery yellows to contemplative purples, like the pansy I have chosen for this project. In this tutorial, we will explore how to capture a balance between striking contrasts of color, with subtle gradient changes. You'll learn to build rich layers of pigment while keeping the petal edges and the leaves light and fluid.

Materials Needed

1 sheet of cold-press 140-pound (300-gsm) aquarelle/watercolor paper

HB pencil

A piece of paper towel

Brushes

- > Size 1
- > Size 3/0
- > Size 4

Watercolor paints

- > Chinese white
- > Raw umber
- > Yellow ochre
- > Burnt sienna
- > Dioxazine violet
- > Prussian blue
- > Ivory black
- > Hooker's green light

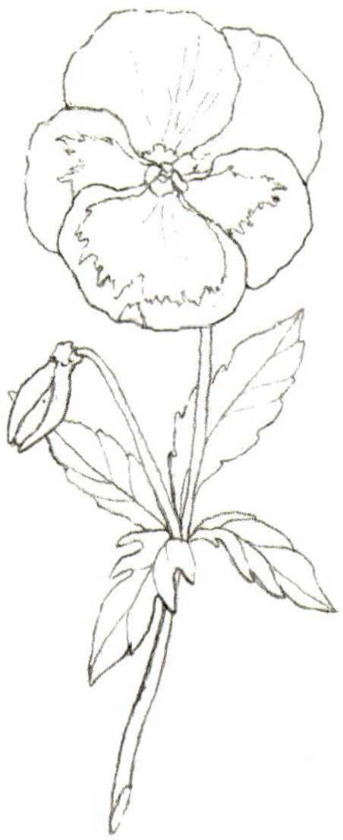

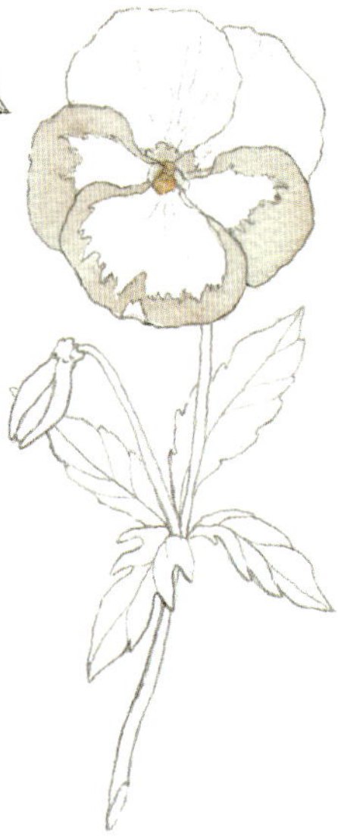

Step 1: Draw the Outline

Starting on a sheet of cold-press watercolor paper, draw the pansy's outline with a sharp HB pencil using the template provided on page 185. The inner sections of the pansy are quite delicate, so keep your line work soft and practice strong, confident lines for the stem and leaves, as they are more flowing and uniform.

Step 2: Paint the Base Layer

Using a size 1 brush, mix a mid-toned solution of Chinese white with a tiny hint of raw umber. We want this color to be a warm cream tone and not a cool-toned white. Glaze this color onto the outer section of the lower three petals, and the tiny section at the top two petals where they meet the others in the center. Allow this layer of paint to dry and clean the brush.

Switch to a size 3/0 brush, and mix a mid-toned solution of yellow ochre with a tiny dab of burnt sienna. We want to create a warm, rusty mustard yellow. Load the bristles with this color and paint the inside of the flower where all the petals meet. Let this layer dry and clean the brush.

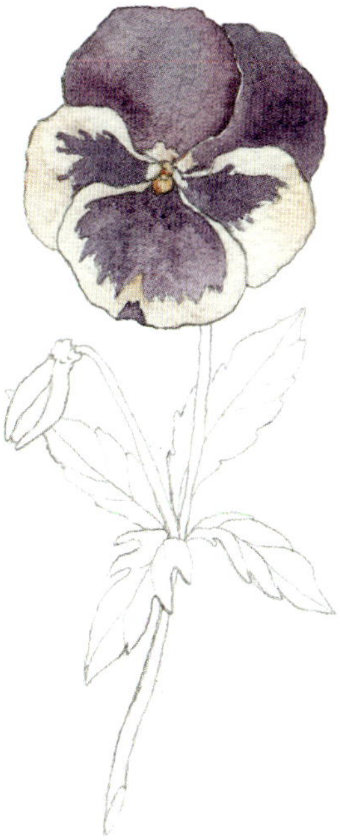

Step 3: Add Color

Using a size 4 brush, mix a mid-toned solution of dioxazine violet with water. We want this color to be a rich purple. Load the bristles and flood the upper two petals with this mixture, and do the same for the center of the lower three petals. Take note that there is a small lower section on the center bottom petal also to be filled in with this rich purple mixture.

While these layers are still damp, mix in a tiny dab of Prussian blue to the mid-toned purple mixture to create a deeper hue. Drop this mixture onto the center of the back right-hand petal, the left-hand side of the back left petal, and along the center of the bottom three petals where they come to join in the center. As these layers dry, they will create a natural, soft gradient in between the different layers of purple.

Swap to a clean size 3/0 brush and mix a light-toned solution of burnt sienna and water. Gently glaze this mixture onto the bottom of the lower central petal, just where the two purple sections meet. Then dab a tiny amount of this burnt sienna mixture into the left-hand side of the very yellow center of the bloom, creating a subtle shadow. Clean the brush.

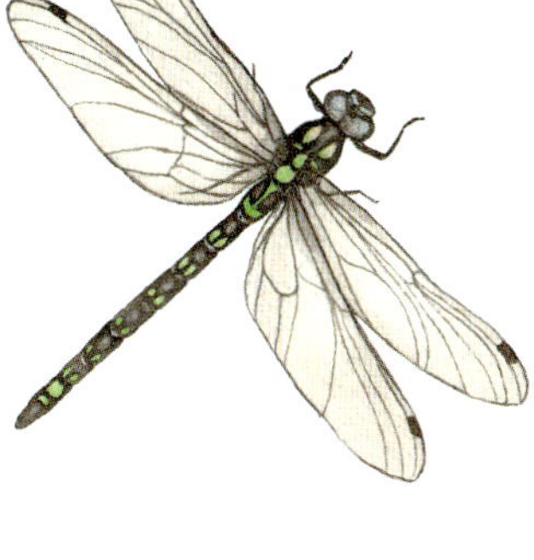

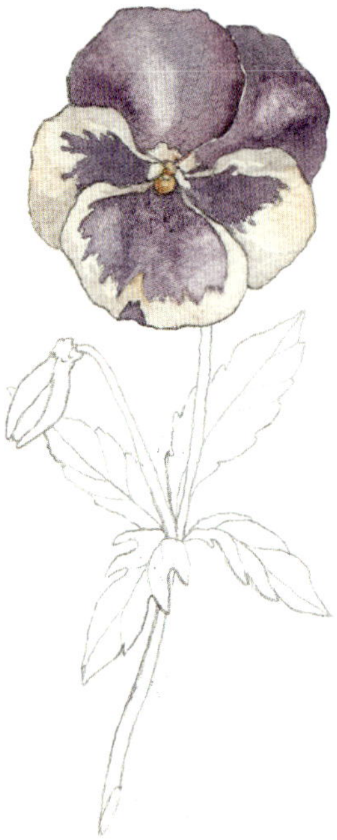

Step 4: Add Highlights and Shadow

To create highlights on the petals, swirl a clean size 1 brush into water, then wiggle the bristles on the center of both of the upper petals, and the lower-section left and right edges on the purple segment of the middle bottom petal. The pigment will lift onto the bristles. Press a piece of paper towel firmly onto these areas, then lift up. Underneath will be a subtle, luminous highlight. Clean the bristles of the brush.

For the shadows on the petals, use the clean size 1 brush to mix a simple light-toned solution of ivory black and water to create a very watery gray. Carefully paint the sections of the petals where they almost overlap with each other, on the tops and bottoms, and at the central section where all the petals meet. Clean the brush.

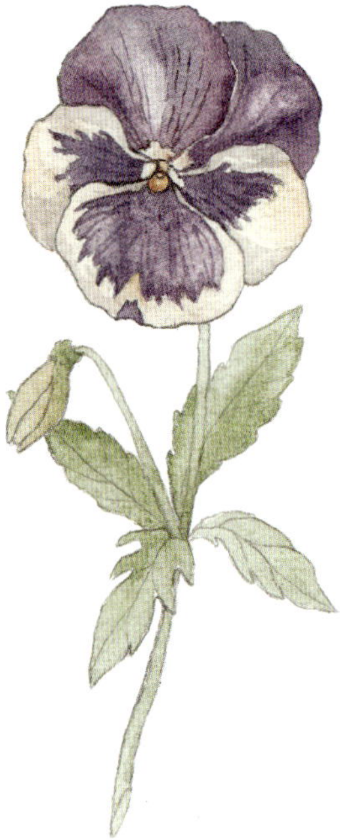

Step 5: Add Color and Detailing

For the stem and leaves of the pansy, use a clean size 1 brush to mix a mid-toned solution of Hooker's green light and water. Load the bristles and fill the stem, bud, and leaves with this color. While this layer is still damp, drop in another coating of this mixture to the tip of the bud where it meets the stem, the outer sides of the leaves, and also where the leaves join to meet at the center of the stem. Clean the brush.

To add definition to the pansy blossom, with a clean size 3/0 brush, mix a simple mid-toned solution of dioxazine violet and water. Load the bristles and gently trace the outline of each petal and its inner colored sections of purple. Take note to also trace the inner section of the pansy where all the petals grow from. Finally, gently paint flowing lines that naturally grow outward along the purple sections of the petals from the inside, splaying out in a V shape.

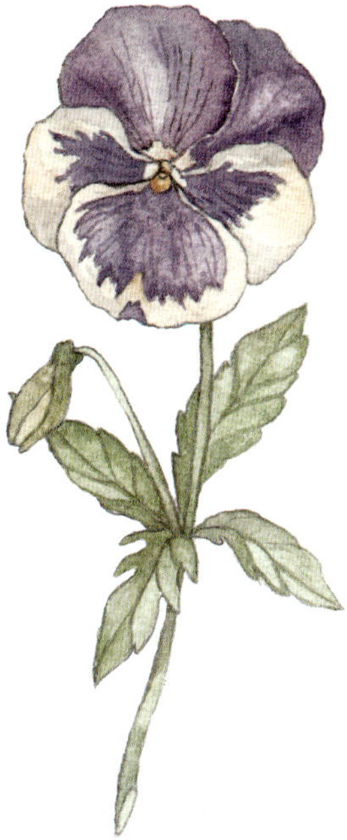

Step 6: Define the Leaves

We now want to define the detailed areas that surround the veins on the leaf and divide it into different sections of darker green. First, using a clean size 1 brush, glaze an extremely thin layer of clean water over each of the leaves. We do not want the water to be sitting and pooled on top of the paper; we want the paper to be slightly damp but not wet.

Clean the bristles of the brush and use it to mix a mid-toned solution of Hooker's green light with a swirl of raw umber to create a deep, warm green hue. While the paper is still damp, use the tip of the brush to drop color along the edges of the leaf and also following the curves of the veins inward toward the center rib, creating a concentration of color at the center where the leaves all flow to meet at the stem.

Use the very tip of the brush to paint this same color along the very bottom of the stem and also where it meets the head of the pansy, seamlessly blending the color into the green. Add a layer of this green onto the outer layer of the bud. The pansy is now complete. Well done!

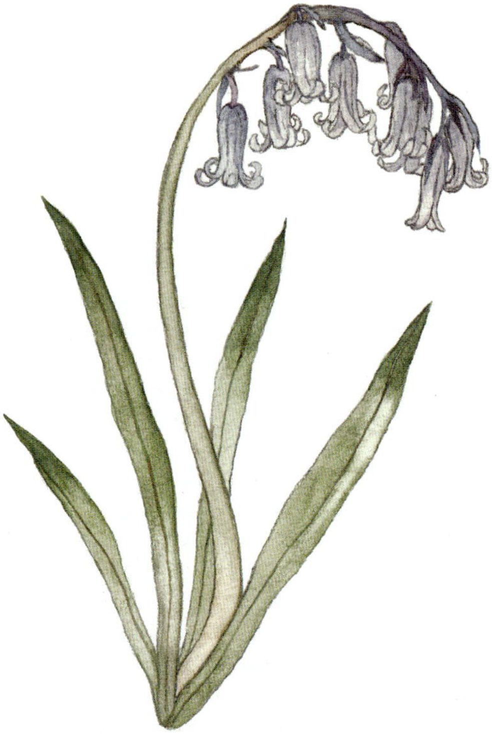

Bluebell

Each year, a sudden lush, vibrant display of bluebells appears. They are one of the last blooming flowers of spring, a welcome reminder that summer is soon on its way. In this tutorial, we will focus on layering and creating gentle transitions between colors. Subtle additions to color mixes can have great effect, and this can be very useful when portraying subtleties in the different green hues found on leaves or the violets of its petals.

Materials Needed

1 sheet of cold-press 140-pound (300-gsm) aquarelle/watercolor paper

HB pencil

A piece of paper towel

Brushes

- Size 1
- Size 3/0
- Size 4

Watercolor paints

- Dioxazine violet
- Prussian blue
- Raw umber
- Sepia
- Hooker's green light

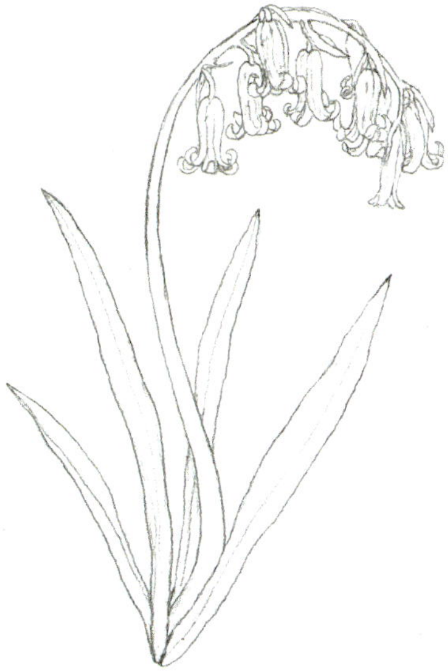

Step 1: Draw the Outline

Starting on a sheet of cold-press watercolor paper, draw the bluebell's outline with a sharp HB pencil using the template provided on page 189. The blossoms on the bluebell are quite intricate with many curls and fine details, so do make sure to take your time and trace slowly and carefully.

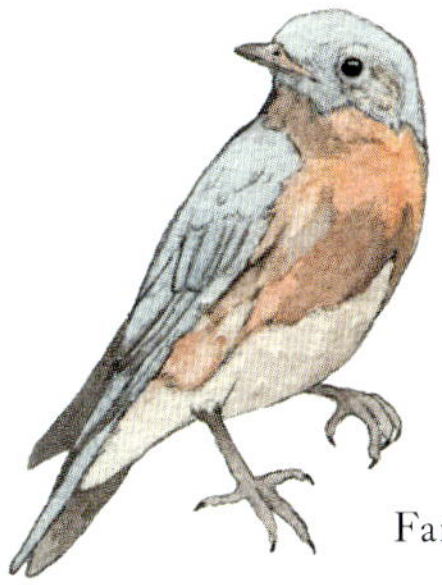

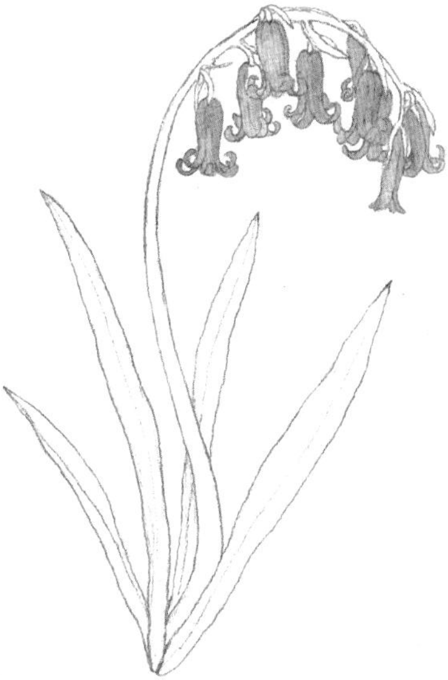

Step 2: Paint the Base Layer

For the base layer of color for the flowers of the bluebell, use a size 1 brush to mix a light-toned solution of dioxazine violet with a tiny dab of Prussian blue. We want this to be a watery pale violet with a cool-toned hue. Load this mixture onto the bristles and fill in each of the blossoms. Let this layer dry and clean the brush.

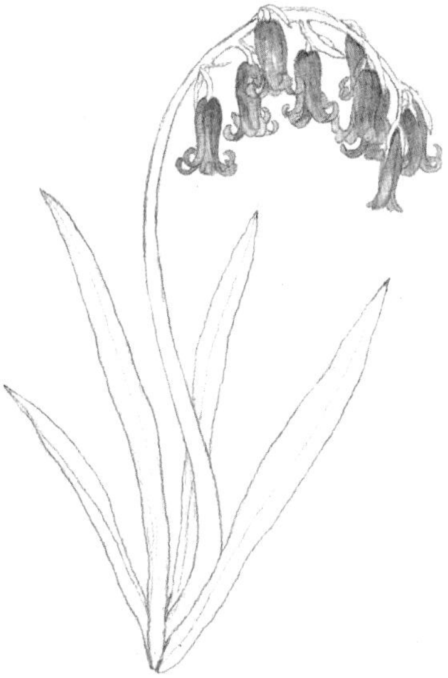

Step 3: Add Definition

Using the same light-toned violet mixture we mixed in step 2 but switching to a size 3/0 brush, mix in a delicate swirl of dioxazine violet with a tiny hint of the Prussian blue to lift this mixture to a mid-toned solution that has slightly more pigment and is less watery. Load the bristles with this cool-toned violet and carefully glaze the tops of the blossoms where they meet the stem, gently dragging the paint downward to midway along the petals, then at the lower section of the petals; gently paint only the outer edges, avoiding the middle. This will create a subtle shadow and sense of dimension at the top of the blossoms, and a delicate outline to each of the petals while still preserving the lighter violet toward the tips.

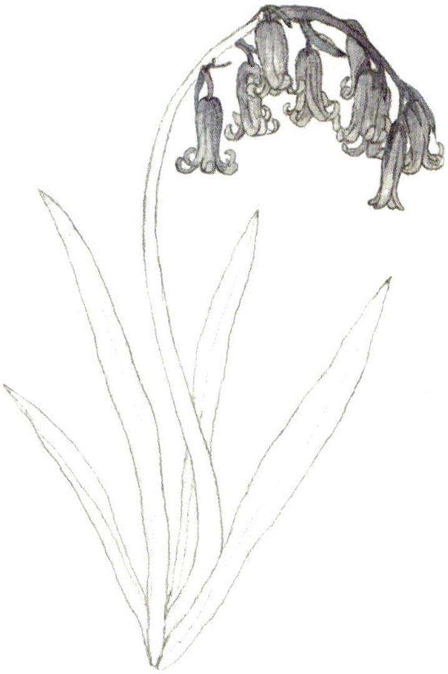

Step 4: Create Depth and Shadow

We are now going to deepen the colors of the mid-toned violet that we mixed in step 3 using the same size 3/0 brush. Swirl the bristles into dioxazine violet and mix this into the mid-toned solution, heightening the deep purple hues and creating a richer color. Load the brush with color and gently fill in the top of the stem that meets and extends from the blossoms, not forgetting the little tendrils that sit on top of some of the blossoms. Allow this layer to dry. Dip back into your deep purple solution and brush the very tips of these tendrils to create deeper shadows. Clean the brush.

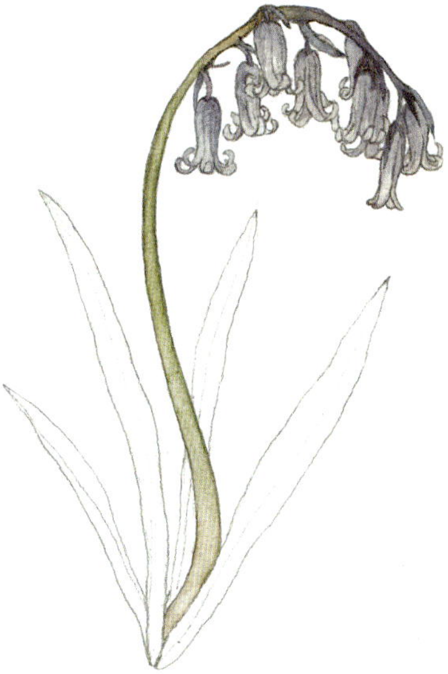

Step 5: Paint the Stem

For the first layer of the stem, use a clean size 1 brush to mix a light-toned solution of raw umber with a tiny dab of sepia. We want to create a warm caramel color. Load the bristles with this watery warm solution and glaze the entire stem.

While this layer is still damp, swirl your size 1 brush into pure sepia and drop this pigment at the top of the stem where the brown color transitions into the deep violet where the blossoms are growing. Gently soften the edges by dragging the paint slowly into the violet, creating a soft and natural transition between the two colors once they are dry.

When the initial caramel layer is dry, clean your size 1 brush and mix a simple mid-toned solution of Hooker's green light and water. Glaze this solution on the stem while avoiding the very bottom and very top, allowing the green glaze to transition into the caramel and earthy brown at either end by gently softening any hard edges with the brush. Allow this layer of green to dry and clean the brush.

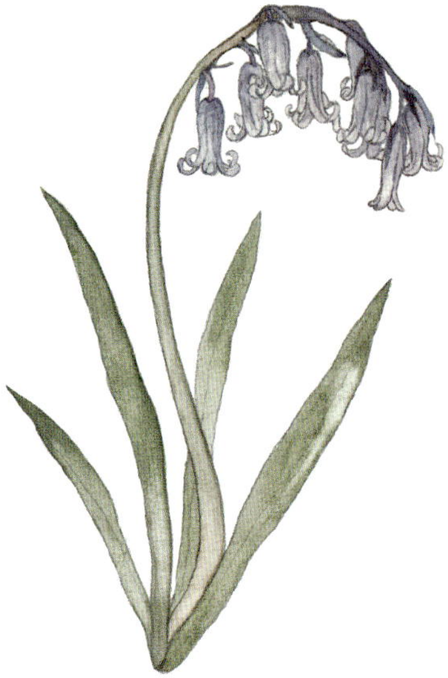

Step 6: Paint the Leaves

Using the same simple mid-toned Hooker's green light solution, use a size 4 brush to glaze each of the four leaves of the bluebell. While this layer is still damp, drop another coat of this green mixture to the tip of each leaf, softly dragging the paint downward to blur any hard edges and creating a gentle transition between the layers of dark to light. Allow these coats to dry.

Next, create highlights. Swirl a clean size 1 brush into water, then wiggle the bristles on the upper right-hand side of the right leaf and the lower section of the two leaves on the left of the stem. The pigment will lift onto the bristles. Press a piece of paper towel firmly onto these areas, then lift up. Underneath will be a subtle, luminous highlight.

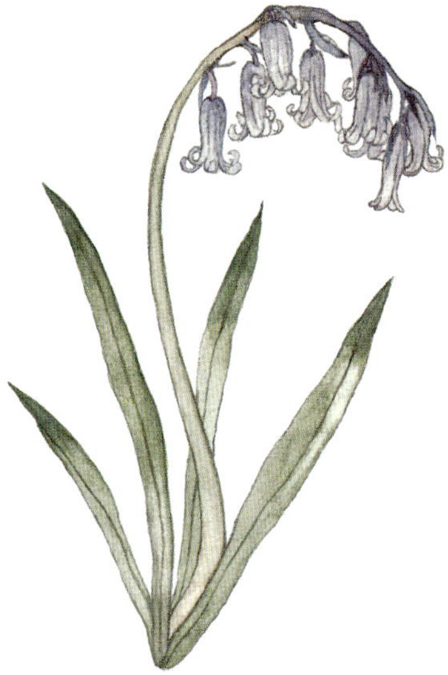

Step 7: Add Final Details

For the final details on the bluebell, use the size 1 brush to mix a mid-toned solution of Hooker's green light with a tiny hint of sepia. Load this color onto the bristles and gently glaze the very tip of each leaf with this darker green color, softening the edges to create a gentle transition from darker to lighter green as it travels down the leaf of the bluebell. Allow this layer to fully dry.

Finally, using a clean size 3/0 brush, mix a mid-toned solution of sepia and water. Load the bristles and gently and slowly trace the central line of each leaf and the outline of the stem. Allow this paint to dry. The bluebell is now complete. You did a great job!

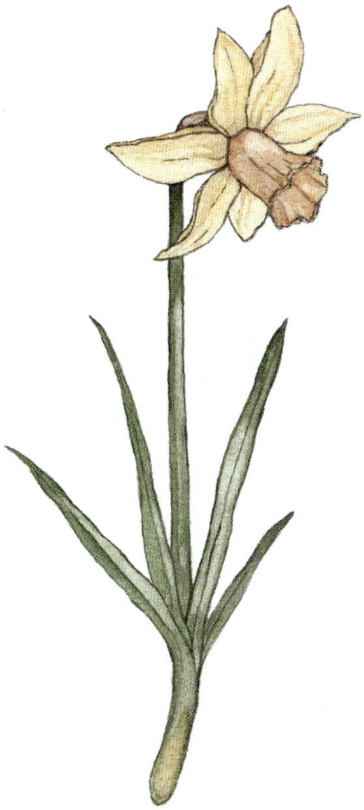

Daffodil

In the garden, few flowers announce springtime as joyfully and symbolically as the daffodil. Their cheerful trumpet-shaped blossoms seem to embody the sunlight itself. I am always so grateful to see them pop up from the soil after the darkness and reflection of wintertime.

In this project, you will learn how to paint daffodils in a way that captures their delicate yet flowing lines. You'll discover how to balance vivid sunshine yellows with soft rustic shadows, and how to let the layers of paint underneath shine through to create a sense of natural light.

Materials Needed

1 sheet of cold-press 140-pound (300-gsm) aquarelle/watercolor paper

HB pencil

A piece of paper towel

Brushes

- > Size 1
- > Size 4
- > Size 3/0

Watercolor paints

- > Raw umber
- > Burnt sienna
- > Raw sienna
- > Yellow ochre
- > Hooker's green light
- > Sepia

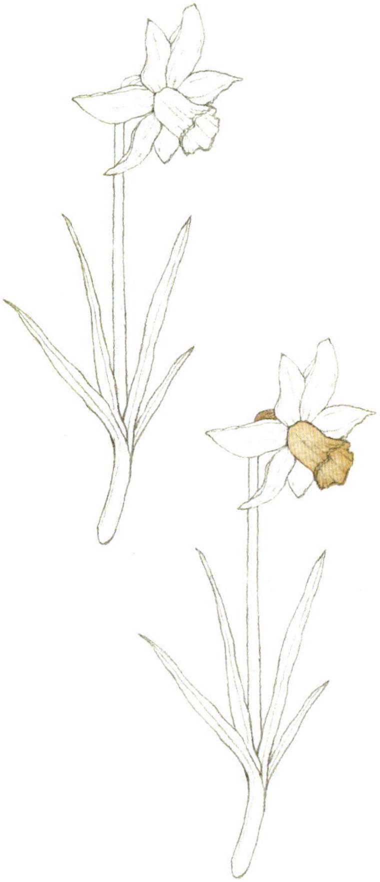

Step 1: Draw the Outline

Starting on a sheet of cold-press watercolor paper, draw the daffodil's outline with a sharp HB pencil using the template provided on page 187. The flower and leaves of the daffodil are elegant and curved, so do make sure to take your time and trace slowly and carefully to ensure that your lines remain smooth and flowing.

Step 2: Paint the Inner Blossom

Using a size 1 brush, mix a mid-toned solution of raw umber and water. Load the paint onto the bristles and paint a thin layer of this warm caramel color onto the inner blossom at the head of the daffodil, and also the back part at the top of the stem where it meets the petals.

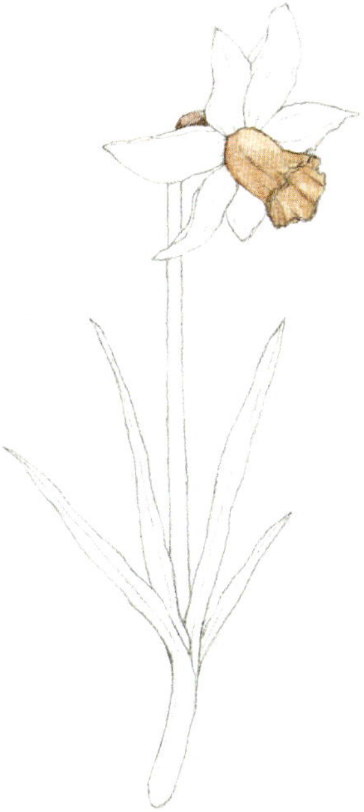

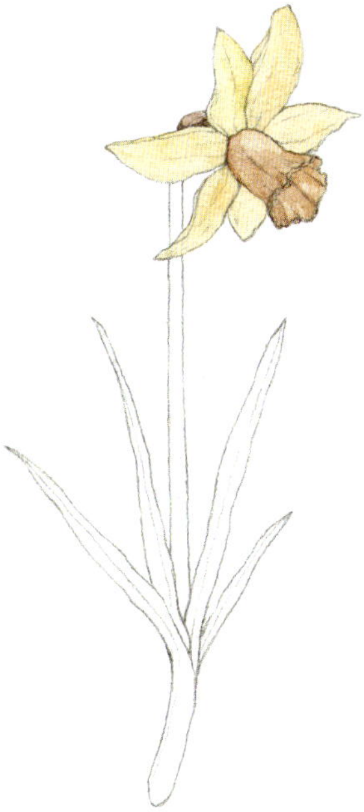

While this layer is still damp, take another swirl of the same mid-toned solution and drop it onto the tip of the blossom's outline on the right-hand side. While this layer disperses and dries, it will create a natural gradient of color from darker to light. Add another layer of this mid-toned caramel to the top of the stem and allow to dry. Clean the brush.

Step 3: Create Depth with Color

Using a clean size 1 brush, mix a mid-toned solution of burnt sienna and water. We want this color to be a rusty orange color. Load the bristles and paint a thin layer on the inside of the blossom, leaving some small patches on the inside of the blossom unpainted to create a sense of light hitting the inside of the petal.

Paint a layer of this rusty orange on the outside of the blossom, beginning with the tips of the petal and gently brushing upward along the center of the flower, and finishing toward the left-hand side of the central blossom where it meets the surrounding blooming petals.

While this paint layer is drying, load the bristles with the same rusty orange color, and using the tip of the brush, paint a thin layer at the top of the stem on the bottom outline where it comes to meet the blooming petals at the head. Clean the brush.

Step 4: Paint the Blooming Petals

Using a size 4 brush, mix a simple mid-toned solution of raw sienna and water. Load the bristles with this warm, sunny yellow color and glaze each of the surrounding petals that are blooming around the inner blossom at the head of the sunflower. Allow this paint layer to dry and clean the brush.

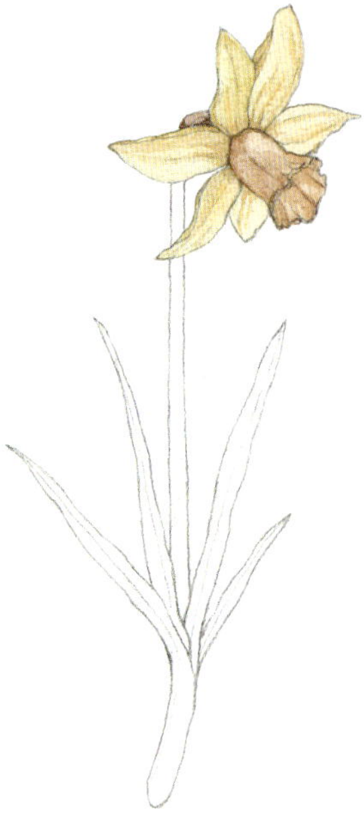

Step 5: Create Definition

Using a clean size 1 brush, mix a simple mid-toned solution of yellow ochre and water. We want this color to be a rich, sunny yellow that is not too watery. Load the bristles with the solution, and using the tip of the brush, begin at the bottom outline of each petal where it's growing from the central blossom and paint a thin glaze that softly splays outward to the tips of the petals, splitting into delicate lines of two. Each line will have a richer saturation of color at the bottom, but the lines will gradually become softer and extend downward to the tips of the petals.

Use the same sunny yellow glaze to paint the underside of each of the petals. Finally, use the tip of the brush to paint a thin layer of this deep yellow color right at the outline of the inner blossom at the left-hand side where the petals extend out and grow from. Clean the brush.

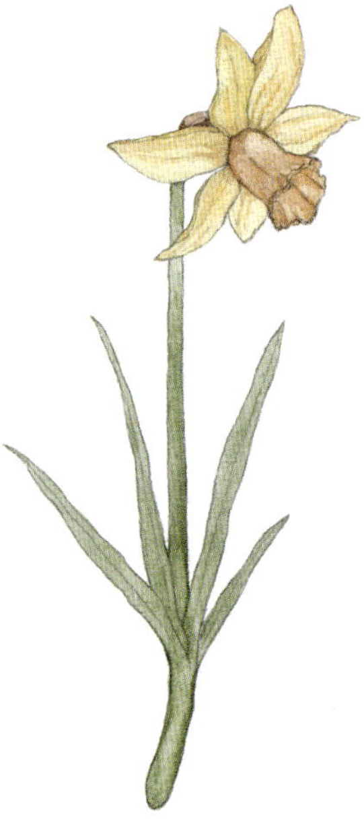

Step 6: Paint the Stem and Leaves

Using a clean size 4 brush, mix a simple mid-toned solution of Hooker's green light and water. Load the paint onto the bristles, and glaze the stem and bottom leaves with this warm, earthy green color.

While this first layer is still damp, load the bristles at the tip of the same brush with the same mid-toned solution and paint a thin layer of green on the left and right sides of the bottom of the stem to where they meet the growing leaves. Allow these layers to fully dry.

Step 7: Add Finishing Touches

Dip a clean size 1 brush into water and wiggle the bristles onto the very bottom of the stem, extending the wiggling effect slightly upward to the midway point. This agitation of the paint layer underneath will cause the pigment to lift up onto the bristles.

Next, press a dry paper towel onto this dampened section on the bottom of the stem, then lift the paper towel off. Underneath will reveal a luminous highlight. Dip the tip of the size 1 brush back into water and paint a very thin layer of water onto this lifted highlight section, then swirl the bristles into yellow ochre. Drop this yellow ochre pigment onto the thin water layer on the bottom of the stem and allow it to dry. This will create a subtle color layer that adds realistic depth and tonality to the stem. Clean the brush.

For the shadows on the stem, use a clean size 1 brush to mix a mid-toned solution of Hooker's green light with a tiny dab of sepia to create a dark, earthy green. Paint a layer of this warm green shadow from the top of the green section of the stem toward the head of the flower, extending down toward the left-hand side, down to the bottom where the leaves grow. Paint another layer of this deep, rich green at the tip of each leaf, softly extending the paint downward toward the stem, creating a gentle gradient on the leaves as they go from tip to stem.

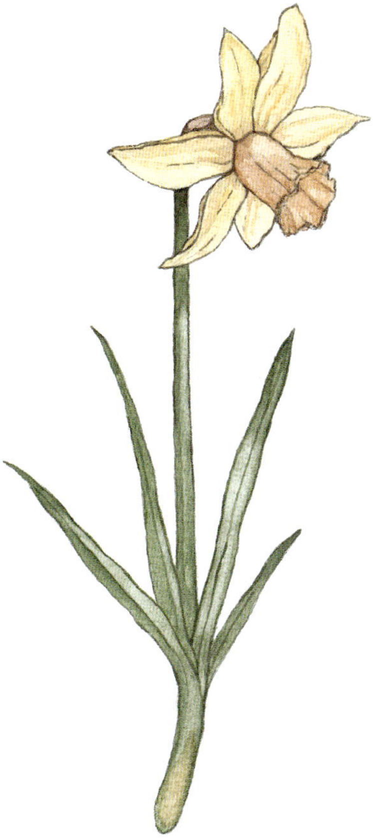

Finally, use a size 3/0 brush to mix a mid-toned solution of sepia and water. Carefully trace the outlines of the central rib of each leaf and the outlines of the stem, leaves, and petals, especially keeping the lines soft at the folds of the head of the central bloom. The daffodil is now complete. You did a great job!

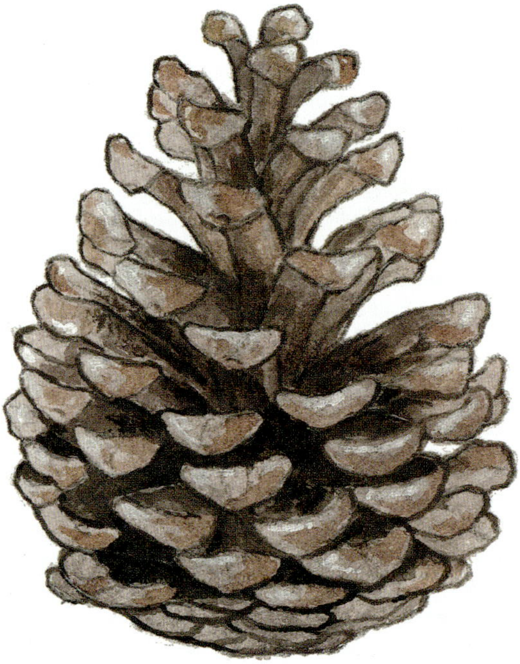

Pine Cone

Pine cones, the woody fruits of pine trees, are nature's way of packaging seeds for the next generation. One of their most remarkable features is their spiral arrangement of scales, which provide a protective covering for the seeds within. I love to collect them from the garden and dry them out indoors to use as decoration around the house throughout the year!

Materials Needed

1 sheet of cold-press 140-pound (300-gsm) aquarelle/watercolor paper

HB pencil

Brushes

- > Size 4
- > Size 1
- > Size 0
- > Size 3/0

Watercolor paints

- > Sepia
- > Vandyke brown
- > Burnt umber
- > Ivory black

Acrylic white

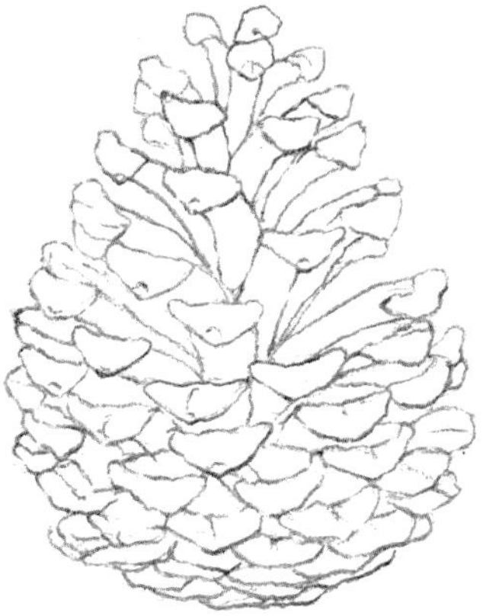

Step 1: Draw the Outline

Starting on a sheet of cold press watercolor paper, draw the pine cone's outline with a sharp HB pencil using the template provided on page 189.

Step 2: Paint the Base Layer

To prepare the color that will fill the entire base layer of the pine cone, use a size 4 brush to mix a mid-toned solution of sepia with a small swirl of Vandyke brown. We want this color to be a warm, earthy brown. Load this color onto the bristles and fill the entire shape of the pine cone from top to base. Let this paint layer dry and clean the brush.

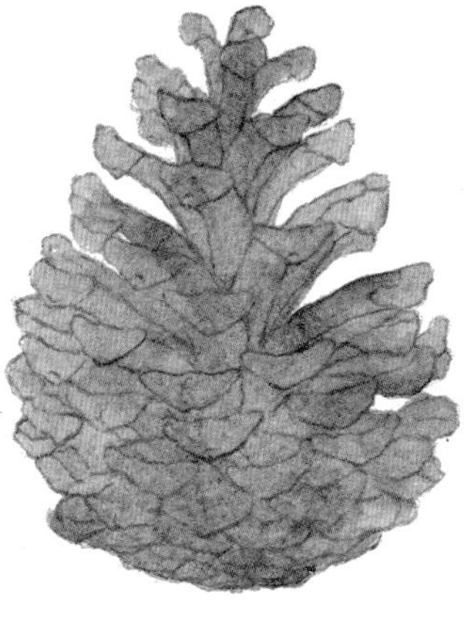

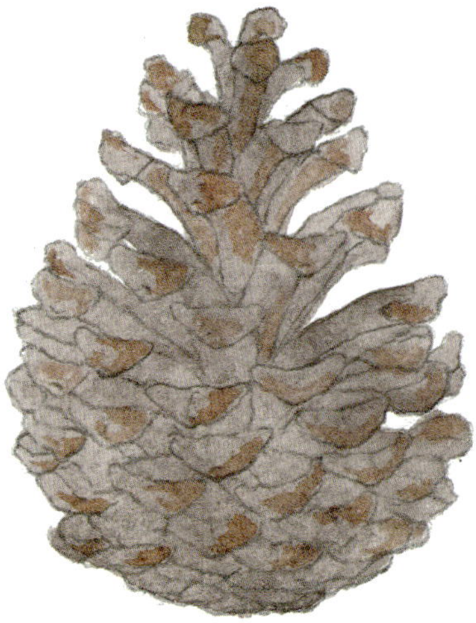

Step 3: Give the Pine Cone Scales Definition

Using a size 1 brush, mix a mid-toned solution of Vandyke brown with a swirl of burnt umber to give the color a rusty, copper brown undertone. Load this color onto the bristles and gently glaze the right-hand side of each of the scales on the pine cone. The scales will appear more compact and tightly packed together, and also more sprawling and open toward the top where woody stalks appear, so be sure to paint along the right-hand sides of any visible part of the scales. Allow these layers to dry and clean the bristles of the brush.

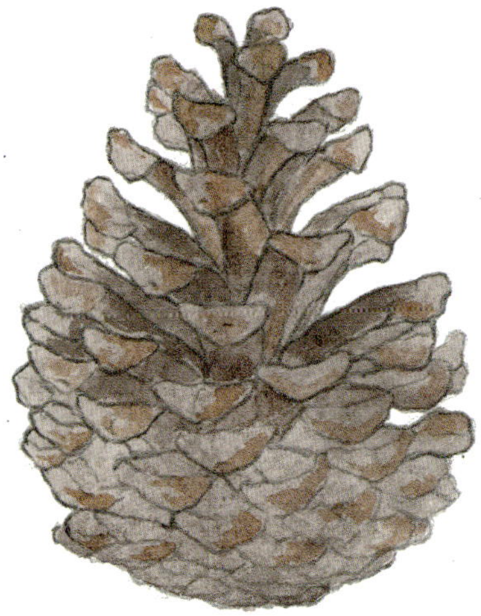

Step 4: Create Shadow

To shade the center of the pine cone, use a clean size 1 brush to mix a simple mid-toned solution of sepia and water to create a wood-shaded shadow. Begin just below the midway point of the pine cone and work upward. Glaze the brush lightly into the crevices where the inner scales tuck under one another along the inner center stalk of the pine cone. The eye will naturally read the center of a pine cone as a deeper pocket of shadow where the light cannot reach, so aim your wash into those narrow overlaps and folds.

Gently drag the dark sepia upward along the stalk and stop at the faces of the scales pointing outward. Continue these steps of beginning in the very inner crevices of the scales where they are growing, softening the paint as you pull it to the face, until you reach the scales at the very top of the pine cone. Allow these paint layers to dry and clean the brush.

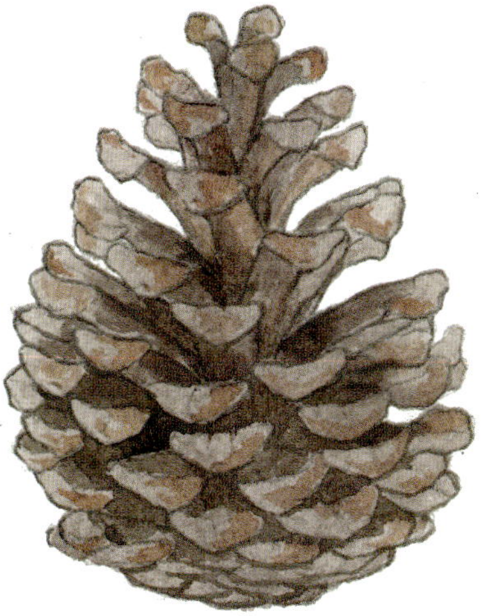

Step 5: Deepen the Shadows

To deepen the shadows on the stalks and scales of the pine cone, first use a size 0 brush to mix a mid-toned solution of sepia with a swirl of ivory black to create a deep, dark earthy brown. Load this color onto the bristles, and beginning at the top of the pine cone and working downward, glaze a layer of deep brown into the very inner crevices of the pine cone from where the scales are growing, dragging the paint up the woody stalk to just below the halfway point.

Once you reach the midsection of the pine cone, start to gradually drag the shadow layer farther up the stalk, and then, just underneath the midway point, bring the shadow layer right up to the face of the scale, as the scales are much denser and more tightly packed here and would have a lot more shadow.

Use the tip of the brush to paint around the faces of the scales at the very base of the pine cone; the shadows are much tighter here, so careful and delicate line work is needed. Allow these layers to dry and clean the brush.

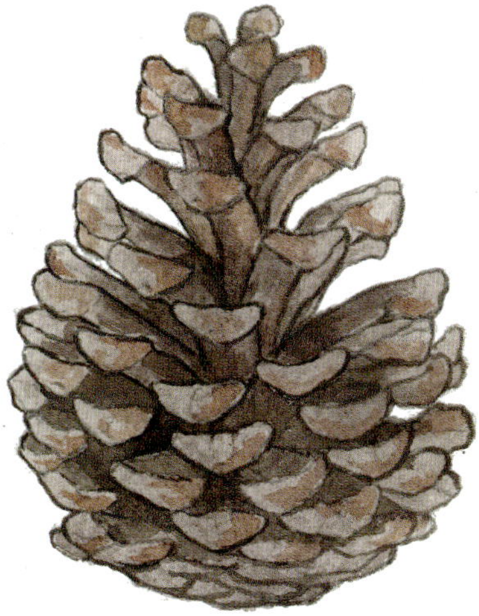

Step 6: Add Definition

Using a size 3/0 brush, mix a mid-toned solution of sepia and a swirl of ivory black to create a warm charcoal hue. Load this color into the bristles, and holding the brush at the ferrule to ensure the most control over the line work, carefully trace the outlines of the woody stalks and faces of the scales on the entire body of the pine cone. Ensure that the lines are flowing and confident. Let these paint layers dry and clean the bristles.

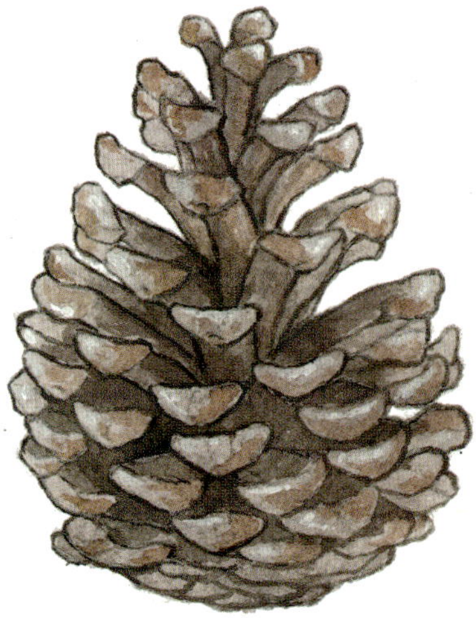

Step 7: Add Subtle Highlights

For the highlights on the front faces of the pine cone, squeeze a small pea-size blob of acrylic white onto the palette. Take a clean size 0 brush and dip the bristles to take a small amount of paint. Carefully dab and trace along the upper edges of each face at the top of the scales with a dappled line of white.

Let the paint curve the upper corners of some of the faces toward the top of the pine cone. As you work downward on the pine cone, tracing the upper edges of the faces, let these highlights begin to lessen as you reach toward the bottom where the scales are very tightly packed together. Clean the bristles and allow the acrylic layer to dry.

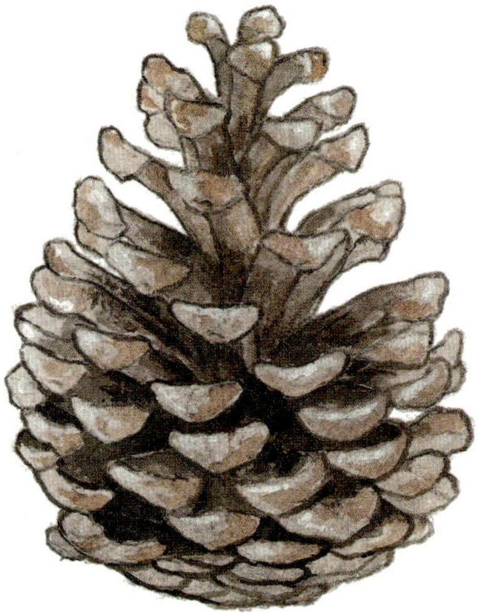

Step 8: Add Finishing Touches

Begin by using a clean size 1 brush to mix a dark-toned solution of sepia with a swirl of ivory black to make a deep brown color. Load this color onto the bristles and repeat the same method as we did in step 5 to paint the initial shadows on the pine cone.

Begin at the top of the pine cone and work downward. Glaze a layer of deep brown into the very inner crevices of the pine cone from where the scales are growing, dragging the paint up the woody stalk to just below the halfway point.

Once you reach the midsection of the pine cone, start to gradually drag the shadow layer farther up the stalk, and then, just underneath the midway point, bring the shadow layer right up to the face of the scale, as the scales are much denser and more tightly packed here and would have a lot more shadow. Use the tip of the brush to trace around the faces of the scales that are tightly stacked and dense at the very base of the pine cone. Allow these paint layers to dry. The pine cone is now complete; well done!

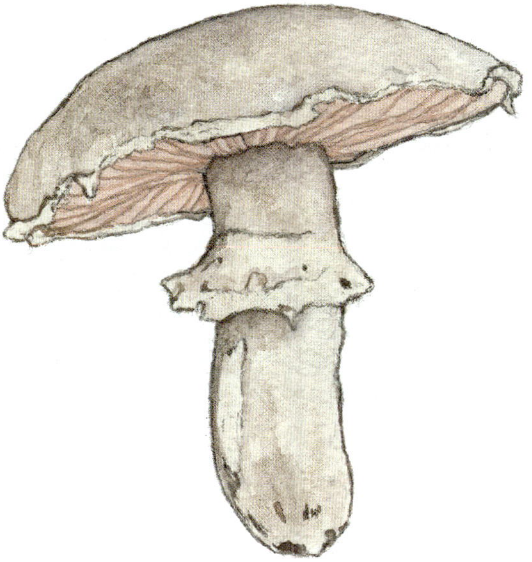

Field Mushroom

The field mushroom is always a pleasant joy to see popping up in the garden, like a fairy left it there overnight! Not often found growing in rings, these little mushrooms appear as singletons from the soil or occasionally in groups scattered randomly among the grass. Meadows and grass grazed by sheep, cattle, or horses sometimes help spread vast quantities of these fungi of summer and early autumn. Sometimes, if the weather conditions are right, it is not uncommon to be able to pick in half an hour as many mushrooms as one person can carry home when they are flourishing!

In this tutorial, we'll explore how to capture its velvety cap, the very delicate, gentle folds of its gills, and the way light and shadow play across its pale, rounded form. This will be a tutorial that can teach you an appreciation of subtle, muted earthy colors that can often go unnoticed.

Materials Needed

1 sheet of cold-press 140-pound (300-gsm) aquarelle/watercolor paper

HB pencil

Brushes

- Size 4
- Size 1
- Size 3/0

Watercolor paints

- Chinese white
- Raw umber
- Sepia
- Ivory black
- Light red

Acrylic white

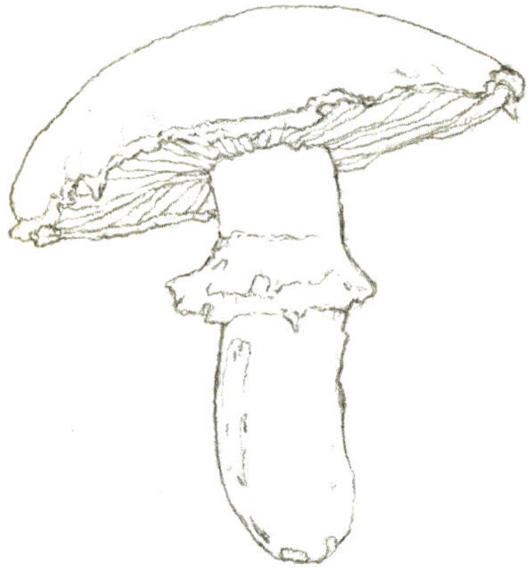

Step 1: Draw the Outline

Starting on a sheet of cold-press watercolor paper, draw the field mushroom's outline with a sharp HB pencil using the template provided on page 189. Lightly sketch in finer details to emphasize the fluffy organic outlines on the flesh of the stem and cap. The gills on the underside of the cap are delicate and flow irregularly, so take care when tracing to create a sense of realism.

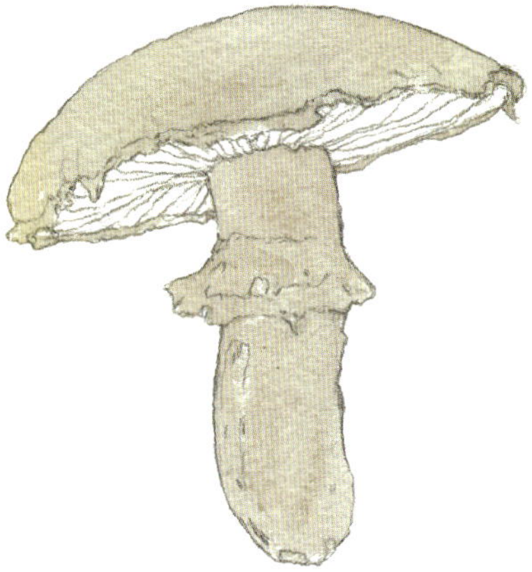

Step 2: Paint the Base Layer

Using a size 4 brush, mix a mid-toned solution of Chinese white with a tiny dab of raw umber. We want to mix a warm cream color rather than a cool-toned pure white, but because raw umber is highly pigmented, only a tiny amount is needed. Load the bristles of the brush and glaze a layer of this cream color onto the upper side of the cap of the mushroom, along the rim, and down the stem. Allow this layer to dry.

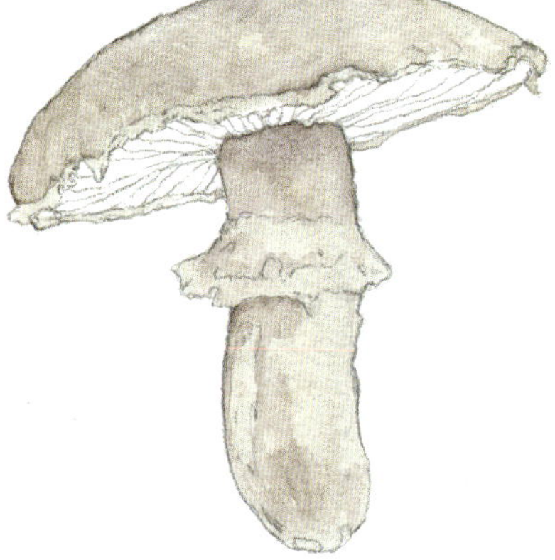

Step 3: Create Shadows

Using the same size 4 brush, clean the bristles in water and mix a light-toned solution of sepia and water. We want this color to be a light earthy brown with a diluted consistency. Load the bristles of the brush with this light brown mixture and paint a thin layer of this paint along the curved outline on the cap of the mushroom, gently pulling the paint downward with the bristles to soften any harsh outlines. Slowly pull the paint to the fluffy flesh along the bottom of the head of the mushroom.

Use the same brush and paint mixture for the stem, beginning from the top where it joins to meet the gills and gently pulling the brown paint downward along the top of the stem, then tapering to the left-hand side as it reaches the middle of the stem, and along the underside of the peeling "skirt" on the stem, down along the left-hand side toward the very bottom. There will be a small patch of flesh on the bottom-left section of the stem that will act as a highlight, so do not fill this in. Allow these layers of paint to dry.

Then, add one more layer of this light-toned earthy brown to the very top outline of the stem and underside of the stem skirt; this is where shadow would fall most naturally and be the most concentrated. Clean the brush.

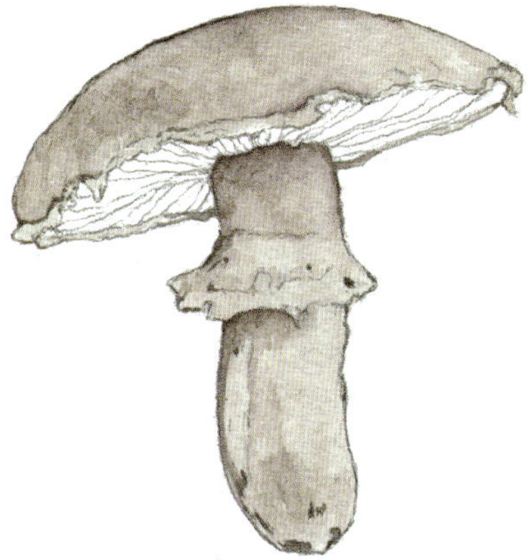

Step 4: Add Further Depth

Using a size 1 brush, mix in a swirl of sepia with a tiny dab of ivory black to the light-toned brown we previously made in step 3. This will elevate its texture and richness of color from a watery and light-toned mixture to a mid-toned solution.

(continued)

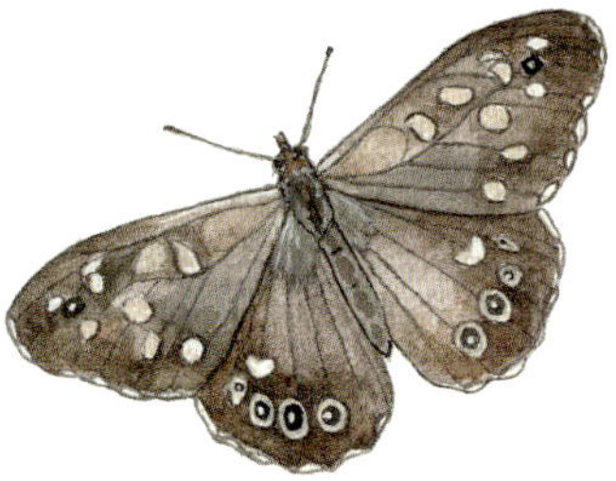

Load this color onto the brush and paint a thin glaze over the areas of the mushroom where the shadows would be more intense and rich, along the upper edge of the top section of the mushroom where it meets the gills, letting the paint flow gently down to the left-hand side of the skirt, and along the underside of the skirt, gently flowing down to the left-hand side of the bottom of the stem. Clean the brush.

Next, swap to a size 3/0 brush, and using the same mid-toned earthy brown solution, load the bristles, ensuring the brush is at a fine point. Hold the brush at the ferrule and gently trace along the outlines of the cap and stem, focusing on the little clumps of clay along the skirt and bottom of the stem, and the fluffy organic outlines of the flesh on the upper trim of the head of the mushroom. Clean the brush.

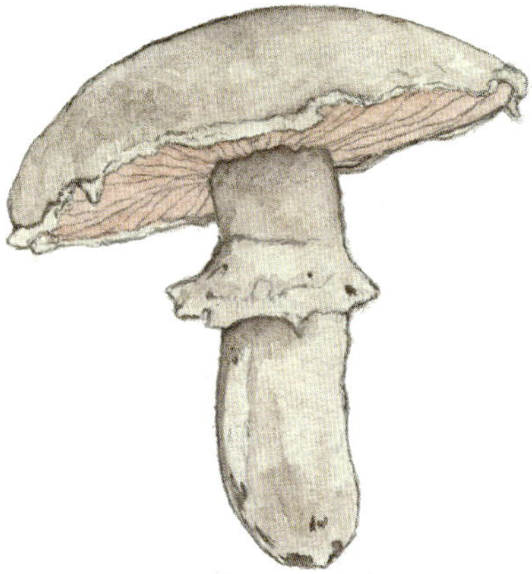

Step 5: Paint the Base Layer of the Gills

Using a clean size 4 brush, mix a light-toned solution of light red with a swirl of Chinese white to create a warm dusky pink. Coat the bristles with this solution and glaze the entire underside of the cap of the mushroom, covering all the gills. Allow this paint layer to dry.

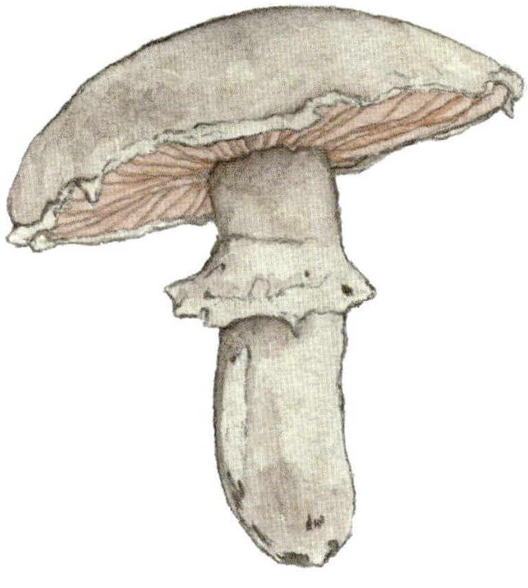

Step 6: Define the Delicate Lines

Use a clean size 3/0 brush to mix a mid-toned solution of light red and a tiny hint of sepia. We want the color to be a rich maroon.

Begin at the base of the gills near the stem, where the lines are closer together and slightly darker. With a steady hand and holding the brush at the ferrule, use the very tip of your brush to pull fine, confident strokes outward toward the edge of the cap. Allow this layer to dry and clean the brush.

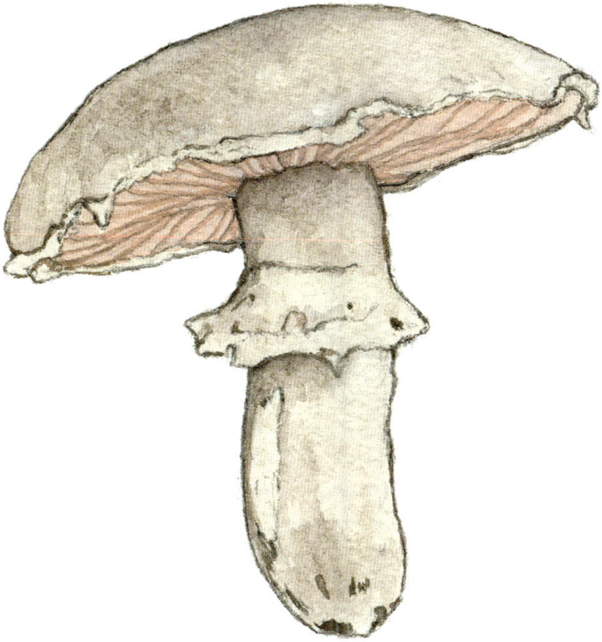

Step 7: Add Finishing Touches

Using a clean size 1 brush, mix a mid-toned solution of sepia and water, and gently glaze one more shadow layer along the upper edge on the cap of the mushroom, gently pulling the glaze down to blend the paint seamlessly into the dry layers beneath it.

Repeat this step using the same brush and solution to add another shadow layer on the top of the stem at the underside of the cap, and along the left-hand side of the stem, traveling softly toward the bottom.

Swap to a clean size 3/0 brush and dip into the same mid-toned earthy brown, and carefully outline the fluffy organic lines of flesh that run along the center of the stem skirt and the bottom of the stem.

Finally, clean the size 3/0 brush and squeeze a small dab of acrylic white onto the palette. Dip the brush into the paint and dab small organic lines along the folding flesh on the cap of the toadstool and along the right-hand side of peeling flesh on the left-hand side of the stem. Allow this acrylic white to dry. The field mushroom is now complete. You did a great job!

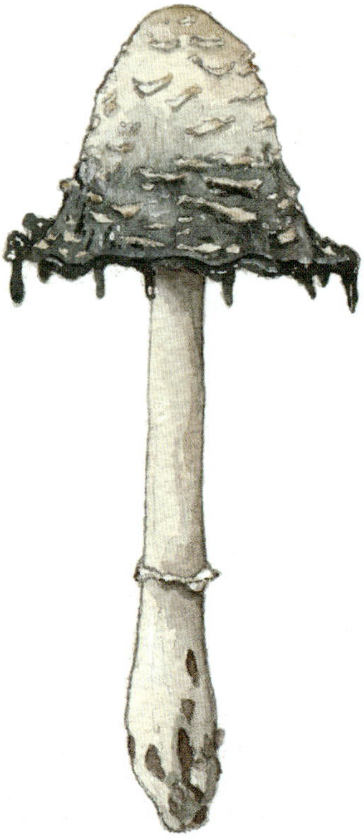

Shaggy Inkcap Toadstool

A rare and exciting find in the garden, this visually striking toadstool can be appreciated for its otherworldly beauty, earthy tones, and magical scales that make it look like it was picked straight out of a fairy tale. Otherwise known as a lawyer's wig or a shaggy mane, the inkcap inspired this tutorial, which will give you the opportunity to practice illustrative outlines using fine-tipped brushes and steady hands to create realistic line work.

Materials Needed

1 sheet of cold-press 140-pound (300-gsm) aquarelle/watercolor paper

HB pencil

Brushes

- Size 4
- Size 0
- Size 1
- Size 3/0

Watercolor paints

- Chinese white
- Raw umber
- Indigo
- Payne's gray
- Ivory black
- Burnt umber
- Sepia

Acrylic white

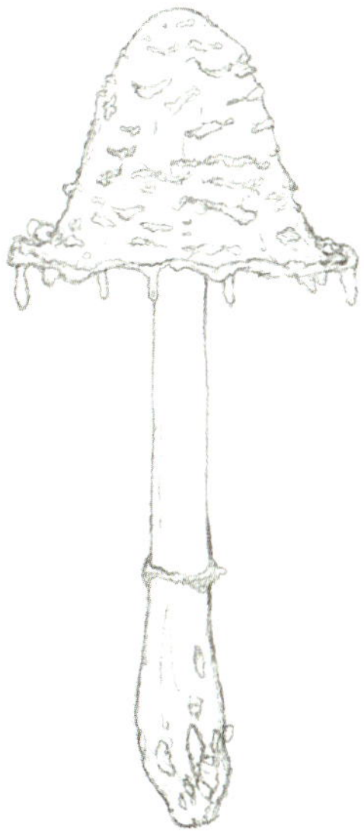

Step 1: Draw the Outline

Starting on a sheet of cold-press watercolor paper, draw the shaggy inkcap toadstool's outline with a sharp HB pencil using the template provided on page 187. Sketch in finer details, using your pencil lightly to emphasize the soft, fluffy organic outlines on the flesh of the stem.

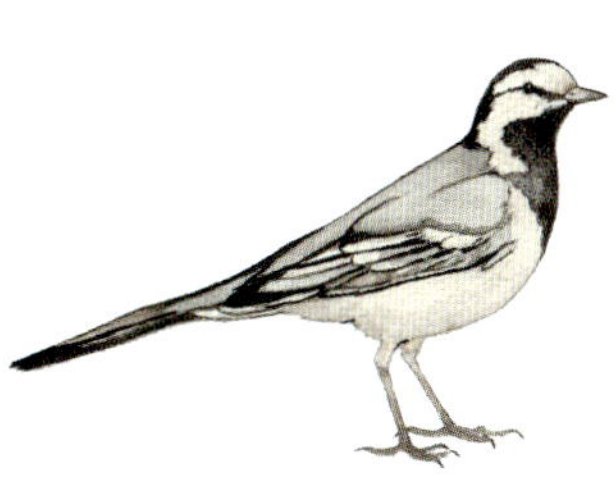

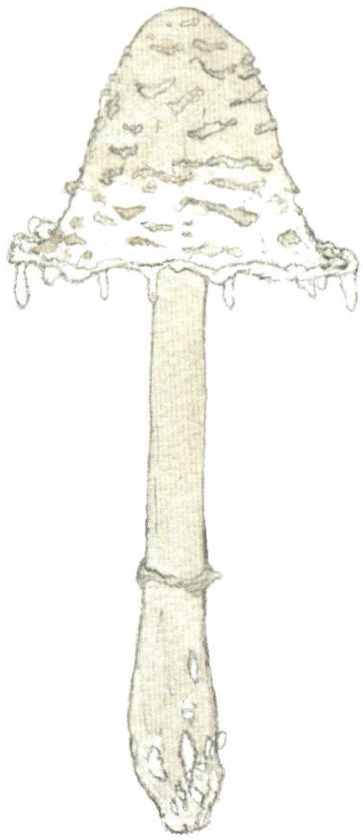

Step 2: Paint the Base Layer

Using a size 4 brush, mix a mid-toned solution of Chinese white with a tiny dash of raw umber to create a warm cream color that has a very slight caramel undertone. Load the bristles with this color and carefully paint a layer onto the upper cap of the toadstool, filling it in from the top to the midway point.

Using the same brush and color, paint a layer of this warm cream color onto the stem, being careful not to fill in the clumps of soil at the base. Clean the bristles of the brush.

Next, swap to a size 0 brush and load the bristles with the warm cream mixture. Fill in the scales on the cap of the toadstool from the top to the base of the cap. Allow this paint to dry and clean the brush.

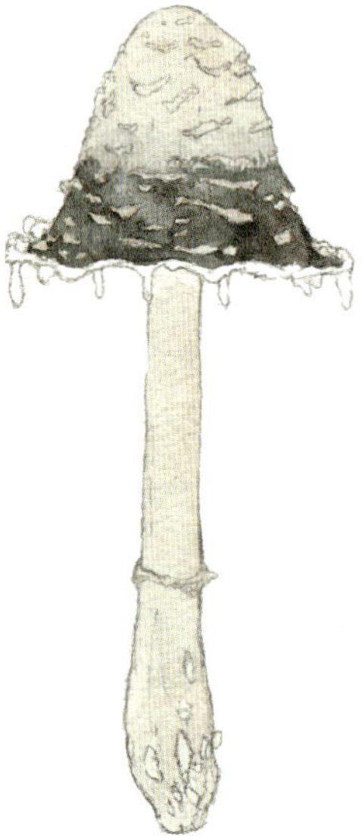

Step 3: Add Darker Colors

For the dark, inky navy color that will fill the midway to the base of the cap of the toadstool, use a size 1 brush to mix a mid-toned solution of indigo with a small swirl of Payne's gray. Load this mixture onto the bristles, and beginning at the base near the outer lip at the bottom of the toadstool, fill in the base section of the cap, gradually dragging the paint upward to the midway point, causing the color to have a subtle gradient as it blends seamlessly into the cream color when they meet at the midway point. Be cautious not to fill in the cream-colored scales on the cap of the toadstool that we painted in step 2.

While this deep navy layer is still damp, swirl the bristles back into the deep navy color and glaze a layer along the base of the cap where it meets the outer lip to deepen the saturation toward the bottom. Allow the paint to dry and clean the brush.

Step 4: Add Dimension

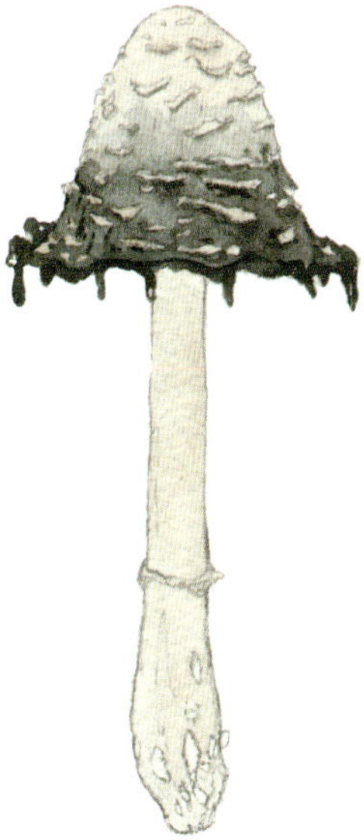

Using a clean size 0 brush, mix a mid-toned solution of indigo with a swirl of ivory black to create a deep, inky navy color. Load this color onto the bristles and carefully paint along the outer lip at the base of the cap of the toadstool. This will look like inky, dripping-liquid flesh. Clean the bristles of the brush.

Next, swap to a size 3/0 brush and load this same deep, inky color onto the bristles. Paint a layer of this dark color onto the underside of the scales on the cap, which will look like a shadow layer underneath each of the peels. Paint some small downward strokes on the left-hand side of the cap to create a sense of ragged texture. Allow these layers to dry and clean the bristles of the brush.

Step 5: Paint Shadows and Outlines

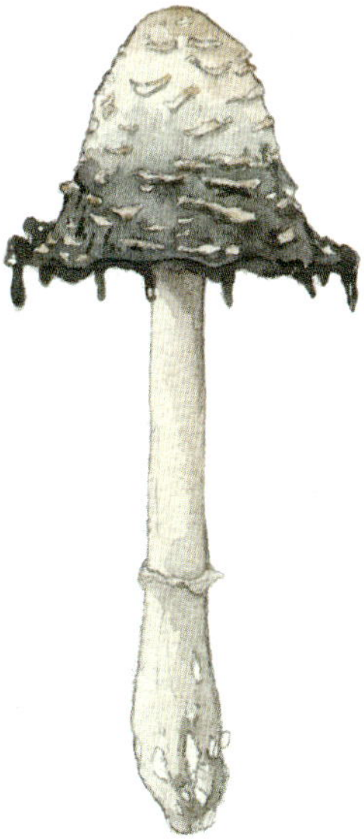

To prepare the color that will make the shadows along the stem of the inkcap, use a clean size 1 brush to mix a light-toned solution of Payne's gray and water. Load this color onto the bristles of the brush and paint a thin layer of shadow along the right-hand side of the flesh on the stem. Glaze the underside of the cap where it meets the stem and along the underside of the skirt on the midway point of the stem. For the very bottom, slightly bulbous section of the stem, paint along the curvature on the outer edge and carefully around the clumps of soil gathered at the bottom.

(continued)

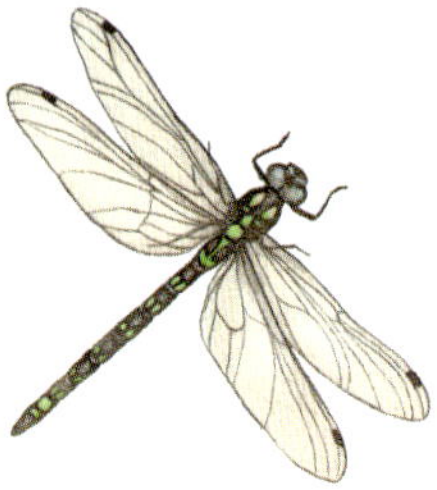

While this gray shadow layer is still damp, glaze another wash of the same color at the very top of the stem where it meets the cap for a darker shadow where the cap is, creating a canopy effect. Add another layer of gray shadow along the very bottom of the stem around the clumps of soil. Clean the bristles of the brush.

As these layers of shadow are drying, use a clean size 0 brush to mix a light-toned solution of burnt umber and water. Glaze a layer of this watery warm brown along the curvature at the very top of the toadstool cap, softening the edges down into the cream layer underneath it.

Using the very tip of the brush, paint a thin layer of warm brown along the upper outlines of each of the peeling gills on the cap, then apply the same method of using the very tip of the brush to outline the entire cap. Allow these layers to dry and clean the brush.

Step 6: Create Deeper Shadows

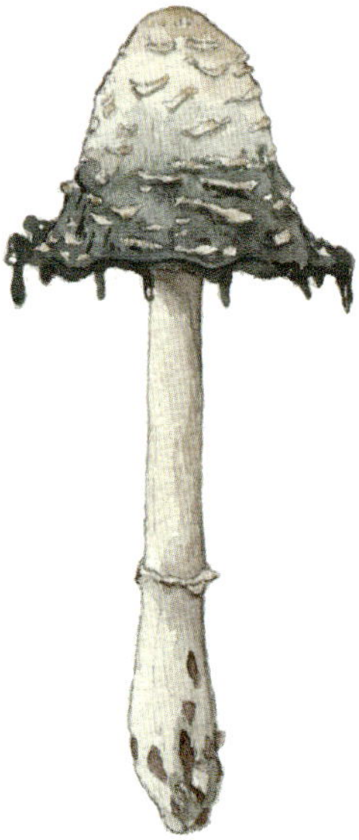

Using a clean size 0 brush, mix a light-toned solution of sepia and water to make a warm, earthy brown color. Load this mixture onto the bristles, and following along the layers of shadow we painted in step 5, glaze a layer of this along the right-hand side of the stem, along the underside of the cap, skirt, and where the stem meets the base section of flesh on the stem. Gently paint a layer of small downward dashes on the midsection of the cap on the middle to left-hand side to create a sense of subtle textured markings. Allow these layers to dry.

Next, we want to paint the soil clumps on the base of the stem. Using the same brush and warm brown mixture, swirl the brush into sepia and mix this into the watery light-toned brown to elevate its texture and saturation to a mid-toned solution. Load this color onto the bristles and carefully fill in the clump of soil at the bottom of the stem. Allow these layers to dry and clean the brush.

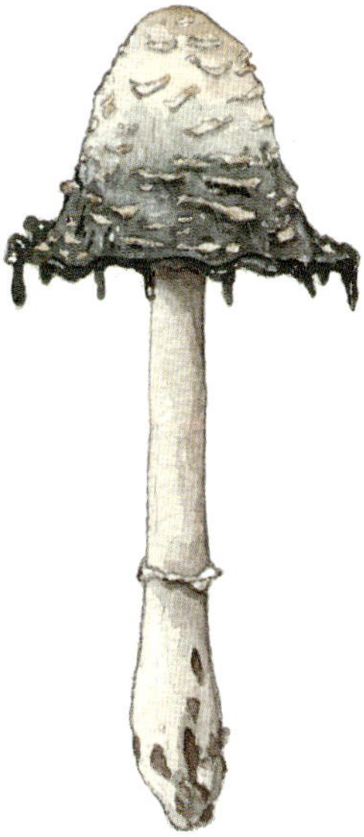

Step 7: Add Finishing Touches

Using the same mid-toned solution of sepia that we mixed in step 6, use a clean size 3/0 brush to load this color onto the bristles and carefully outline the stem, soil clumps, and the fleshy skirt that sits along the midway point of the stem. Allow these layers to dry and clean the brush.

Next, squeeze a pea-size amount of acrylic white onto your palette. Using the same size 3/0 brush, load some of this acrylic onto the bristles and paint some small downward dash brushstrokes along the midway to bottom section of the cap on the toadstool. Paint a small highlight along the outer lip toward the right-hand side to create the appearance of shine and moisture. Paint a thin layer of acrylic white along the midway skirt on the stem. The shaggy inkcap toadstool is now complete. Well done!

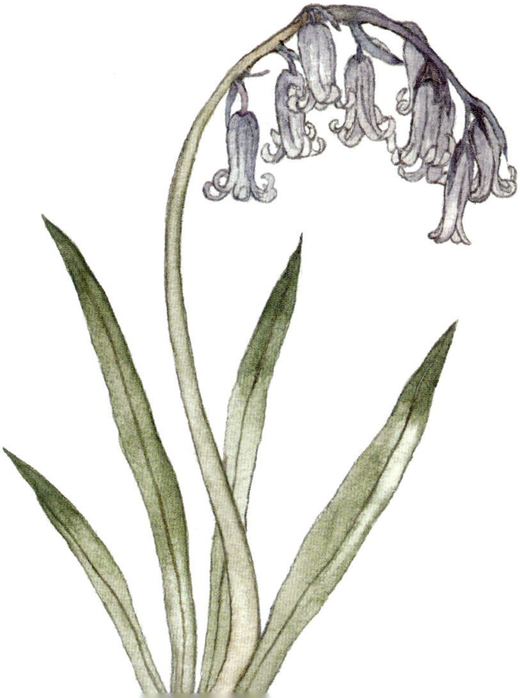

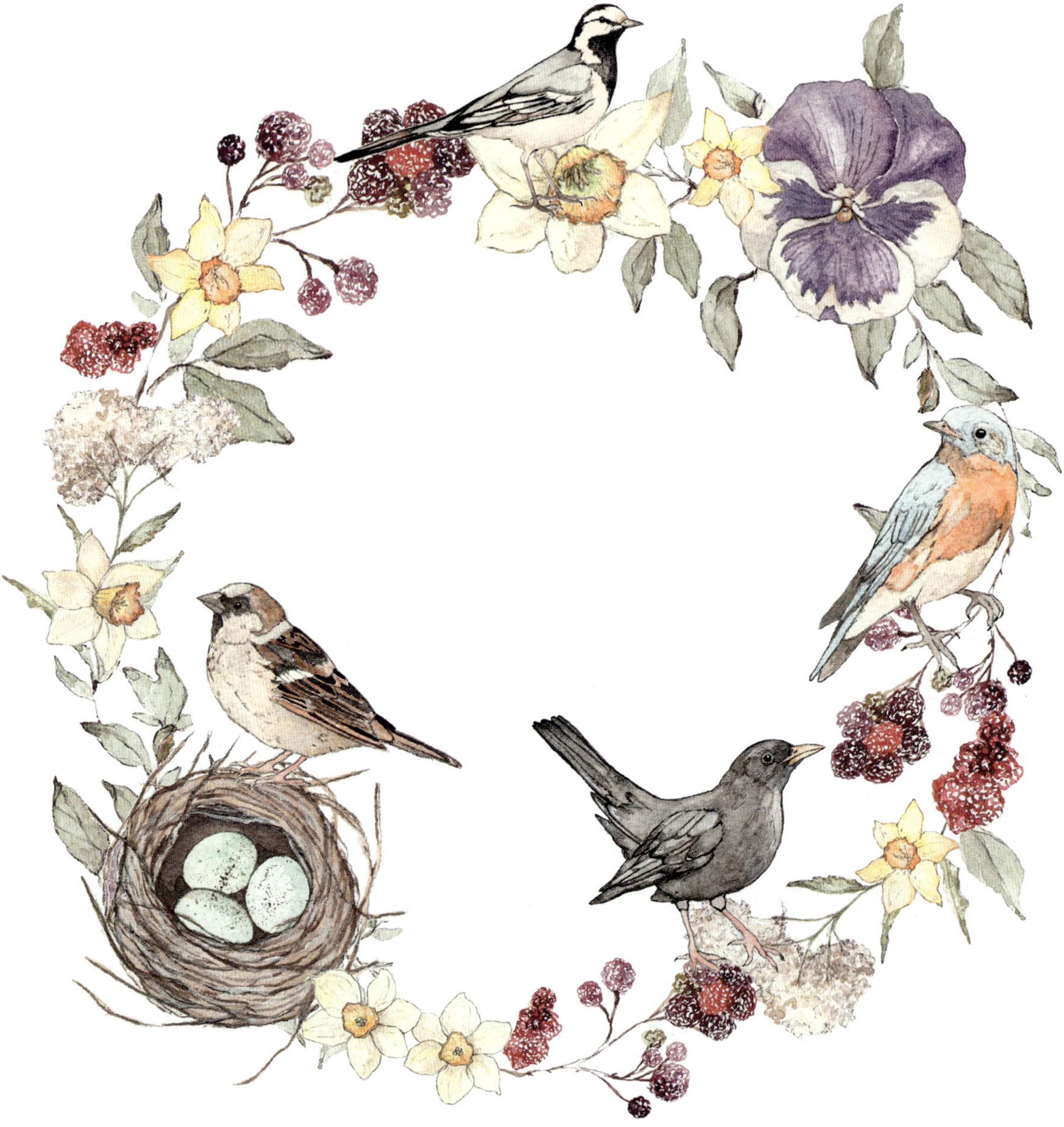

Birdsong Brushstrokes

Lift your eyes to the branches and listen to the soft chorus that gathers there. This chapter centers on birds and the colors and structures held in their feathers and beyond. From the careful construction of a nest woven with patience and purpose, you will also learn how to create the delicate texture of a tiny bird's egg. You will learn to capture the warm, familiar presence of a regular garden companion, the blackbird, and the bright, lively charm of the bluebird.

In these tutorials, you will find a steady development of your confidence with texture and detail, showing how delicate marks can create a surprisingly strong structure from materials such as interwoven twigs, grasses, and leaves, while also challenging yourself with a brighter, more vibrant palette to capture the bursts of color from a delicate wing moving through the sky or a bird sitting on a branch. So let's grab our brushes and get to work!

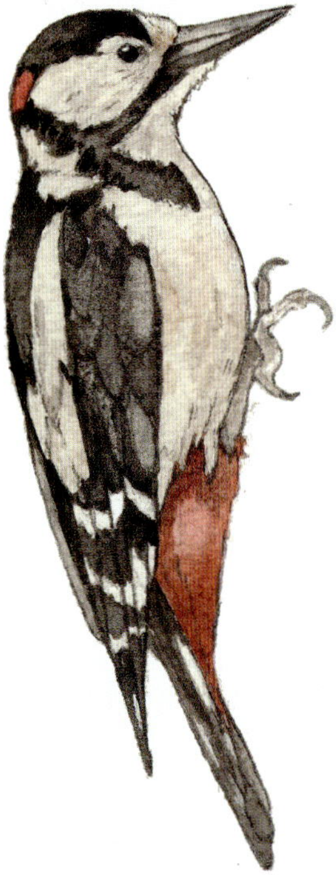

Woodpecker

Woodpeckers are certainly lively subjects to watch and paint! With bold colors and even bolder personalities that you may be able to quite literally hear from a mile away, woodpeckers are amazing birds to have in the garden. Their unique vertical foraging on trees is always entertaining to watch. Because woodpeckers eat plenty of grubs, beetles, ants, and other insects, they also provide top-notch pest control for gardeners! They make very rewarding subjects for watercolor painting; their bold patterns, crisp markings, and bright flashes of color invite you to practice clean edges, controlled layering, and confident brushstrokes.

Materials Needed

1 sheet of cold-press 140-pound (300-gsm) aquarelle/watercolor paper

HB pencil

A piece of paper towel

Brushes

- Size 4
- Size 1
- Size 0
- Size 3/0

Watercolor paints

- Chinese white
- Raw umber
- Ivory black
- Sepia
- Light red
- Lamp black

Acrylic white

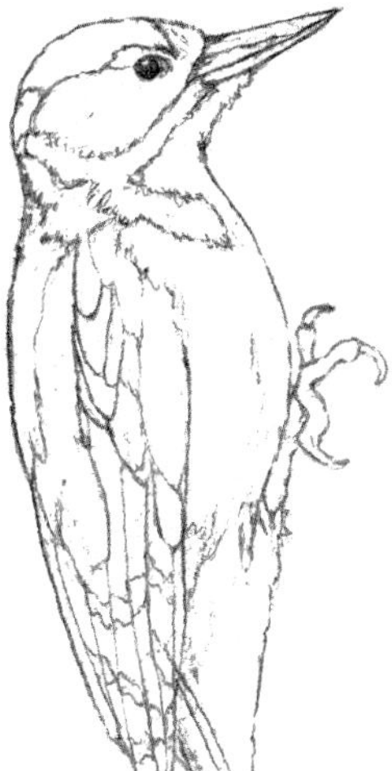

Step 1: Draw the Outline

Starting on a sheet of cold-press watercolor paper, draw the woodpecker's outline with a sharp HB pencil using the template provided on page 191. Make sure to fill in the eye, but leave a small dot on the upper center uncolored for a highlight, which will be added later. The feathers on the wings of the woodpecker are quite intricate, so do take your time in tracing each one carefully.

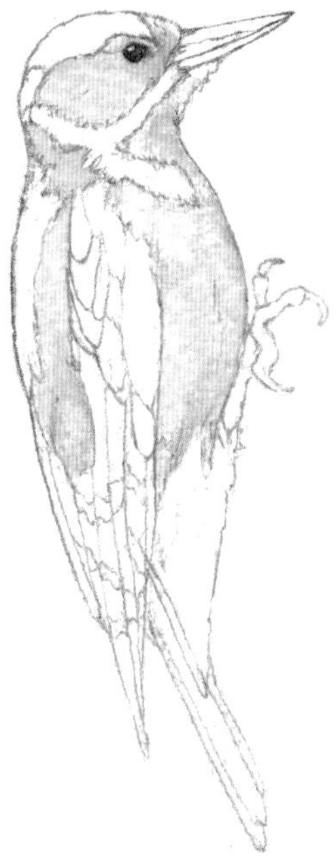

Step 2: Paint the Base Layer

To prepare the color that will fill the feathers on the face and plumage, use a size 4 brush to mix a mid-toned solution of Chinese white with a dab of raw umber to create a warm cream mixture. Load this color onto the bristles and glaze a layer of cream onto the feathers of the central section of the face, along the central segment on the left-hand side of the wing, and on the feathers flowing down the underside of the chin and neck to the front feathers on the plumage on the chest down to the lower side of the body where the feathers join to meet the bent leg. Clean the brush.

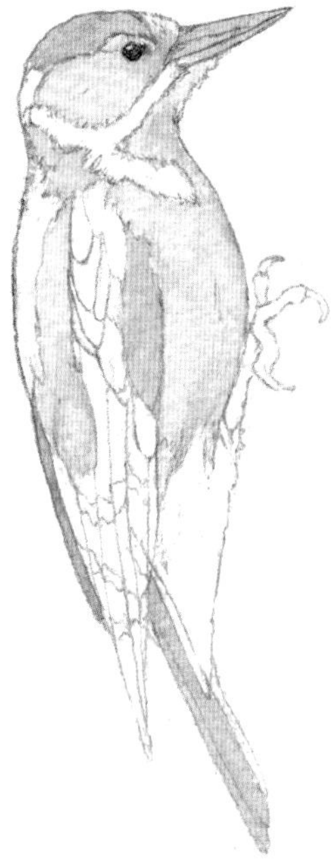

Step 3: Add Gray

Next, using a size 1 brush, mix a light-toned solution of ivory black with a tiny dab of sepia and water to create a light, earthy gray. Load this color onto the bristles and paint a layer of this wash onto the beak, the feathers that run on the top section of the head, and the feathers on the upper right-hand side of the wing.

Glaze a layer of gray on the feathers on the back of the wing at the left-hand side, and on the left and central feathers of the tail. Let these layers dry and clean the bristles of the brush.

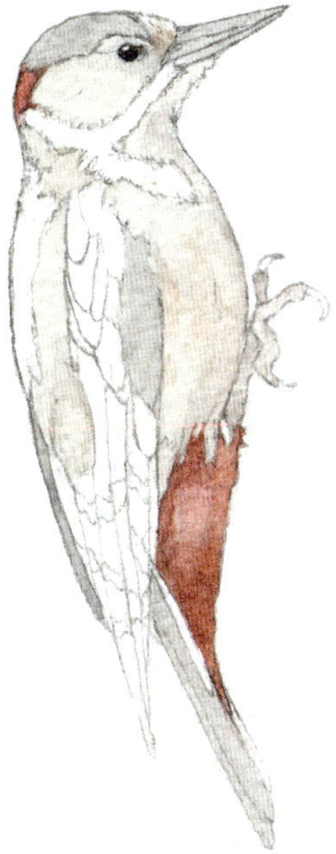

Step 4: Add Pops of Color

Using a clean size 0 brush, mix a light-toned solution of raw umber and water. We want this mixture to be quite thin and diluted. Load the pale umber mixture onto the brush and gently glaze a wash onto the feathers of the chest and a thin layer on the feathers between the eye and beak. Once these layers are dry, repeat the step on the face feathers between the eye and beak to deepen the tone slightly. Allow these layers to dry and clean the bristles.

Next, use a clean size 4 brush to mix a mid-toned solution of light red and water. Load this color onto the bristles and fill the rectangular section of feathers at the back of the head, and the feathers just below the central body and just above the tail.

Once dry, clean the size 4 brush with water, then wiggle the bristles on the center of this red-feather section. The dry pigment will begin to lift up onto the brushes and leave a damp patch underneath. Press a dry paper towel onto this damp patch and lift up, revealing a luminous highlight of lighter red underneath. Clean the brush.

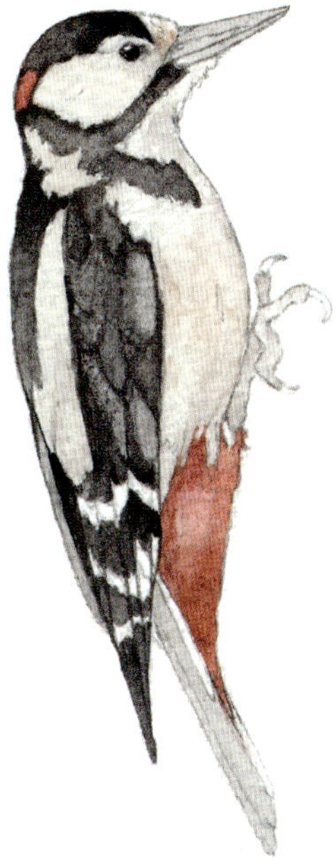

Step 5: Add Black

Using a clean size 1 brush, mix a mid-toned solution of ivory black and water to create a warm charcoal black that is not too thick or pigmented. Load this color onto the bristles and paint a layer onto the feathers that run along the top of the forehead, along the center of the face and between the neck and chest, on the feathers on the left-hand side of the back of the wing, and on the main cluster of overlapping feathers that run down along the right-hand sides and tip of the wing, but avoid the three lined patterns of feathers that are close to the end of the wing.

(continued)

While this layer of ivory black is still damp, use a clean size 0 brush to mix a mid- to dark-toned solution of lamp black and water, and paint a layer of darker-toned inky black along the right-hand side of the black forehead feathers, along the top of the black feathers at the beginning of the back of the upper wing where it meets the neck, along the upper outline of the black feathers that cross the face from the beak to the back of the head, and on the black feathers in the dense cluster of the wing toward the tip between each of the three unpainted line patterns. Allow these layers of feathers to dry.

Next, take a size 3/0 brush and swirl it into the mid- to dark-toned lamp black solution, and carefully fill in the eye, leaving unpainted the white dot highlight, which will be added in later. Clean the brushes.

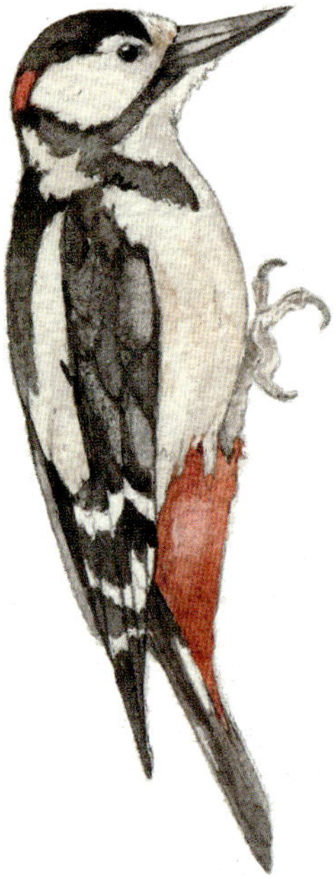

Step 6: Add Subtle Details

Using the same mid-toned solution of ivory black and water that we mixed in step 5, swirl in the clean size 3/0 brush and paint a layer to the underside and at the tip of the beak, softening the outlines to seamlessly blend the darker black into the gray layer underneath. Paint a wash of the same warm black onto the feathers of the tail, leaving a small unpainted section toward the top of the feather closest to the red feathers on the lower body.

Next, swirl the bristles into the mid- to dark-toned lamp black solution that we also mixed in step 5 and outline the nostril running down the center of the upper beak. Add some small dash brushstrokes to give texture to the black upper wing feathers where they meet the neck, and along the black feathers that run along the top of the head. Paint a layer of dark black at the corner of the beak on the left-hand side where it joins to meet the black feathers running across the center of the face. Clean the brush and allow these layers to dry.

Next, using a clean size 3/0 brush, mix a light-toned solution of sepia and water, and glaze a wash on the foot and claws of the woodpecker. Allow the layers to dry and clean the bristles.

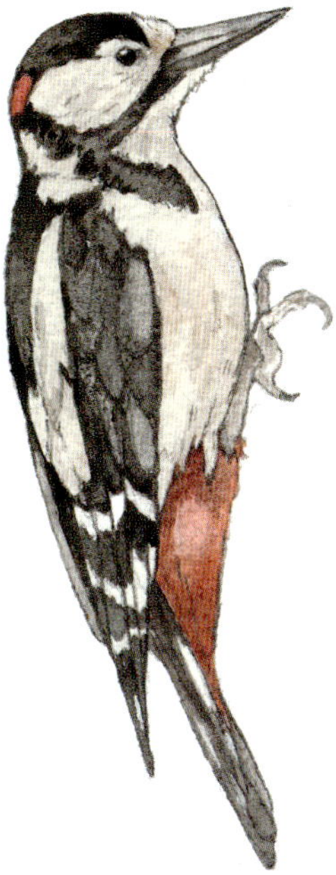

Step 7: Add Finishing Touches

Using a clean size 3/0 brush, mix a light-toned solution of ivory black and water to create a watery pale gray. Load this color onto the bristles and paint some quick and short dash-like brushstrokes that flow from the eye along the curvature of the lower face. Paint some dash brushstrokes along the curvature of the central to lower chest, and some small dash brushstrokes on the white section of feathers on the left-hand side of the upper wing.

Using the same size 3/0 brush, swirl some more ivory black into this light-toned solution to elevate its saturation to a midtone. Holding the brush at the ferrule, trace along the outlines of the feather on the face, beak, tail, individual feathers of the wing, and claws on the end of the foot. Clean the bristles.

Finally, squeeze a pea-size amount of acrylic white onto your palette. Dip the clean size 3/0 brush into this and add a tiny dot of white in the unpainted center of the eye, which creates character and luminosity. Paint the white line patterns that are on the lower tip of the wing, and the small white feather on the tail that meets the red feathers on the lower body. The woodpecker is now complete. Well done!

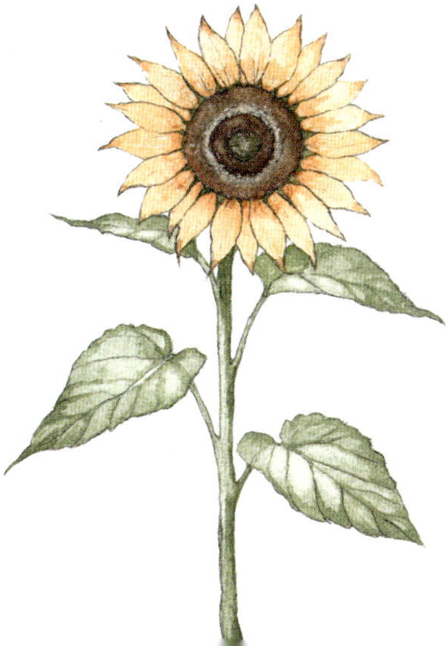

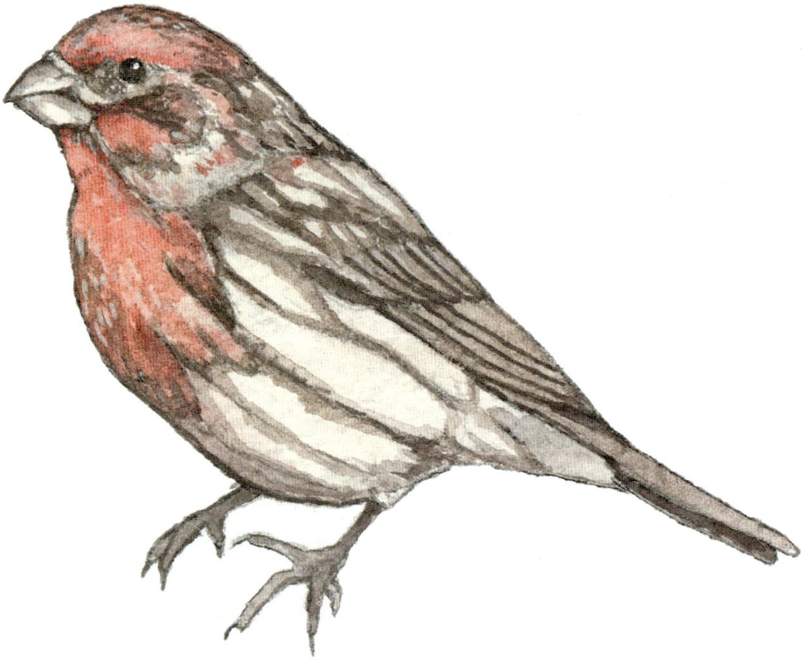

House Finch

In this tutorial, we'll paint the cheerful little house finch. For a garden bird, it has an almost exotic color palette of feathers that consists of lively and vibrant reds paired with warm browns. As it has quite fluffy, dense feathers, it's a wonderful subject for exploring texture and learning techniques on how to suggest a soft surface without having to overwork the painting.

Materials Needed

1 sheet of cold-press 140-pound (300-gsm) aquarelle/watercolor paper

HB pencil

Brushes

- Size 4
- Size 1
- Size 3/0

Watercolor paints

- Chinese white
- Raw umber
- Light red
- Indian red
- Vandyke brown
- Sepia
- Ivory black

Acrylic white

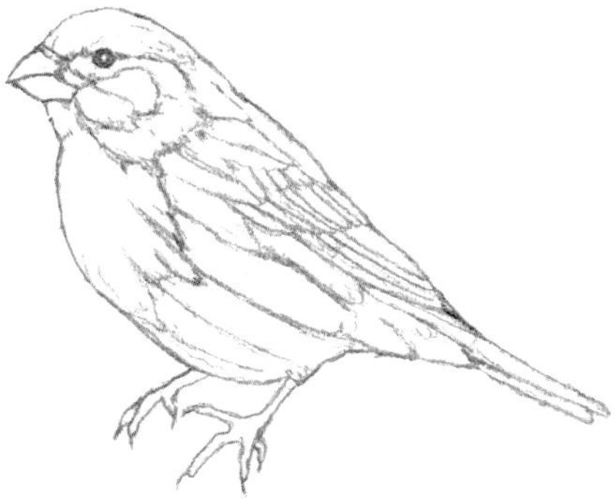

Step 1: Draw the Outline

Starting on a sheet of cold-press watercolor paper, draw the house finch's outline with a sharp HB pencil using the template provided on page 191. Make sure to fill in the eye, but leave a small dot on the upper center uncolored for a highlight, which will be added later. The feathers on the wings of the house finch are quite intricate, so do take your time in tracing each one carefully.

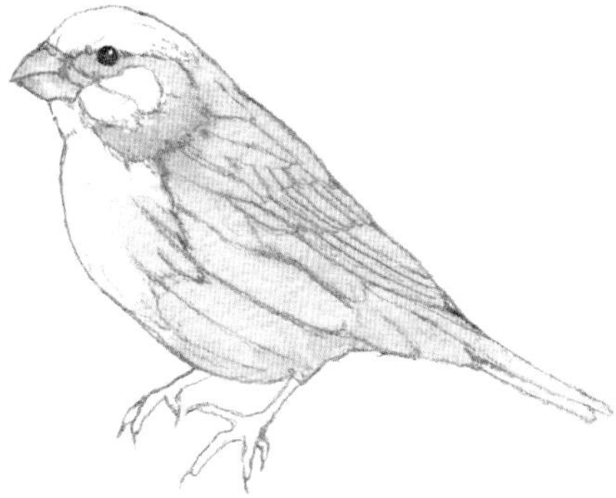

Step 2: Paint the Base Layer

Using a size 4 brush, mix a mid-toned solution of Chinese white with a swirl of raw umber to create a warm cream color. Load this solution onto the bristles and glaze the beak and the feathers along the underside of the eye, down along the cheek, the lower plumage along the belly, and the wing and upper feathers of the tail. Allow this paint layer to dry.

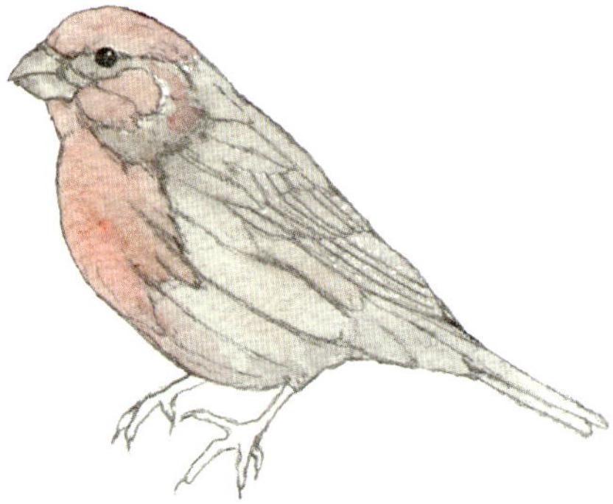

Step 3: Add a Pop of Color

Clean the bristles of the size 4 brush with water, then use it to mix a light-toned solution of light red and water. Load the paint onto the bristles and paint a thin layer of this light reddish pink on the feathers on the top section of the head, upper cheek, lower section of the cheek on the upper right-hand side, section of feathers below the beak at the front of the face, lowering along the neck, and filling in the front of the plumage.

Extend a thin layer of paint to the lower underside of the belly, just past the left leg. Allow this paint layer to dry.

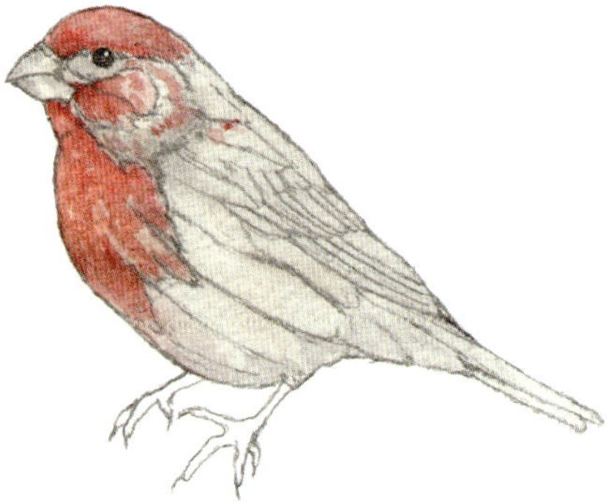

Step 4: Create Depth

Using a size 1 brush, mix a mid-toned solution of light red with a small swirl of Indian red to create a deeper maroon-toned hue. Load this color onto the bristles, and using short dabbing brushstrokes to emulate the growth pattern and shape of small, fluffy feathers on the face and the plumage of the finch, fill in the sections of the body that we coated with a layer of light red solution in step 3: the feathers on the upper head, cheek, and neck, and the front plumage along the chest.

As you follow the natural feather growth pattern on the finch, make sure to create more dense, tightly spaced strokes where the feathers meet the beak, in the inner corner of the cheek, and on the underside of the plumage toward the underside of the belly, then as the feathers splay and grow outward, keep the brushstrokes looser and slightly more spaced apart. This will keep areas of light red visible underneath the deeper red tones, giving the feathers a sense of shadow, depth, and fullness.

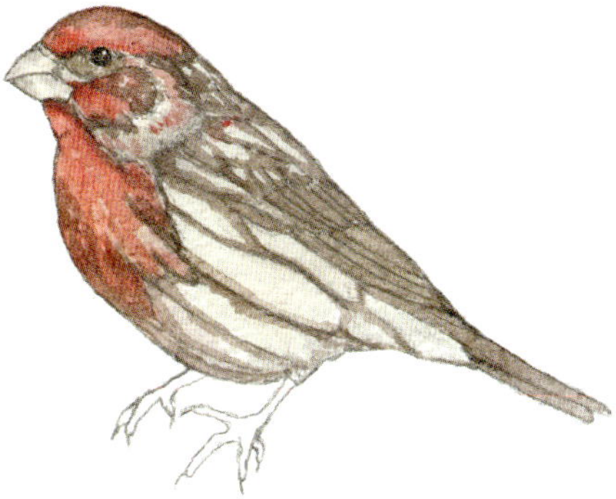

Step 5: Define the Feathers

Clean the bristles of the size 1 brush, then use it to mix a mid-toned solution of Vandyke brown and water. Load the solution onto the bristles, and ensuring that the tip of the brush is at a sharp point, trace the inner outline of each of the feathers on the finch's wing and lower belly. Fill in the entire middle lower section of the wing toward the tip with Vandyke brown to create a feeling of layering of feathers and density.

Paint in the tail feathers with a layer of Vandyke brown, then fill in the section of feathers that surround the eye. Paint a thin layer of short dabbing brushstrokes on the upper-right section and outline of the cheek. Use the same short, spaced brushstrokes to create brown feathers on the lower plumage and upper section of the neck where the feathers meet the beak.

Paint a thin layer of short brushstrokes along the top of the head that gently move downward to trace along the outline of the spine. Finally, fill in a section of short brushstrokes to create a section of brown feathers at the back of the head on the right-hand side where the right-hand side of the neck meets the beginning of the wing feathers.

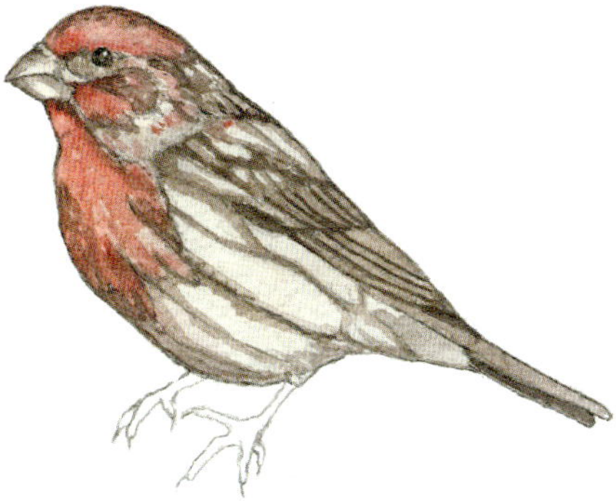

Step 6: Add Shadow and Dimension

Using a size 3/0 brush, mix a mid-toned solution of sepia and water. This color will be used to add shadow and dimension of the sections of brown feathers that we created in step 5. Load the bristles with this deep earthy brown and trace along the outline of the feathers on the upper wing, and fill in the feather on the underside of the tail.

(continued)

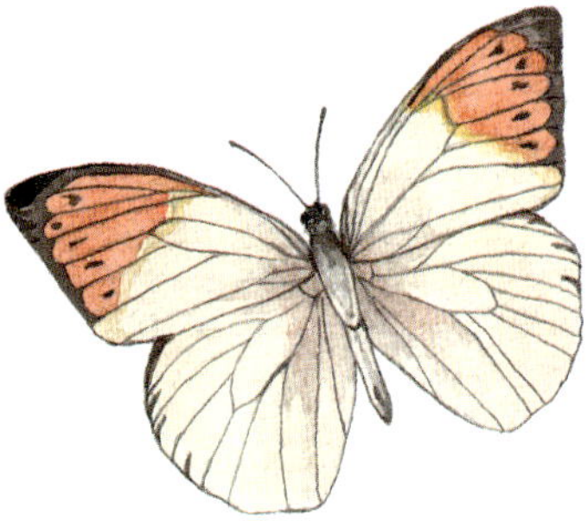

Use the same short brushstroke technique to create little feathers along the upper right-hand side of the back of the head, where the neck meets the top of the wing. Paint short brushstrokes along the curve of the top of the head and the flowing feathers growing from the cheek on the upper right-hand side. We still want to be able to see the Vandyke brown feather layers underneath, so make sure that these sepia feathers are loose, short, and spaced out and not densely packed.

Paint a thin layer of short brushstrokes along the curve of the plumage on the chest. Paint a thin layer of sepia on the outer edges of the beak to create a subtle shadow. Then use the very tip of the brush to trace the outline of both sections of the beak.

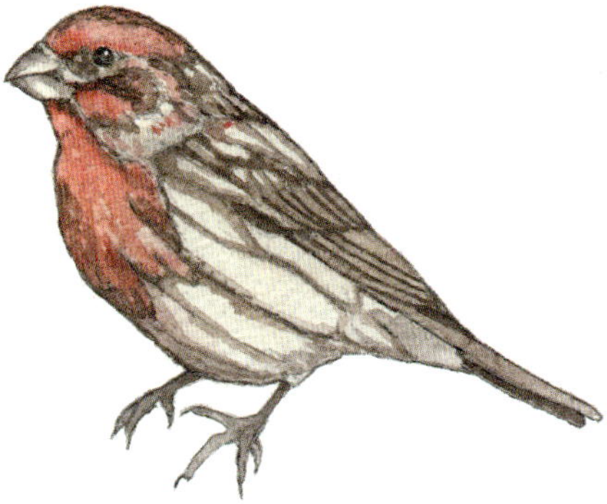

Step 7: Fill In the Feet and Face

Using the same size 3/0 brush and mid-toned solution of sepia and water that we mixed in step 6, we want to deepen this earthy brown to add some extra small details along the feathers and feet and give the finch more realism. Swirl in a tiny dab of ivory black into the mid-toned sepia mixture to give the earthy brown a slightly richer tone.

Load the bristles with this deep earthy mixture, and using the tip of the brush, fill in a tiny section on the right-hand side of the beak where the upper and lower sections meet. Then, fill in tiny, short brushstrokes of deep brown on the feathers around the eye, the right-hand side of the cheek, the curve at the top of the head, and the back of the underside of the tail where the cream gently transitions to the brown feathers at the tip.

Use the tip of the brush to softly outline where the red plumage feathers meet the cream and where the wing feathers meet the feathers of the neck. Swirl back into this deep brown color and gently glaze the feet and claws. Allow this paint layer to dry and clean the brush.

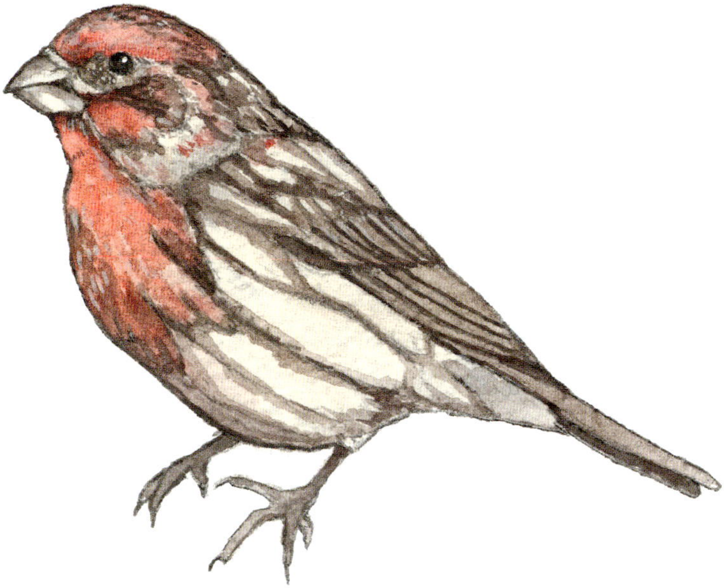

Step 8: Add Finishing Touches

For the eye, use a clean size 3/0 brush to mix a simple dark-toned solution of ivory black and water. Load the paint onto the bristles and fill in the eye, avoiding the dot for highlight, and paint the sharp claws at the tips of the feet. Allow the paint to dry and clean the bristles of the brush again.

Squeeze a pea-size amount of acrylic white onto your palette. Dip the clean size 3/0 brush into this and add a tiny dot of white in the center of the eye, which creates character and luminosity. We will also use this acrylic white to create subtle highlights on the feathers of the bird.

Using the same short brushstroke method that we used before in the tutorial, print tiny, widely spaced feathers that follow the natural growth pattern on the finch along the curve of the top of the head, at the edges of the cheek feathers, and flowing downward along the front red plumage of the finch and along the edge of the red feathers where it transitions into cream feathers of the body. Trace a small line of white on the two sections of the beak, above the central outline where they join. The house finch is now finished! Well done, you did a great job!

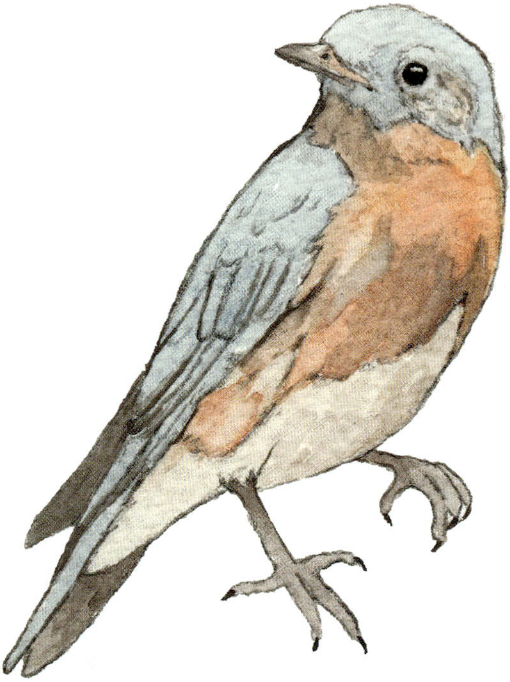

Bluebird

There's something uplifting about the sight of a bluebird, almost like a piece of sky that decided to take flight, or decided to take a rest and perch in the branch of a tree. Though they're not as common here in Ireland as some other birds, there is something incredibly magical about the shifting colors on their wings, from blues to iridescent oranges.

In this tutorial, we will focus on the play of tonal dilution and saturation with color that will give the bluebird the distinctive glow to its plumage. This project will be a delicate balance between vibrancy and subtlety.

Materials Needed

1 sheet of cold-press 140-pound (300-gsm) aquarelle/watercolor paper

HB pencil

Brushes

- Size 4
- Size 1
- Size 3/0

Watercolor paints

- Chinese white
- Raw umber
- Ivory black
- Prussian blue
- Burnt sienna
- Sepia

Acrylic white

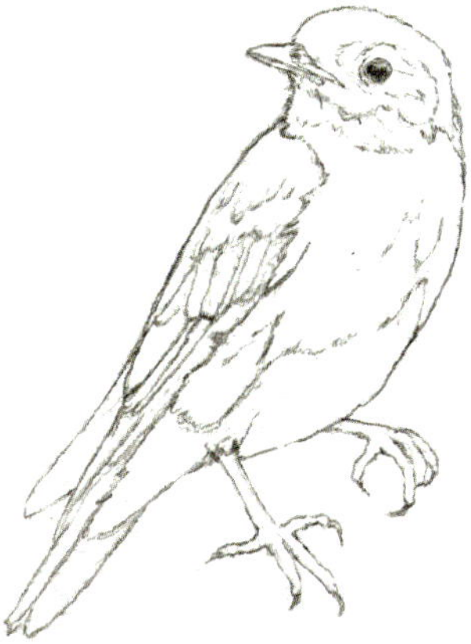

Step 1: Draw the Outline

Starting on a sheet of cold-press watercolor paper, draw the bluebird's outline with a sharp HB pencil using the template provided on page 189. Make sure to fill in the eye, but leave a small dot on the upper center uncolored for a highlight, which will be added later.

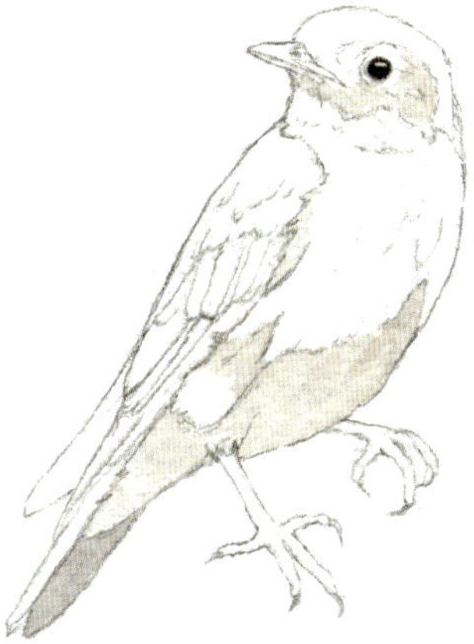

Step 2: Paint the Base Layer

For the cream color that will fill the lower belly and face, use a size 4 brush to mix a mid-toned solution of Chinese white with a small dab of raw umber. We want this color to be a warm-toned cream rather than a cool-toned pure white.

Load this mixture onto the bristles and glaze the feathers of the middle to lower belly, following the plumage down to the back feathers where they meet the beginning of the base of the tail. Fill in the feathers on the lower face underneath the beak and eye with this same cream color.

(continued)

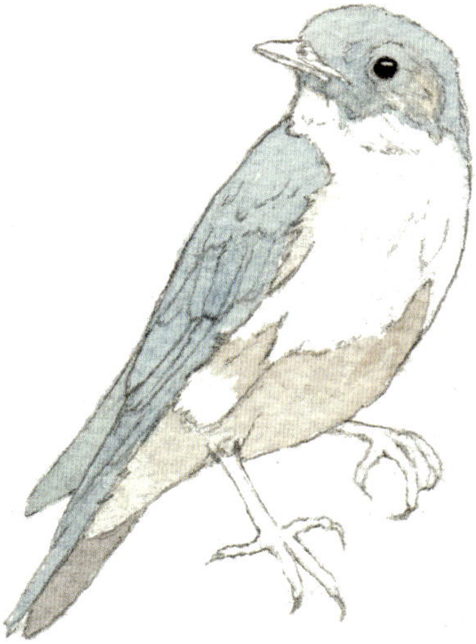

While this layer of paint is drying, switch to a size 1 brush and mix a light-toned solution of ivory black and water. Fill in the feather at the very underside of the tail, from the tip to where it meets the body. Clean the brushes.

Step 3: Paint the Blue Feathers

Using a clean size 4 brush, mix a light- to mid-toned solution of Prussian blue and water. Load the delicate cool-toned blue onto your bristles and glaze over the feathers on the head of the bluebird, gently painting around the feathers that sit under the right side of the eye. Glaze the wing feathers, following down to the tail, and the back tail feather to the left of the wing. Allow this layer of blue to dry.

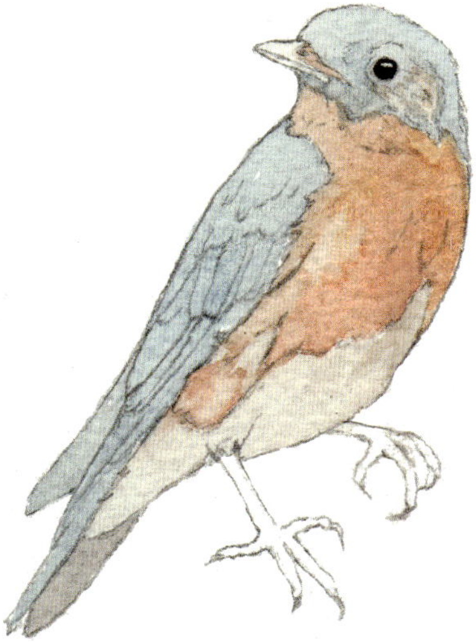

Step 4: Add Color

Using the same size 4 brush in step 3, clean the bristles and mix a light-toned solution of burnt sienna and water. Load the bristles with this light orange solution and gently paint in the feathers on the entire midsection on the body of the bluebird, following down on the left-hand side close to the left foot, avoiding a small patch in this section, which will be left cream toward the lower left-hand side. Switch to a size 3/0 brush and fill the bristles with the same light-toned orange, and carefully fill in the upper beak to the right of the nostril.

Finally, paint some small feathers of orange on the cream section of the face on the undersection of the eye, creating some tonal depth. While these first orange layers are still damp, dip the size 4 brush back into the orange solution and paint another layer of orange on the plumage of the bluebird, gently letting the paint travel across the chest to the left. Add another layer of orange at the section of orange feathers near the left foot. Allow these sections to dry fully and clean the brushes.

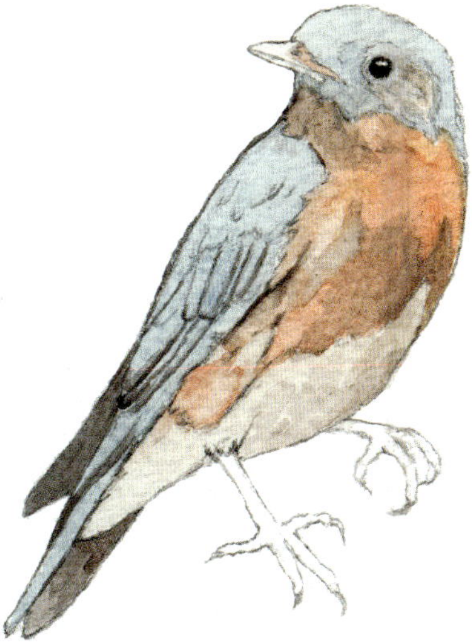

Step 5: Create Shadow and Depth

For the color that will be used to create the shadows on the feathers, use a clean size 1 brush to mix a light-toned solution of sepia with a small dab of ivory black. This color should be a watery, dark earthy brown rather than a light, inky black, so make sure that you do not add too much black. Load the bristles with this solution and glaze a layer of light brown onto the feathers on the neck of the bluebird, following downward to where they meet the top of the wing. Fill in the feathers on the mid to lower section of the orange plumage, following to the left where the midsection feathers meet the blue wing.

Gently paint a layer of light brown onto the lower right-hand side of the cream plumage, following downward to meet the feathers on the right-hand side of the left leg. Switch to a clean size 3/0 brush, dip into this same light-toned brown, and gently paint some small strokes on the feathers that surround the eye to the right-hand side.

For the shadows on the wing feathers, we want to deepen this light-toned solution by using the same size 1 brush and adding in a swirl of sepia and a tiny dab of ivory black to elevate it to a mid-toned solution that has slightly more pigment and a deeper tone. Use the tip of the bristles to paint the outlines of the wings, focusing a thicker line along the tips. Finally, paint a layer of this mid-toned brown onto the back wing at the leftmost part of the body, and a subtle shadow at the top of the underside of the tail where it meets the body. Clean the brushes.

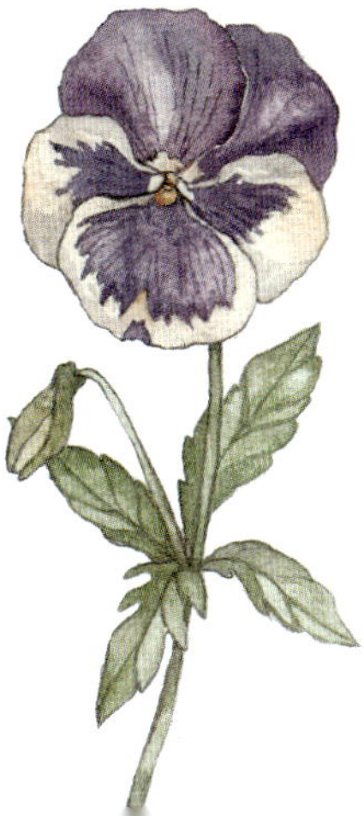

Step 6: Add Finishing Details

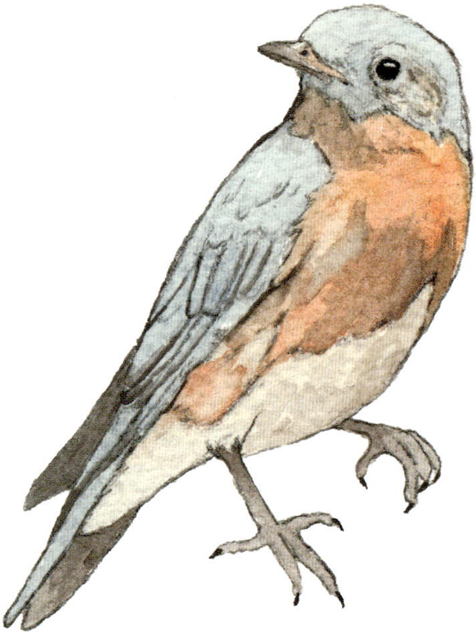

To create definition on the fine details of the bluebird, use a clean size 3/0 brush and dip into the same mid-toned earthy brown mixture that we used in step 5. Glaze a thin layer of this mixture at the tip of the beak, gently moving the paint to the right toward the nostril to soften the edges, creating a natural gradient from dark earthy brown at the tip to orange toward where the beak meets the feathers. Use the tip of the size 3/0 brush, holding it at the ferrule to have the most control over the bristles, to create a delicate outline of the bluebird and various outlines on the body that separate the colored feathers: from blue at the head, transitioning to orange in the midsection, to cream at the bottom to the underside of the body.

Use this same method to gently outline each of the feathers on the wing. Fill in tiny strokes for the feathers that surround the eye and travel down to the right-hand side.

For the claws of the bluebird, switch to a clean size 1 brush and use it to add a few droplets of water to dilute the mid-toned earthy brown solution to a light-toned solution. Load the bristles with this solution and glaze both of the feet of the bluebird. While this layer is still drying, swirl the bristles of the brush into pure sepia and drop this pigment into the very tops of the feet where they meet the feathers of the body. Allow both layers to dry fully. This will create a subtle and soft gradient shadow on the legs of the bluebird as the color transitions from dark to light toward the tips of the claws.

Finally, swap back to the size 3/0 brush and clean the bristles. Then mix a simple dark-toned solution of ivory black and water. Load the paint onto the bristles and fill in the eye, leaving the dot in the center uncolored for a highlight, and fill in the sharp claws at the tip of the feet. Allow the paint to dry and clean the bristles of the brush again.

Squeeze a pea-size amount of acrylic white onto your palette. Dip the clean size 3/0 brush into this and add a tiny dot of white in the center of the eye, which creates character and luminosity. The bluebird is now complete. Good job!

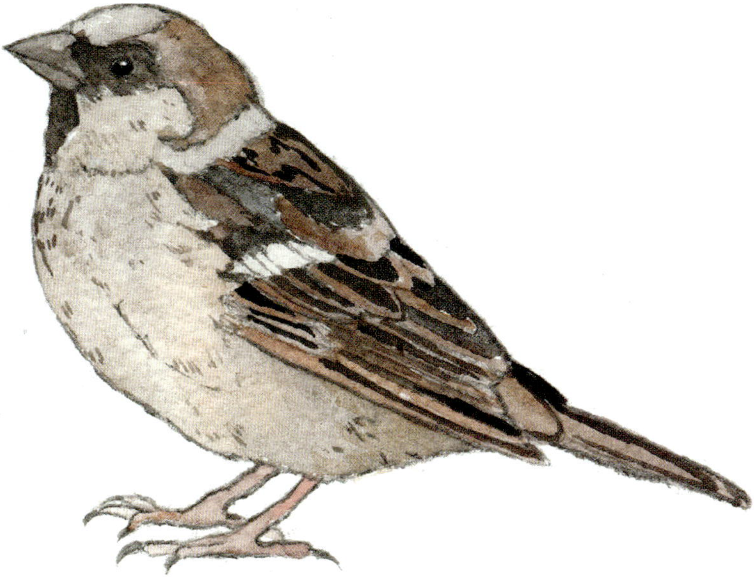

House Sparrow

Though they're common garden birds, house sparrows are always a joy to hear singing an active symphony of noisy chirping! They can make for very entertaining groups to watch at a garden bird feeder. If you provide seeds, grain, and scraps, large groups can swarm and flutter in a mass of brown-feathered chaos! They are year-round garden companions, so no matter the season, you will always see their friendly faces hopping along the grass or chirping away in the hedgerow.

Materials Needed

1 sheet of cold-press 140-pound (300-gsm) aquarelle/watercolor paper

HB pencil

Brushes

- > Size 4
- > Size 1
- > Size 3/0
- > Size 0

Watercolor paints

- > Chinese white
- > Raw umber
- > Sepia
- > Vandyke brown
- > Ivory black
- > Burnt umber
- > Indian red

Acrylic white

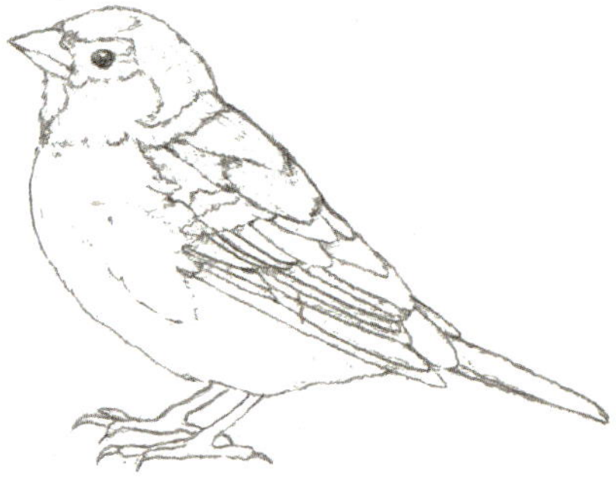

Step 1: Draw the Outline

Starting on a sheet of cold-press watercolor paper, draw the house sparrow's outline with a sharp HB pencil using the template provided on page 193. Make sure to fill in the eye, but leave a small dot on the upper right-hand side uncolored for the highlight, which will be added in later. The wing of the sparrow has many little intricate feathers, so do make sure to take your time carefully tracing in each segment.

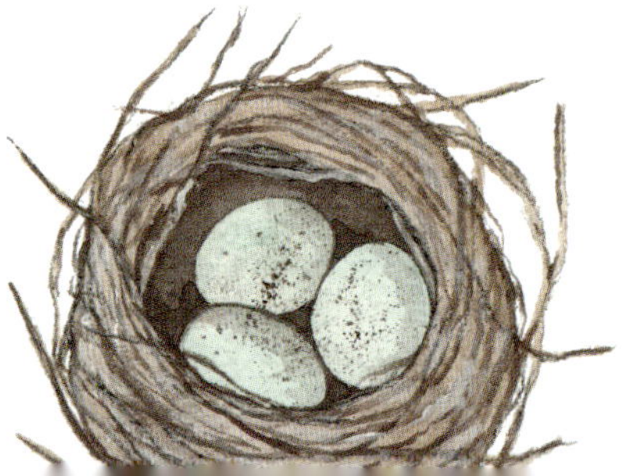

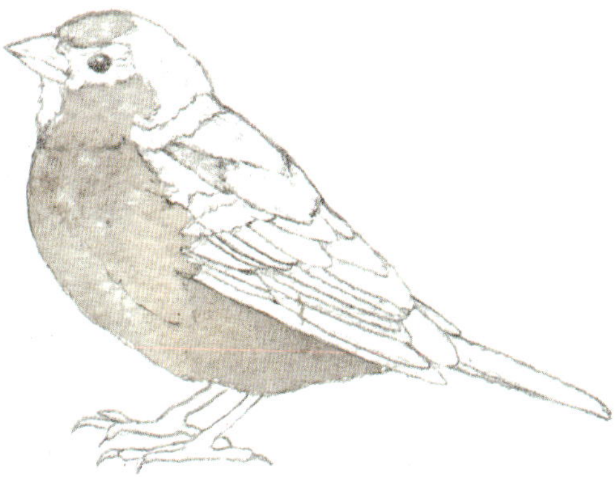

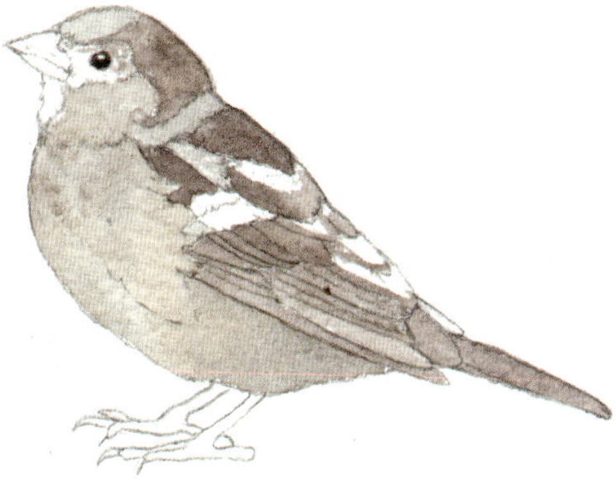

Step 2: Paint the Base Layer of the Feathers on the Body

To prepare the color that will fill the feathers on the face and plumage, use a size 4 brush to mix a mid-toned solution of Chinese white with a dab of raw umber to create a warm cream mixture. Load this color onto the bristles and glaze a layer of cream onto the feathers of the forehead and lower face below the eye, flowing down along the neck to the chest plumage, to the lower body on the underside of the wing.

While this layer is still damp, use a size 1 brush to mix a light-toned solution of sepia and water. Load this watery earthy brown onto the bristles and drop the pigment at the lower right-hand side of the feathers on the body where they meet the underside of the wing, and at the top of the plumage where the chest meets the neck. Fill in a tiny section of feathers on the upper wing toward the left-hand side. Allow these layers to dry and clean the brushes.

Step 3: Fill In the Wing Feathers

Using a clean size 1 brush, mix a mid-toned solution of sepia with a tiny dab of Vandyke brown to create a warm brown solution. Gently glaze this color onto the feathers on the right-hand side of the head and add small dabs of brown feathers surrounding the eye.

Fill in the feathers on the upper wing of the sparrow, and the cluster of feathers on the midsection and left-hand side. Leave some feathers untouched by brown along the mid to upper section of the wing, and some individual feathers along the outer right-hand side of the wing flowing toward the tail. Glaze a layer of this warm brown solution along the tail feathers, and then using the very tip of the brush, paint some short dash brushstrokes on the front plumage of the sparrow to create individual soft feathers on the chest. Allow these layers to dry and clean the brush.

(continued)

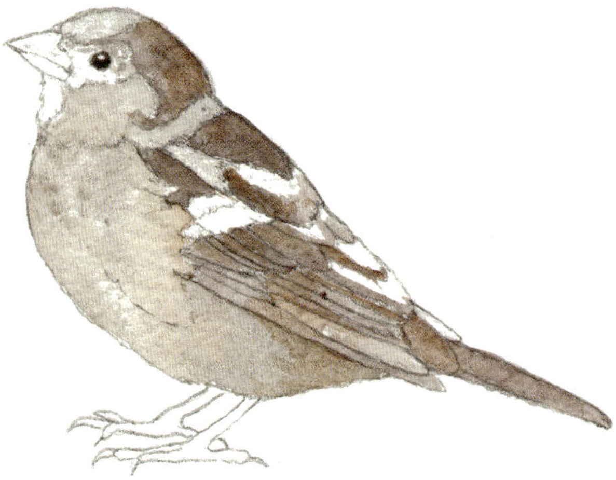

Next, we will fill in the eye. Using a size 3/0 brush, mix a dark-toned solution of ivory black and water. We want this color to be very thick and pigmented. Using the tip of the brush, paint black in the eye, but leave a small dot on the upper right-hand side unpainted for the highlight, which will be added in later. Allow this layer to dry and clean the brush.

Step 4: Create Subtle Gradients of Color

Next, we will be adding some subtle brown color variation to the feathers on the body and wing of the sparrow. Using a size 0 brush, mix a mid-toned solution of Vandyke brown with a swirl of burnt umber to create a warm, rusty brown. Load this color onto the brush and gently glaze a thin layer of warm, rusty brown on each of the brown feathers on the head and wings of the sparrow that we painted on in step 3. Glaze a thin wash of this rusty brown onto the tail feathers and allow these layers to dry.

Next, we want to also create some subtle rusty feathers on the cream sections of the body. We want this mid-toned earthy brown to be slightly lighter, so use the size 0 brush to swirl in some water to dilute the pigment. This will bring the color from a mid-toned solution to a light-toned solution.

Load this lighter rusty brown onto the bristles and glaze a thin layer using the tip of the brush along the right-hand side of the cream feathers on the body, along the outlines of where they meet the brown feathers on the wing. Paint a layer of lighter brown on the underside of the wing, flowing down to the bottom of the body to where it comes to meet the tail. Allow this layer to dry, and then apply another layer of light wash to deepen its tone and create a sense of shadow. Clean the brush.

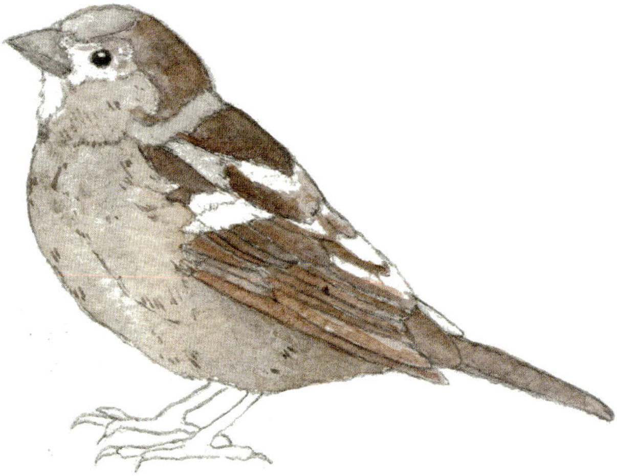

Step 5: Add Definition

Now we will prepare the color that will add some more subtle brown color gradients to the feathers on the wing. Using a clean size 3/0 brush, mix a mid-toned solution of burnt umber with a small swirl of raw umber. Glaze a layer of this warm, rusty brown along the cluster of feathers along the left to middle sections of the lower wing. Glaze a layer of this solution onto the right-hand side of the brown feathers on the head. Allow these layers to dry and clean the brush.

Next, using a clean size 1 brush, mix a simple mid-toned solution of ivory black with a tiny dab of sepia. Load this color onto the bristles and fill in the beak. Allow this to dry and clean the brush.

Next, swap back to the clean size 3/0 brush and load the bristles with this mid-toned warm, earthy gray color. Create small, quick dash brushstrokes that are sparse, and follow the natural curvature of the cream feathers on the face and body. These little brushstrokes will portray tiny soft feathers on the face and plumage. They should not be tightly packed and dense but are looser and more widely spaced. Clean the brush.

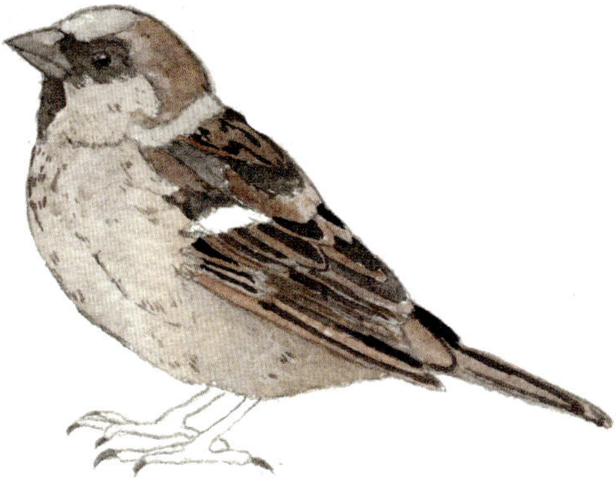

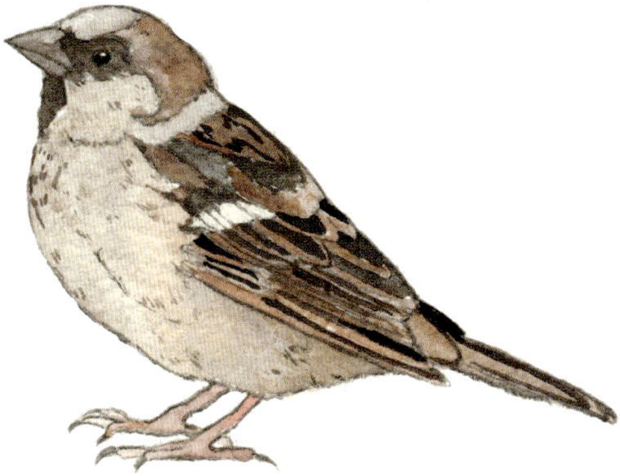

Step 6: Add the Black Feathers

Next, we will fill in the black feathers on the sparrow. Use a clean size 1 brush to mix a mid-toned solution of ivory black and water. We do not want this color to be overly inky and thick and overbearing. Gently use the tip of the brush to paint a glaze of black on the feathers that surround the eye and meet the beak, and on the left-hand side of the neck, and add some small, quick dash brushstrokes down the upper plumage on the front of the chest.

Next, fill in all the remaining feathers on the wing and tail that were not painted in the previous steps, with the exception of one small section of wings on the midsection on the left-hand side of the wing. For the feathers on the upper wing where they meet the back of the neck, paint some small, fluffy dashes that flow downward to create a sense of texture and volume. Allow these paint layers to dry.

Step 7: Add Finishing Touches

Using a clean size 0 brush, mix a light-toned solution of Indian red and water, and fill in both of the sparrow's feet with the light pink color. Next, swap to a clean size 3/0 brush and mix a mid-toned solution of sepia and water. Load this mid-toned solution onto the bristles and carefully trace over the outlines of the beak, body, different color sections of feathers on the face and body, individual feathers on the wings, and feet and claws to create sharp definition. Clean the bristles.

Finally, squeeze a small amount of acrylic white onto your palette, and using a clean size 3/0 brush, paint in a tiny dot on the upper right-hand side in the eye for a highlight. The house sparrow is now complete. Well done, you did a great job!

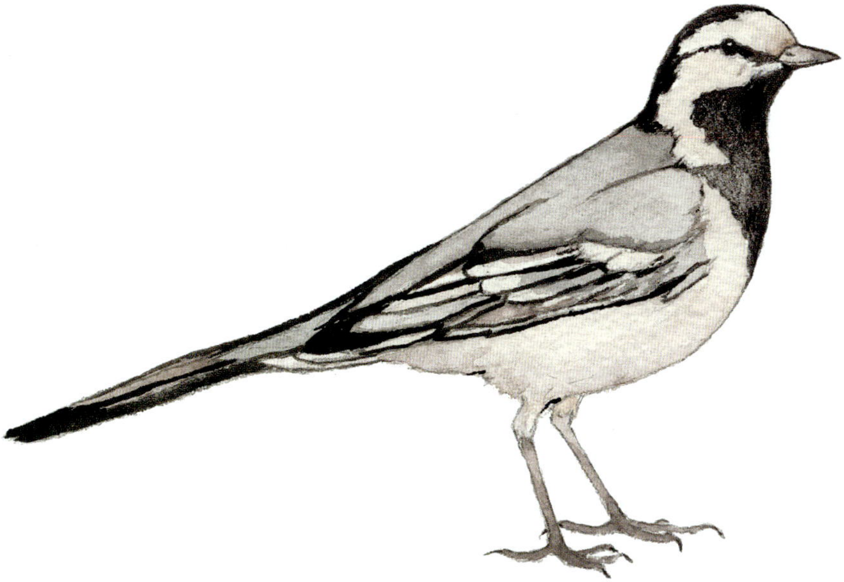

Pied Wagtail

The pied wagtail is a delightful small, long-tailed, and rather sprightly black-and-white bird often found as a companion in the garden. I absolutely love to watch them out the window, whether it's standing, pecking at crumbs and tiny insects, or doing its iconic dance by enthusiastically wagging its tail up and down!

Although the colors used in this tutorial are quite simple, this will be a lesson on how to create contrast, which in turn can create wonderful vibrancy even if the palette is not inherently saturated!

Materials Needed

1 sheet of cold-press 140-pound (300-gsm) aquarelle/watercolor paper

HB pencil

Brushes

- Size 4
- Size 1
- Size 3/0

Watercolor paints

- Chinese white
- Raw umber
- Sepia
- Ivory black

Acrylic white

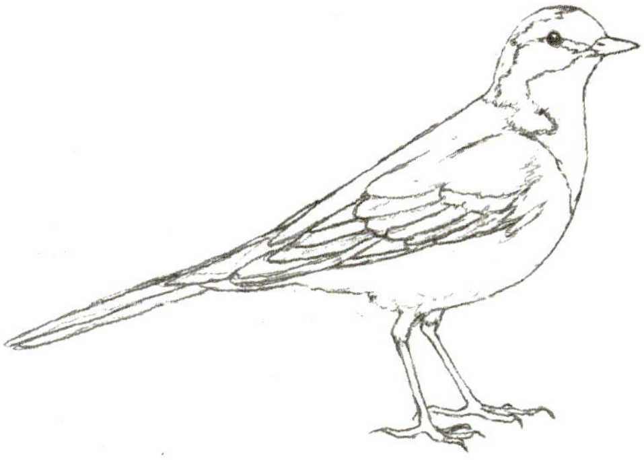

Step 1: Draw the Outline

Starting on a sheet of cold-press watercolor paper, draw the pied wagtail's outline with a sharp HB pencil using the template provided on page 191. Fill in the eye (we will deepen this with black paint later), making sure to leave a dot on the upper center uncolored for a highlight. The layered feathers on the wing of the wagtail are quite intricate, so do take your time in tracing each one carefully.

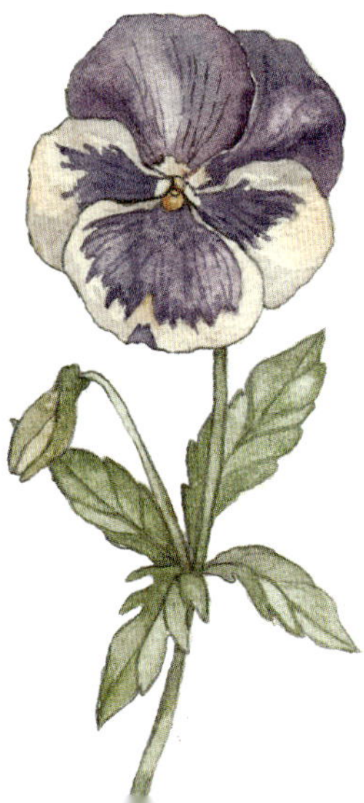

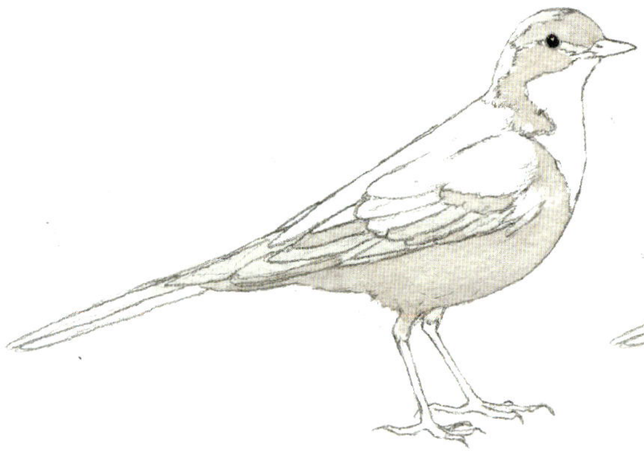

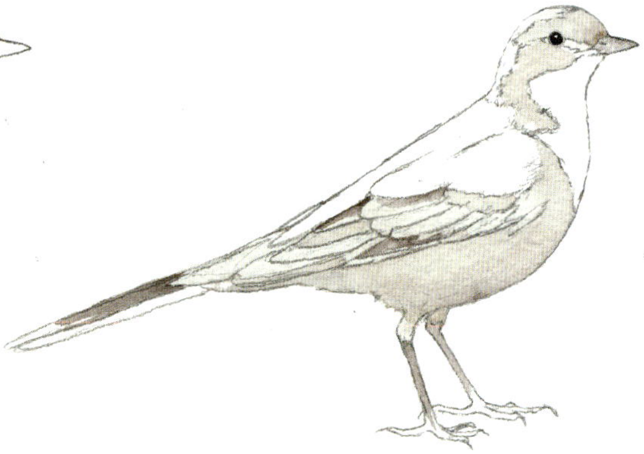

Step 2: Paint the Cream Base Layer

For the cream color that will fill the lower belly, lower wings, and face of the wagtail, use a size 4 brush to mix a mid-toned solution of Chinese white with a small dab of raw umber. We want this color to be a warm-toned cream rather than a cool-toned pure white. Load this mixture onto the bristles and glaze the feathers on the face, avoiding the small section that runs from the beak to the eye, down along the neck to the mid to lower plumage. Continue along the curve of the front plumage, across the mid to lower belly, and following down the plumage to the lower back feathers where they meet the beginning of the base of the tail.

Step 3: Create Subtle Shadows

Using a size 1 brush, mix a mid-toned solution of sepia and water. Load the bristles of the brush and gently fill in the beak, three feathers in the wing (two feathers on the upper section of the wing feather cluster, and one on the lower section), and the upper feather on the upper tail. Dip your brush into water and add a droplet or two to the mid-toned sepia mixture. This will lighten the color and create a lighter dilution of brown. Gently paint a thin coat along the curve of the lower belly and down the legs. Soften the edges of the paint layers to ensure subtle blending and gradients of color, creating a realistic shadow. Allow these paint layers to dry and clean the brush.

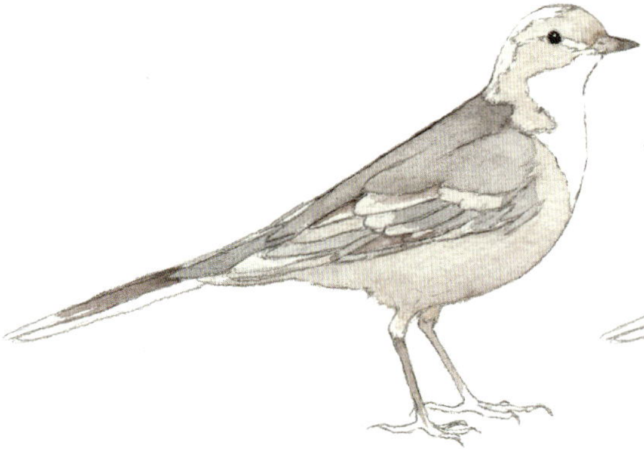

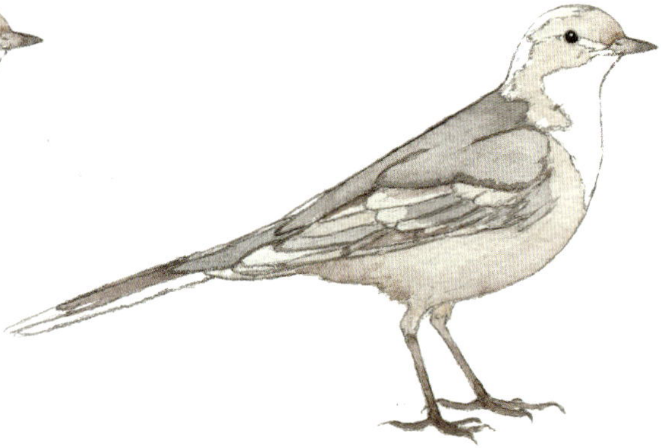

Step 4: Paint the Wings

Using a clean size 1 brush, mix a light-toned solution of ivory black and water. This color should be a pale gray. Load the mixture onto the brush and drop a small amount using the tip of the brush at the very tip of the beak. Paint a thin glaze on the entire upper section of the wing, extending the paint downward to the tail, filling in the cluster of feathers to the right-hand side, moving across to the left, and filling in the feathers in the middle to lower section of the wing. Paint a thin glaze along the outline of the plumage of the wagtail, following the curve of the belly across to the left to the underside of the wing.

Finally, add a thin layer of gray to the face and on the upper section of feathers where they join the beak. Clean the brush.

Step 5: Add Definition to the Feathers

Using a size 3/0 brush, mix a mid-toned solution of sepia with a small swirl of ivory black. We want this to be a deep brown color that is not too thick yet not too pale and watery. Load this solution onto the bristles and paint along the inner edges of each of the feathers on the wing. Extend the glaze upward along the curve of the wing and into the top of the back where the feathers join the cream of the neck. Fill in the bottoms of the feet and claws.

Next, deepen the shadow at the feathers at the front of the upper face where they join to meet the beak by adding a thin layer of deep brown and softening the edges back into the feathers, pushing the paint softly toward the eye. Allow this paint layer to dry, then repeat this process on the bottom of the feet by adding another layer of deep brown. Allow the paint to dry fully and clean the brush.

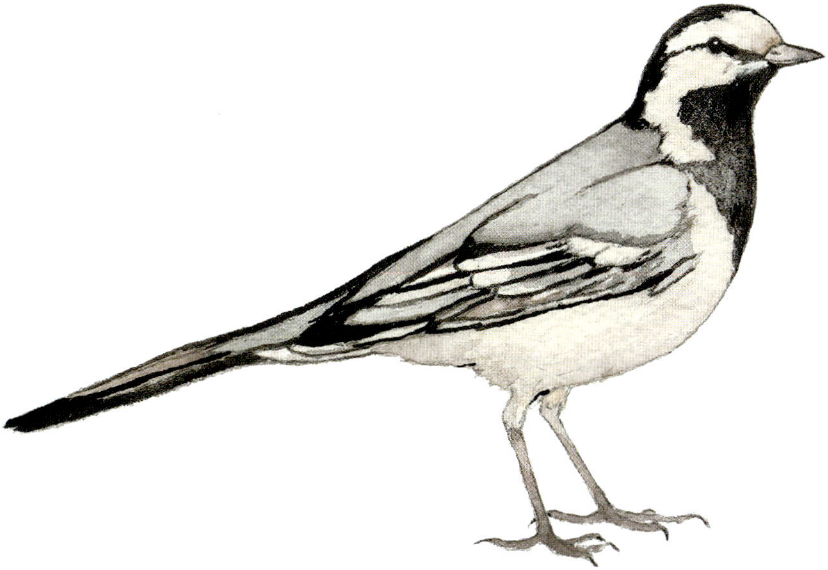

Step 6: Paint the Black and Finishing Touches

Using a clean size 1 brush, mix a dark-toned solution of ivory black and water. This mixture should be heavily pigmented, inky, and thick. Load the bristles with this black mixture and paint a layer on the section of feathers at the top of the head, moving toward the left-hand side to the bottom of the neck, to the front plumage beginning at the bottom of the beak, moving down and across the plumage of the chest and where the feathers meet the top of the right-hand side of the wing, and then to the section of feathers that move across the center of the face. Fill in the remaining feathers on the feather cluster on the wing, and along the spine to the bottom feather of the tail.

Then, switch to a clean size 3/0 brush and swirl back into this thick, dark black solution. Carefully trace the outlines of the feathers on the wing, body, and tail, as well as the claws at the end of the feet, beak, and nostril. Fill in the eye with black but leave the dot unpainted for the highlight. Clean the bristles.

Finally, squeeze a pea-size amount of acrylic white onto your palette. Dip the clean size 3/0 brush into this and paint a tiny dot of white in the center of the eye, which creates character and luminosity. Dab tiny, delicate strokes around the cheek close to where the feathers of the lower face meet the beak. The pied wagtail is now complete. Well done!

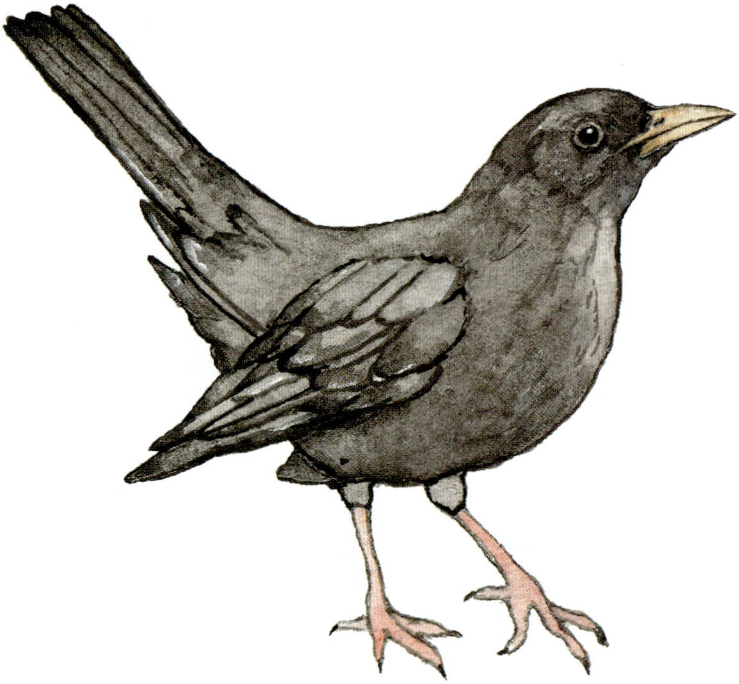

Blackbird

Blackbirds are constant companions in the garden. There's a particular kind of joy in watching them hop across the grass, bold and curious, the flash of their orange beaks catching the light. Every week I buy a bag of apples to cut up and sprinkle outside for them to feast on while I watch from the window!

In this tutorial, we will explore how to build depth and richness with darker pigments. Working with black can be tricky. It's easy for black to look flat or heavy, but with gentle layering and subtle shifts in tone, you'll learn to create feathers that can shine and to capture the lively nature in its eye!

Materials Needed

1 sheet of cold-press 140-pound (300-gsm) aquarelle/watercolor paper

HB pencil

A piece of paper towel

Brushes

- Size 4
- Size 1
- Size 3/0

Watercolor paints

- Ivory black
- Sepia
- Raw umber
- Yellow ochre
- Indian red

Acrylic white

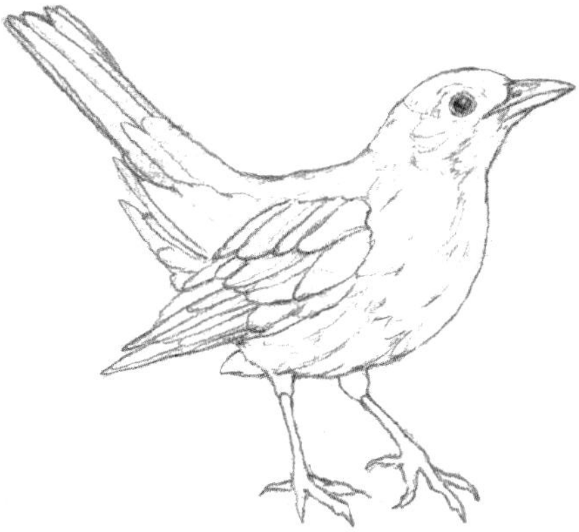

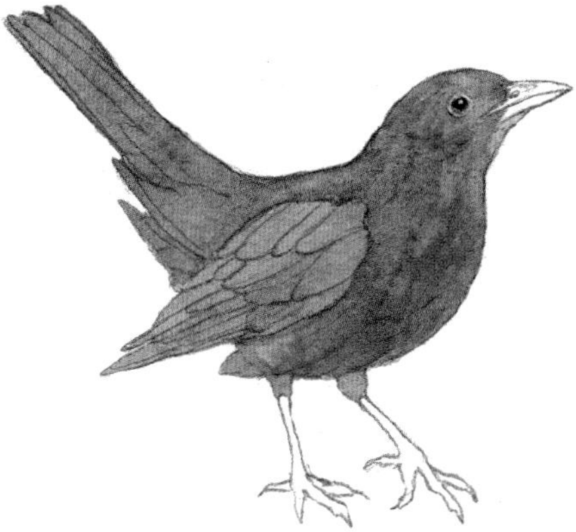

Step 1: Draw the Outline

Starting on a sheet of cold-press watercolor paper, draw the blackbird's outline with a sharp HB pencil using the template provided on page 191. Make sure to fill in the eye, but leave a small dot on the upper center uncolored for a highlight, which will be added later on. The feathers on the wings of the blackbird are quite intricate, so take your time.

Step 2: Paint the Base Layer

For the base layer of the blackbird, use a size 4 brush to mix a mid-toned solution of ivory black with a small swirl of sepia. We want this color not to be pure cool-toned black but to have a warm, earthy undertone. Load this color onto the bristles and fill in the entire body, head, and wing of the blackbird.

While this layer is still damp, load the bristles with another swirl of this dark, earthy color and gently glaze the front plumage of the blackbird. This will give a slight tonal variation and create subtle depth on the feathers at the front. Allow these layers to dry.

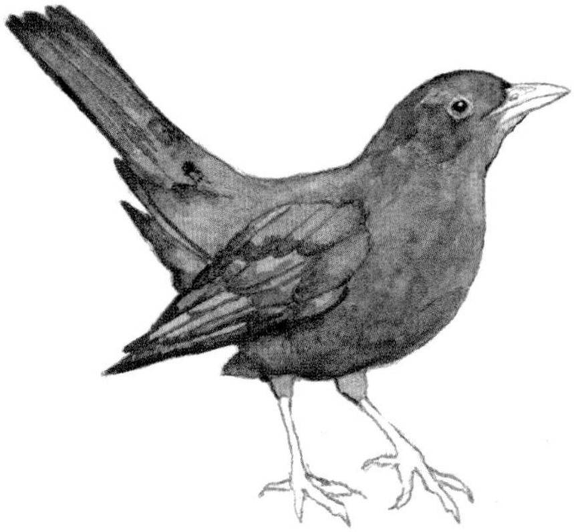

Step 3: Add Shadows and Detailing

Switch to a size 1 brush and mix in slightly more ivory black to the mid-toned earthy mixture we created in step 2 to give the color more of a darker hue. Load this color onto the bristles and glaze the feathers at the very tips of the tail, gently pulling the paint down along the tail toward the body until the edges soften. Repeat this step on the tips of each feather on the wing, concentrating the paint at the collective point of the entire wing where all the feathers meet.

Glaze some of this dark mixture along the feathers on the lower belly and back wing, and on the head on the left-hand side of the eye and where the face meets the beak. Allow this paint layer to dry. Finally, add one more layer of this dark, earthy mixture to the tips of the wing and the tips of the tail. Clean the brush.

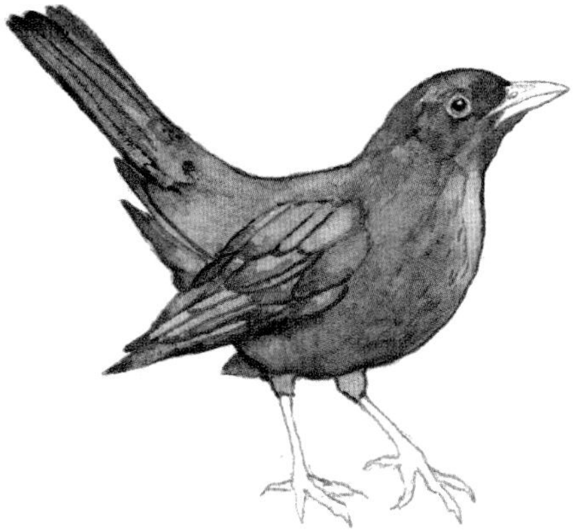

Step 4: Add Highlights and Definition

First, we will create highlights by using a piece of paper towel and a clean size 1 brush. Swirl the brush into water and wiggle the bristles on the right-hand side of the plumage, and on the feathers on the upper section of the wing where it joins to the body. After the paint has been lifted on the bristles, press the paper towel firmly onto each dampened section, revealing the lifted luminous highlight underneath.

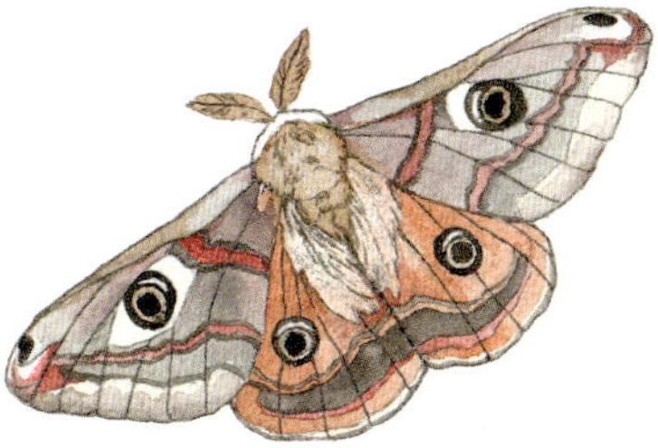

Next, using a size 3/0 brush, mix a simple mid-toned solution of ivory black and water. Load this mixture onto the bristles, and holding the brush at the ferrule to allow the most control over the lines you create, carefully trace the lines on the individual feathers of the wings and at the back and tips of the tail, and the outline of the entire body and upper legs. Do make sure to take your time, as this is quite delicate work and the wing feather has many individual sections. Gently paint delicate, short strokes along the natural curvature of the front plumage down along the lower belly.

While this layer of delicate lines is drying, swirl the brush back into the ivory black mixture and glaze a thin layer at the right-hand side of the face where it meets the beak, softening the edges until the thin paint layer blends seamlessly and softly into the layers underneath, leaving no hard edges. Clean the brushes.

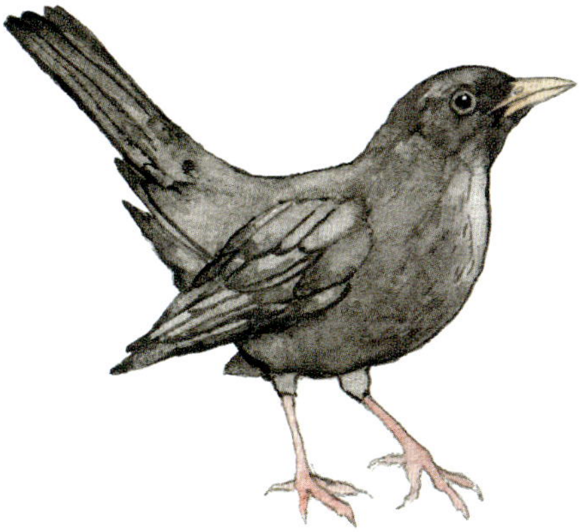

Step 5: Add Color

Using a clean size 1 brush, mix a light-toned solution of raw umber and yellow ochre. We want this to have a warm, rusty yellow color with a watery consistency. Swirl the brush into this mixture and gently fill in the beak. While this layer is still damp, swirl the brush gently into raw umber to pick up a small amount of pigment, and carefully drop this onto the left-hand side of the beak where it meets the face. As the paper dries, it will create a natural, soft gradient between the two layers of warm, rusty colors.

(continued)

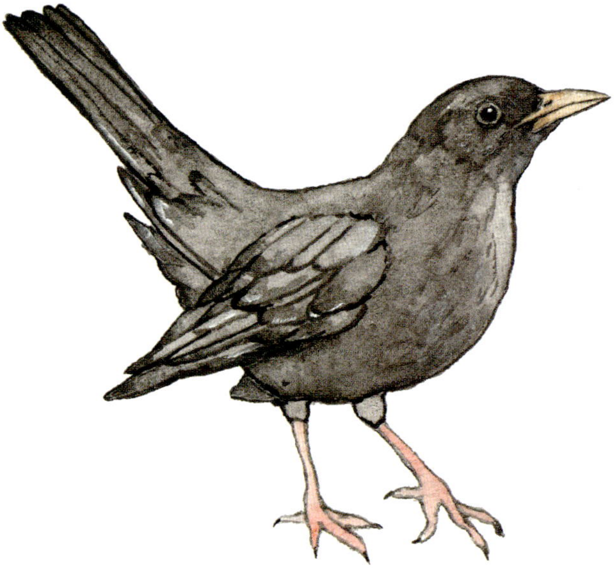

Switch to a clean size 3/0 brush and swirl the bristles into the light-toned raw umber and yellow ochre mixture used as the base layer of the beak, and fill in the outer section of the eye. Allow this paint layer to dry and clean the brush.

For the claws of the blackbird, clean the size 1 brush and mix a simple light-toned solution of Indian red and water. This will have the appearance of a pale pink. Load this color onto the bristles and fill in the left and right feet.

Step 6: Add Finishing Touches

Using a clean size 3/0 brush and the same mid-toned solution of ivory black and water that we mixed in step 4, load the paint onto the bristles. Holding the brush at the ferrule to allow the most control over the bristles, delicately trace the outlines of the beak and feet, filling in the claws at the bottom.

Fill in the eye, leaving the dot in the center unpainted for highlight. Allow this paint to dry and clean the brush.

Finally, squeeze a pea-size amount of acrylic white onto your palette. Dip the clean size 3/0 brush into this and paint tiny highlights following the curved contours on the ends of the wing feathers and lower tail. Add a tiny dot of white in the center of the eye, which creates character and luminosity. Dab tiny, delicate strokes around the cheek close to where the feathers of the lower face meet the eye. The blackbird is now complete. Well done!

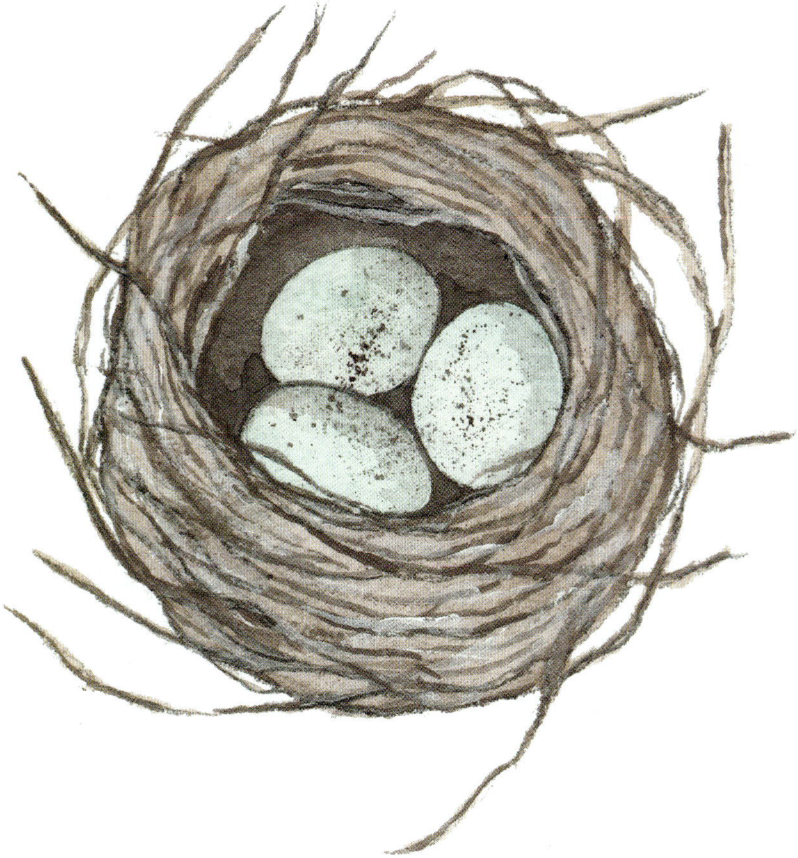

Bird's Nest

In this tutorial, we'll paint a simple bird's nest cradling a cluster of pale eggs. Although this is a quiet subject with an organic structure and calm colors, if you look closer, you can see the paint strokes are full of texture. The beauty of a nest lies in its organized chaos, all those looping strands layered into a soft, protective bowl. We will also learn how to create different textures through splattering techniques to give realistic finishing touches, which are quite interactive and fun to do!

Materials Needed

1 sheet of cold-press 140-pound (300-gsm) aquarelle/watercolor paper

HB pencil

A piece of paper towel

Brushes

> Size 1

> Size 4

> Size 0

> Size 3/0

Watercolor paints

> Emerald

> Cerulean blue

> Sepia

> Vandyke brown

> Ivory black

Acrylic white

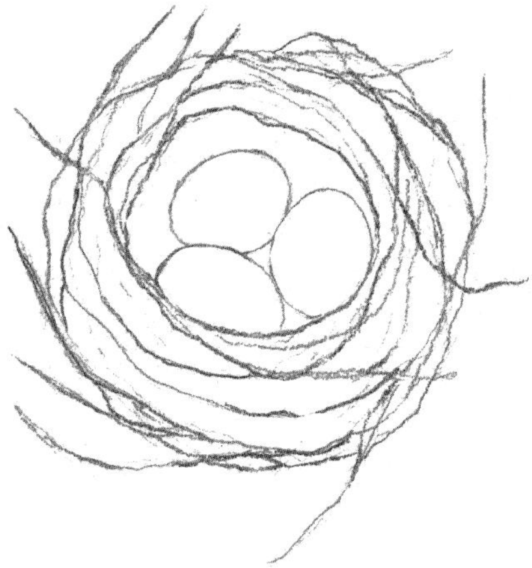

Step 1: Draw the Outline

Starting on a sheet of cold-press watercolor paper, draw the bird nest's outline with a sharp HB pencil using the template provided on page 193. The twigs that build the base structure of the nest have a wispy, organic texture, so you can vary the weight of the pencil on the paper to create a sense of softness and structure.

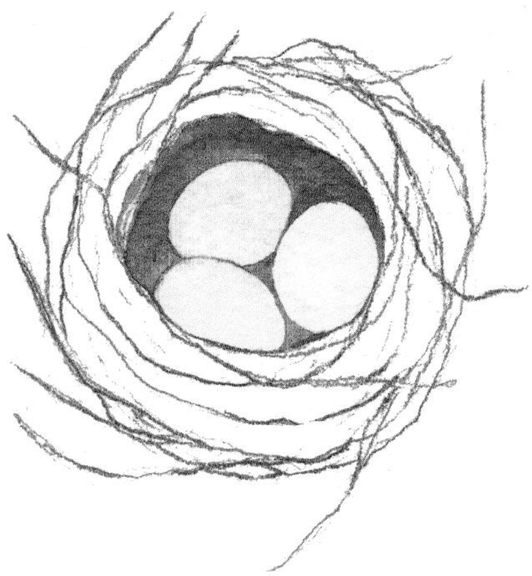

Step 2: Paint the Eggshells and Inner Nest

To mix the color that will be the base layer for the shells of the bird's eggs, use a size 1 brush to mix a light-toned solution of emerald with a tiny dab of cerulean blue. We want this color to be a cool-toned minty green with a watery texture. Load this color onto the bristles and fill each of the three eggs with a layer of this minty green solution. Allow the layers to dry and clean the bristles.

Next, using the same size 1 brush, mix a mid-toned solution of sepia and water to create a rich, earthy brown that is not too watery. Load this color onto the bristles and paint a layer of earthy brown onto the inner section of the nest that surrounds and is in between the eggs. Allow this paint layer to dry and clean the brush.

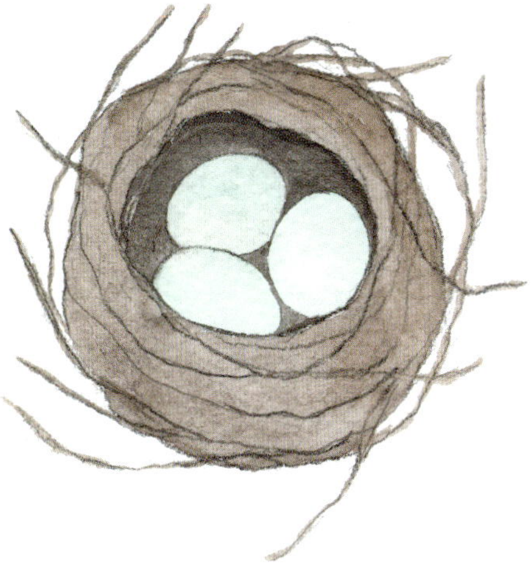

Step 3: Paint the Base Layer for the Outer Nest

Using a size 4 brush, mix a mid-toned solution of Vandyke brown with a small dab of sepia to create a warm, caramel brown color. Load this color onto the bristles and paint a layer of this caramel brown onto the entire outer section of the nest. Swap to a size 0 brush and load the same caramel brown color onto the tip of the bristles, and carefully outline the looser twigs that are coming out from the main structure of the nest. Allow these paint layers to dry and clean the brushes.

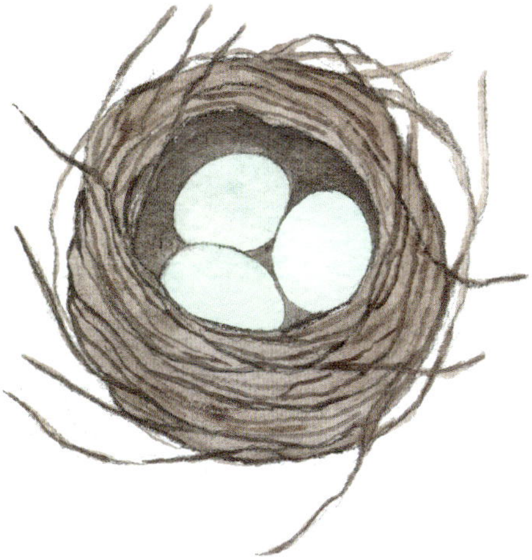

Step 4: Create Organic Structure

The nest's twig structure works best when you think of them as strands, rather than outlines, that will be loose, irregular, and layered. Use a clean size 0 brush to mix a mid-toned solution of sepia and water, and load this earthy brown onto the bristles. We don't want this color to be too watery but also not too thick, as the lines should be crisp but not harsh.

(continued)

Begin by following the natural curve of the nest, letting your wrist move in gentle, flowing arcs. Use light pressure so the brush tip creates thin, tapering strokes. These thin lines mimic the twigs that sit on the surface on the outer structure of the nest. Let some of them wander slightly off course, and occasionally change the rhythm by crossing some lines and overlapping others. Allow these layers to dry and clean the brush. Once dry, these lines may appear chaotic but will have a realistic appearance of densely gathered twigs.

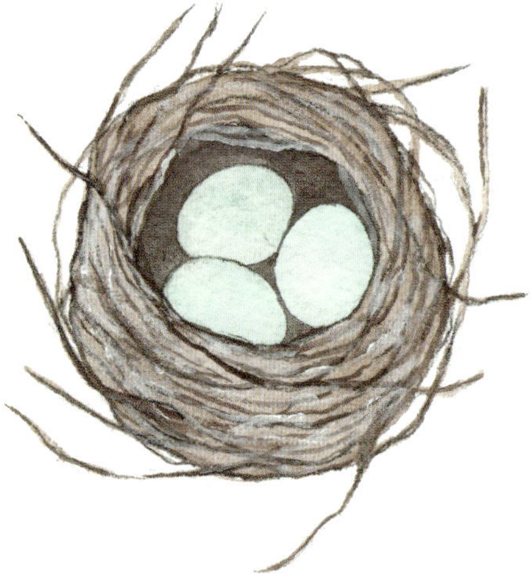

Step 5: Give the Nest Structure Highlights and Density

Next, using a size 3/0 brush, squeeze a small blob of acrylic white paint onto the palette, and load the bristles. Using the same gentle, flowing-arc painting movements as we used in step 4, trace overlapping and crossing lines of white that flow along the natural curvature of the nest structure. Make sure that these lines are quite sparse and irregular, as we want to be able to see the layers of deeper sepia strands underneath. All these tiny variations of strand colors layering on top of one another build the sense of tangled material. Allow the white paint layer to dry and clean the bristles of the brush.

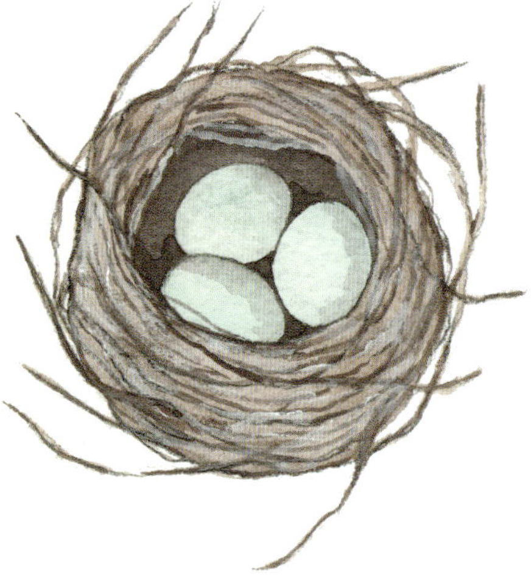

Step 6: Create Shadow Layers

For a shadow layer that will sit beneath the eggs in the inner nest, use a clean size 1 brush to mix a mid-toned solution of sepia with a small dab of ivory black to create a deep, earthy brown. Load this color onto the bristles and gently glaze the inner sections of the nest where the eggs are lying, the mid and bottom sections, and around the base of each of the eggs. This is where shadows would most naturally fall, while the upper section of the inner nest would naturally have more light, so do not paint the section where the light would fall.

Switch to a clean size 3/0 brush and load the bristles with this deep, earthy brown, and carefully trace along the outline of the outer nest and the loose twig strands coming from the main structure. Allow the paint to dry and clean the bristles of the brush with water.

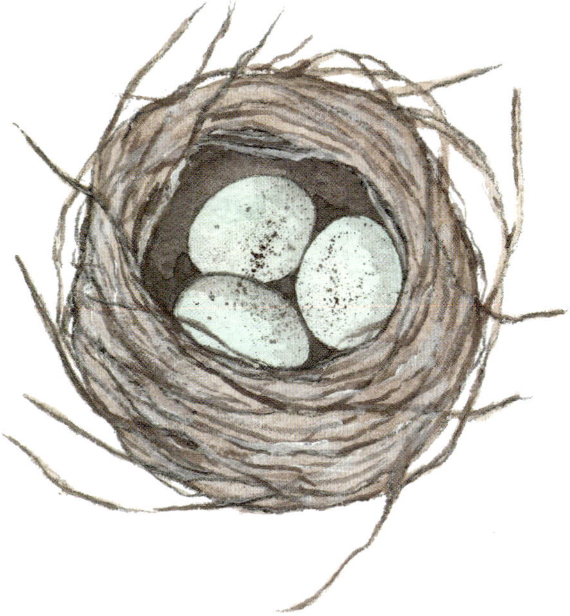

Next, use a clean size 0 brush to mix a light-toned solution of ivory black and water. We want this color to be a watery pale gray. Load this color onto the bristles and glaze the right-hand side of each of the eggs. For the bottom-left egg, glaze along the top, then down along the curve of the shell on the right. Allow these shadow layers to dry.

Step 7: Create Dotted Texture

For the dotted patterns on the eggshells, we will be using a splattering technique. Using a clean size 4 brush, mix a dark-toned solution of sepia and water. We want this to be highly pigmented yet thick and fluid, not too watery.

Load the bristles with this mixture, hold it over the eggshells, and run the tips of the bristles through your finger so that they release minuscule, delicate droplets.

Be careful not to let these droplets release onto any other parts of the nest apart from the eggshells; you can cover the parts you do not want the droplets to land on with dry pieces of paper towel, leaving just the eggs showing. Allow these paint layers to dry.

Switch to a clean size 3/0 brush and load the bristles with the same deep-toned sepia mixture. Paint a final sparse layer of loose, irregular overlapping strands on top of the outer structure of the nest. The bird's nest is now complete. You did a wonderful job!

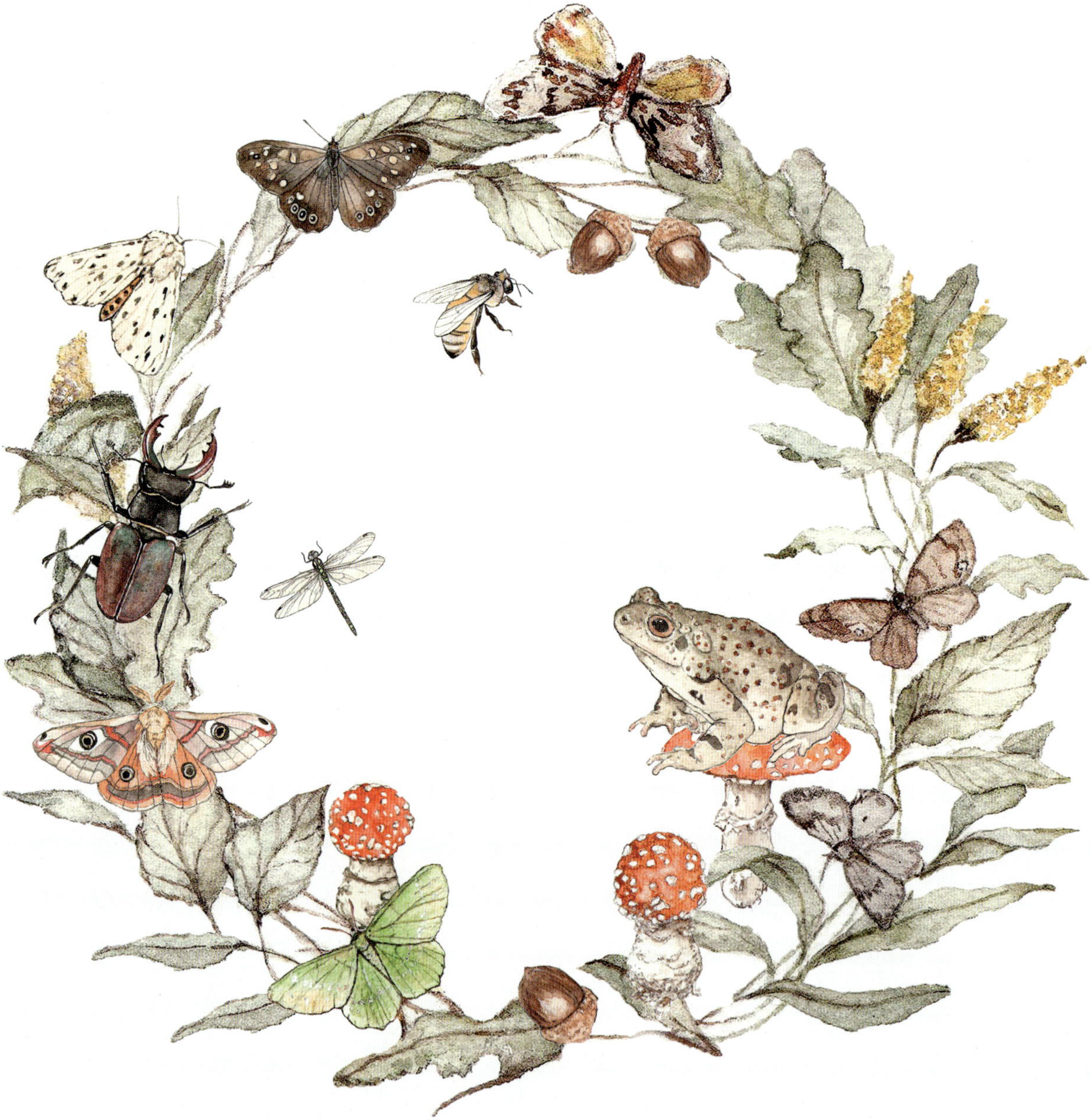

Insect Intrigue

Keep your eyes sharp and your curiosity sharper because this chapter invites you into the miniature garden world where wings glint and colors shift; be prepared to shift your perception that insects are just "creepy crawlies"!

This chapter will be a challenge in symmetry. Butterflies, with patterned wings and drifting movements, are endlessly rewarding subjects. You'll learn how to translate their delicate shapes onto paper, build soft gradations of color, and suggest the lightness of their flight without losing the structure that defines each species. The beetle, with its polished shell, rich, metallic tones, and strong form, will encourage slow, careful observation. The dragonfly, with its translucent wings and slender body, will challenge you to paint subtle veining and crisp shapes, and play with light across its wings.

These tutorials have many interesting and rewarding details to discover. I'm sure you are going to really enjoy painting them!

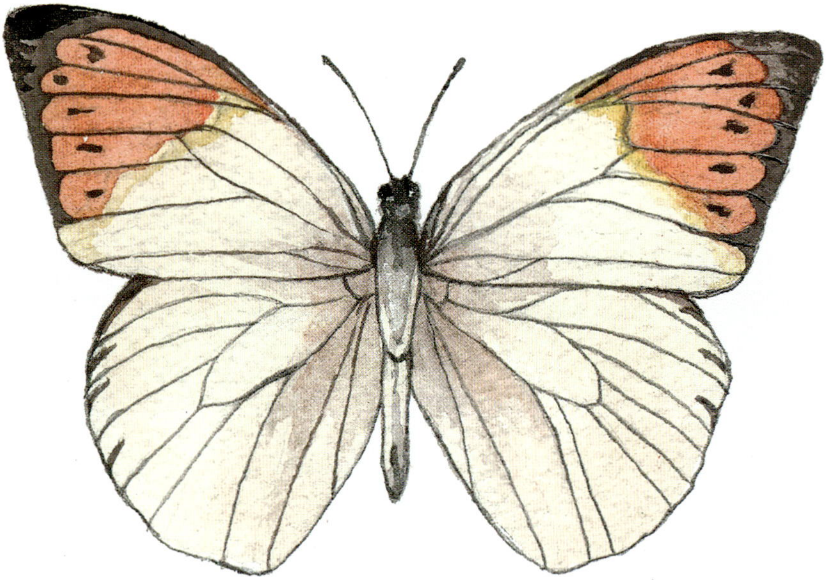

Orange Tip Butterfly

Commonly found in gardens and hedgerows, the orange tip butterfly reveals a bright pop of color on the wings that is always a delightful reminder that there is so much beauty passing us by in our everyday lives, it doesn't even need to be a rare sight to be appreciated!

Although the base layers of their wings are pale with whites and creams, there is a valuable lesson when painting their delicate, segmented bodies. These shapes are perfect for developing control with small brushes and defining form.

Materials Needed

1 sheet of cold-press 140-pound (300-gsm) aquarelle/watercolor paper

HB pencil

Brushes

- > Size 4
- > Size 0
- > Size 1
- > Size 3/0

Watercolor paints

- > Chinese white
- > Raw umber
- > Sepia
- > Ivory black
- > Vandyke brown
- > Cadmium yellow
- > Cadmium orange
- > Burnt sienna

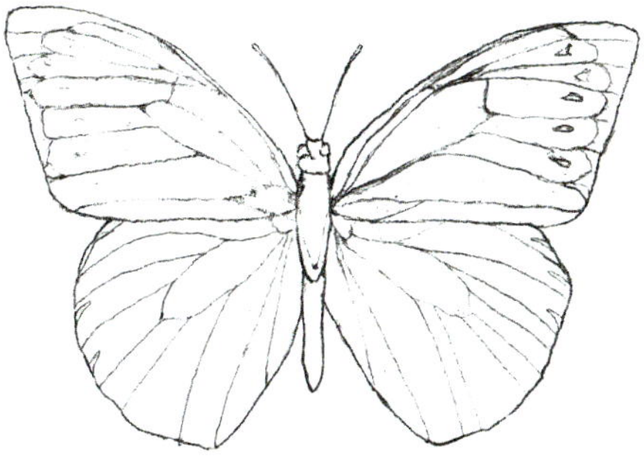

Step 1: Draw the Outline

Starting on a sheet of cold-press watercolor paper, draw the orange tip butterfly's outline with a sharp HB pencil using the template provided on page 193. There are a lot of details in this piece, so make sure to take your time, as butterflies do look their best and most realistic when the patterns of the wings are symmetrical as possible.

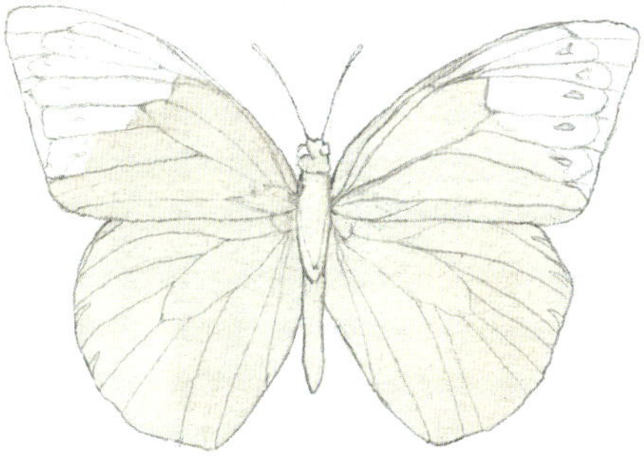

Step 2: Paint the Base Layer

Using a size 4 brush, mix a mid-toned solution of Chinese white with a swirl of raw umber to create a warm cream color. Load this warm cream mixture onto the bristles and glaze a wash over the entire lower wings, the body, and the mid to central section of the upper wings. Allow this paint layer to dry and clean the brush.

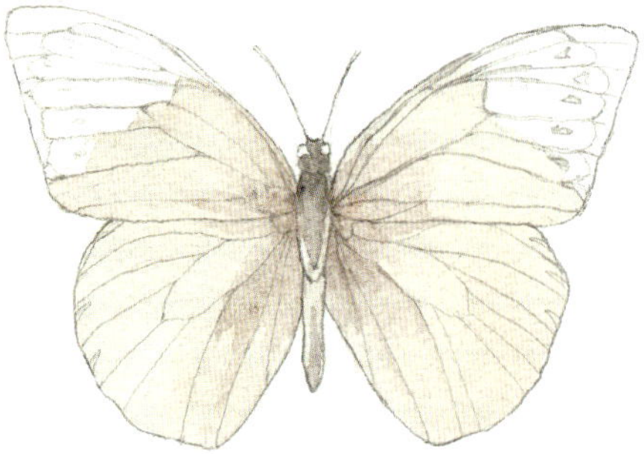

Step 3: Add Depth to the Wings and Body

Using a size 0 brush, mix a light-toned solution of sepia with a dab of ivory black and water to create a watery light brown that is cool toned. Load this color onto the brush and fill in the head, the upper section of the middle of the body, and the line coming from the bottom section of the body with this cool-toned light brown.

While the paint layer is still damp, swirl the brush back into the light brown mixture and drop the pigment at the very top of the head. As this paint layer dries, it will disperse downward, gradually causing a natural gradient from being darker at the head to tapering off into lighter brown toward the center section of the body.

For the inner edges of the wings that meet at the body, use a size 1 brush to mix a light-toned solution of Vandyke brown and water to create a watery warm brown. Paint a light wash of this warm brown hue along the inner edges of each of the wings, dragging the paint gently outward toward the center to soften any harsh lines, blending the brown into the base layer of cream below it. Clean the bristles of the brush.

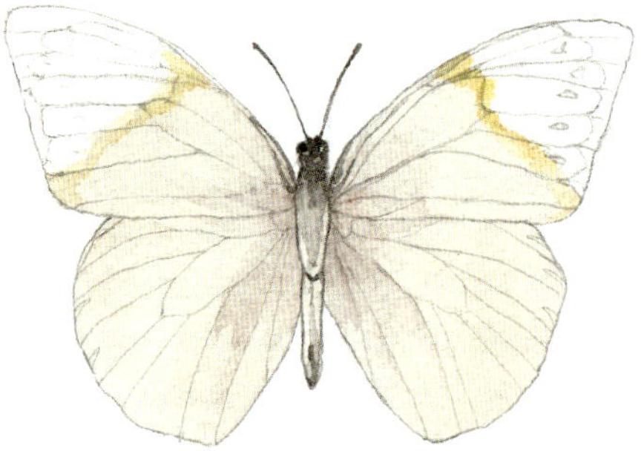

Step 4: Paint a Pop of Yellow and Define the Body

Using a clean size 1 brush, mix a mid-toned solution of cadmium yellow and water. Load this color onto the bristles and paint along the outer edge of the cream sections that we painted on the upper wings in step 2. Follow the curvature of the veins on the wings so the line isn't straight but has an organic flow. Allow the paint layer to dry and clean the brush.

To create definition on the body of the butterfly, swap to a size 3/0 brush and mix a mid-toned solution of ivory black and water. Load the color onto the bristles of the brush and glaze the top of the head of the butterfly, coating the eyes and allowing the paint to disperse downward into the midsection of the body.

Paint the bottom of the body, allowing the black to trail slightly upward. Use the tip of the brush and hold it at the ferrule to have the most control over the lines to trace the outlines of the body and the antennae with this black solution. Clean the brush.

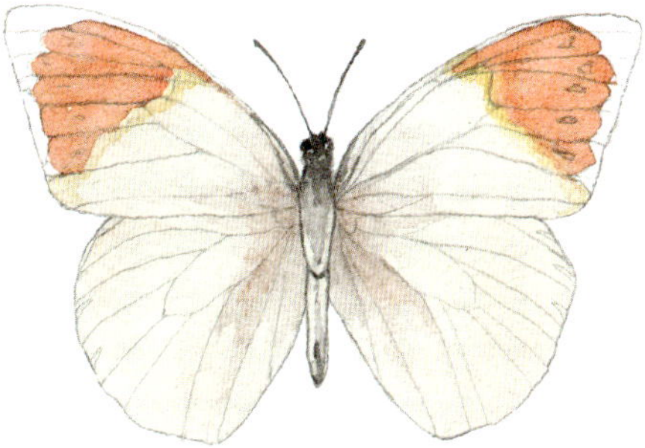

Step 5: Add Orange

Using a clean size 4 brush, mix a mid-toned solution of cadmium orange with a small swirl of burnt sienna. We want this orange to have a warm, sunny appearance yet not be too bright and vivid, rather sitting in a more autumnal, slightly rusty palette. Load this color onto the bristles and glaze the upper middle section of the upper wings, just above the yellow-lined pattern we painted in step 4. Allow this paint glaze to dry.

We now want to add a slight tint of orange to the inner sections of the wings by diluting the mid-toned orange solution to a light-toned solution, which will be a lot more watery and paler. Swirl the clean size 1 brush into water, then mix the watery brush into the mid-toned orange until it has become less saturated with color and now more like a very pale rusty orange. Paint a thin layer of this color onto the center section of each of the wings, gently pulling the paint layer out and to the center to soften the edges and any harsh outlines. Clean the brush.

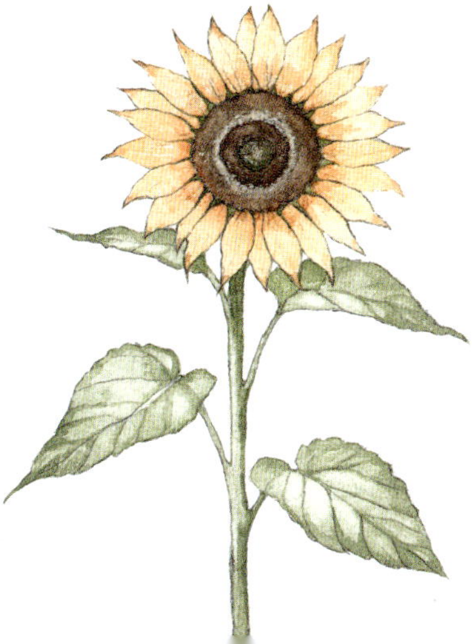

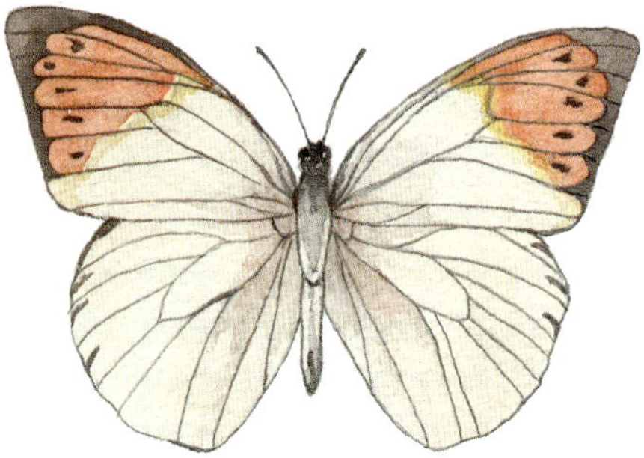

Step 6: Create Definition

Using a clean size 3/0 brush, mix a mid-toned solution of sepia and water. We want this color to be warm, earthy brown. Load this color onto the bristles and outline each of the veins on the wings of the orange tip butterfly using confident flowing lines. Carefully fill in the little markings on the edges of the orange section of the upper wings and along the outer edges of the bottom wings.

Clean the bristles of the brush and swap to a clean size 1 brush, and load the bristles with the same mid-toned sepia solution. Glaze the outer sections of each of the upper wings. Allow these layers to dry and clean the bristles.

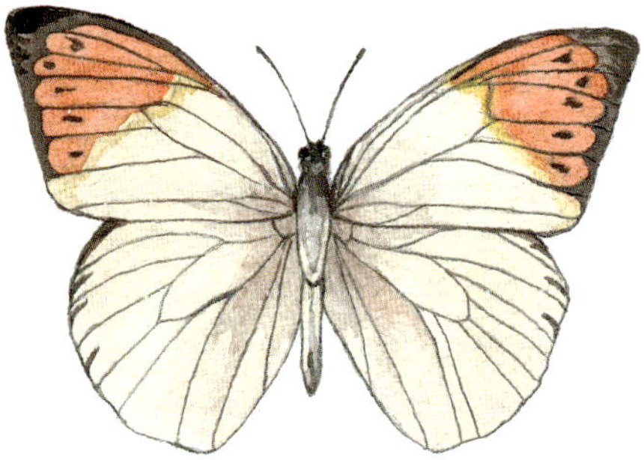

Step 7: Add Finishing Touches

Using the same size 3/0 brush and mid-toned sepia solution, mix in a tiny dab of ivory black to make the color richer and slightly darker. Gently glaze a layer of this dark earthy brown onto the outer edges of the upper wings to create a rich outline. On the upper edges of the lower wings where the wings meet and overlap, paint a thin layer of deep brown just at the top upper edge, letting the paint flow downward and soften as it reaches along the midway outline point. Allow the paint to dry and clean the bristles. The orange tip butterfly is now complete. Well done!

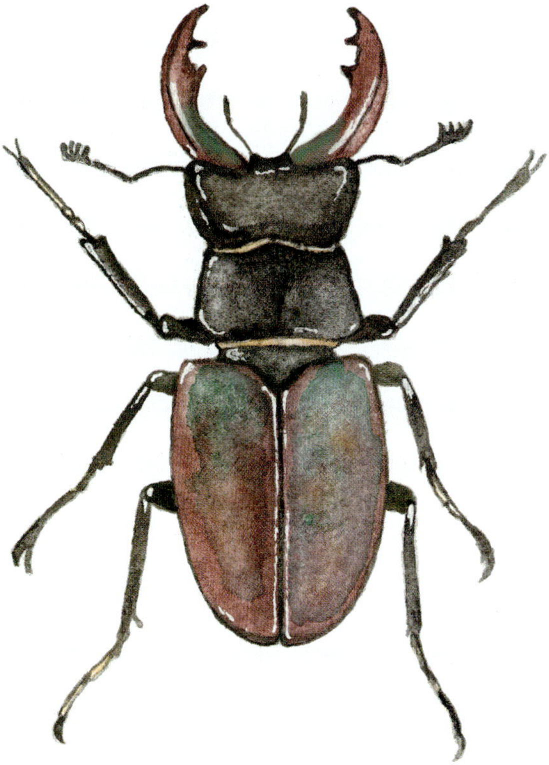

Beetle

In the quiet corners of the garden, under stones and beneath fallen leaves, lives one of nature's most dazzling little creatures: the beetle. I feel as though they can be misunderstood, since many see only a creepy crawly, but if you look closer, you'll find something extraordinary. I often compare them to dazzling gemstones because of how their shells reflect the light; the different shades of jewel and earth tones can be really mesmerizing! In this project, we will focus on how the use of highlights and luminosity can be extremely effective in creating a true sense of realism and dimension, which is very useful when painting something as polished as the armor of the beetle!

Materials Needed

1 sheet of cold-press 140-pound (300-gsm) aquarelle/watercolor paper

HB pencil

A piece of paper towel

Brushes

- Size 4
- Size 0
- Size 3/0
- Size 1

Watercolor paints

- Indian red
- Indigo
- Vandyke brown
- Raw umber
- Ivory black
- Emerald

Acrylic white

Sea salt flakes

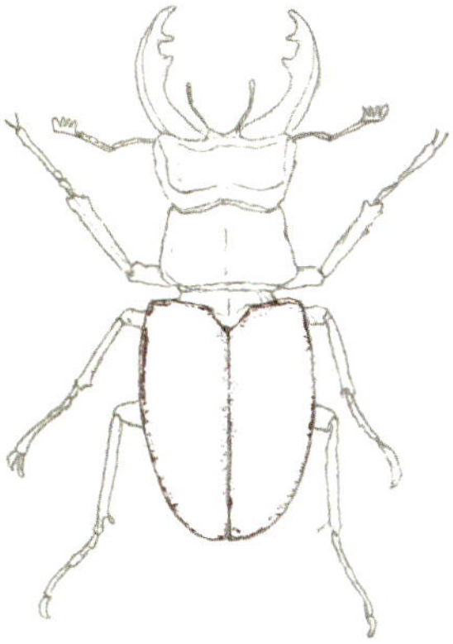

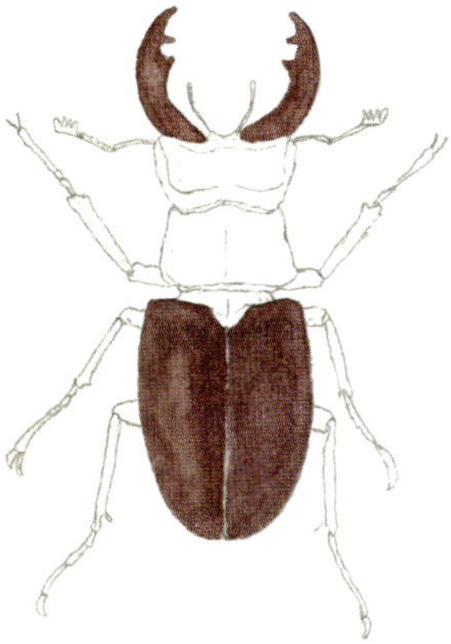

Step 1: Draw the Outline

Starting on a sheet of cold-press watercolor paper, draw the beetle's outline with a sharp HB pencil using the template provided on page 195.

Step 2: Paint the Wings and Horns

To prepare the color for the wings of the beetle, we need to mix a warm, autumnal wine color. Using a size 4 brush, mix a mid-toned solution of mostly Indian red with a tiny swirl of indigo to create a deep maroon tone. Then mix in a tiny dab of Vandyke brown to this mixture for an earthier hue. Load this mid-toned solution onto the brush and glaze over both wings on the back of the beetle, leaving a small line space of white paper in between unpainted to indicate they are separate. Coat the horns of the beetle with the same mixture of deep, earthy maroon. Let this paint coat dry and clean the brush.

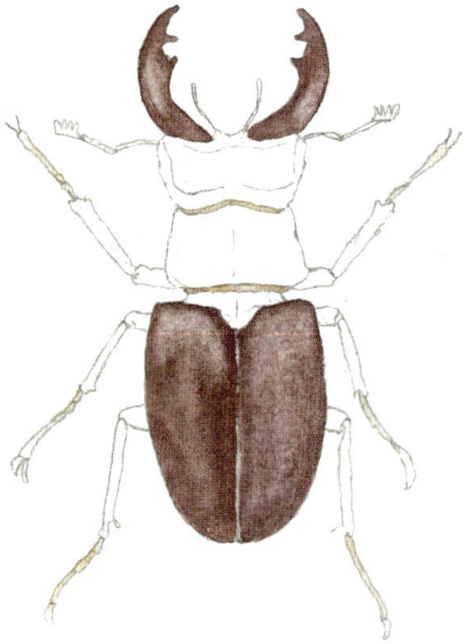

Step 3: Add Color and Highlights

Next, we will create highlights and shine on the wings and horn of the beetle using a paper towel. First, swirl a size 0 brush into water and "wiggle" the bristles along the top of each of the wings, moving gently downward along the center until you reach three-quarters of the way down each wing. As you wiggle the bristles, this will agitate the paint layer underneath and cause it to lift onto the bristles. Next, press a piece of dry paper towel firmly onto these damp areas of the wings that you just worked on, then lift the paper towel. A spot of highlight will be revealed underneath, giving the wings a sense of luminosity. Repeat this step of lifting the paint on the center of the horns.

Now switch to a size 3/0 brush to mix a light-toned solution of raw umber and water. Load the paint onto the bristles and fill in the ends of the lower feet, the middle of the central feet, and the ends of the top feet of the beetle. Use this same brush and raw umber mixture to fill in the sections of the body that separate the beetle's upper anatomy. Clean the brushes.

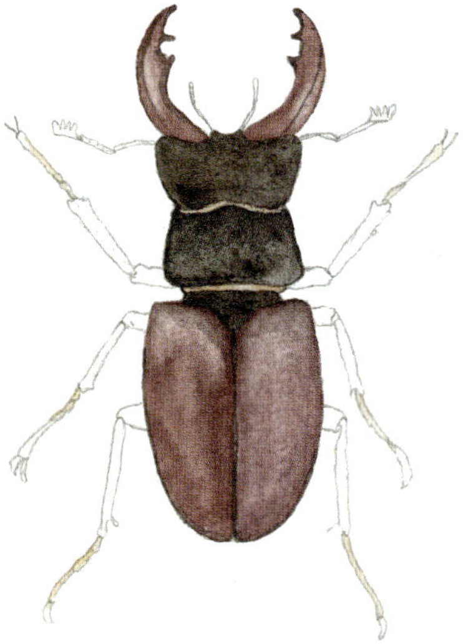

Step 4: Fill In the Anatomy

For the upper body of the beetle, use a clean size 4 brush to mix a mid-toned solution of ivory black with a swirl of Vandyke brown. We want this color not to be cool-toned pure black but to have a warm, earthy undertone. Load this color onto the bristles and fill in the upper anatomy of the beetle. Allow this layer to dry.

(continued)

Switch to a clean size 3/0 brush and dip into this dark earthy color, and gently fill in the line down the center of the wings, then following up along the outside of each wing shell, creating a subtle outline. Dip the bristles of the same size 3/0 brush back into the dark earthy color and trace the outline of the horns, carefully drawing in a central line that flows down to meet the top of the head. Clean the brush.

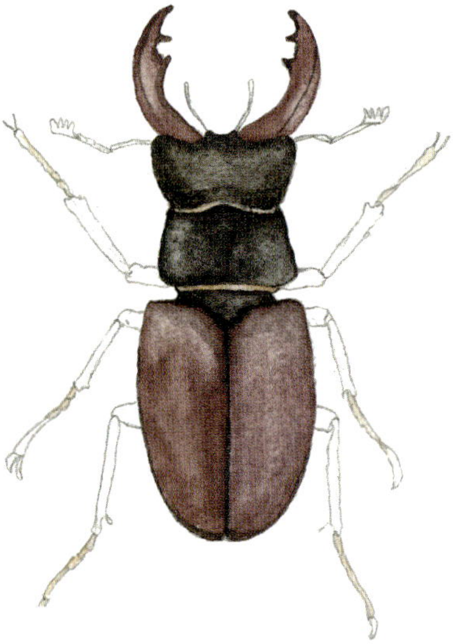

Step 5: Create Upper Anatomy Highlights and Detailing

To create the highlights on the upper body of the beetle, we will use the same lifting method used in step 3. Swirl a clean size 0 brush into water, then wiggle the bristles on the center of the head, on the left- and right-hand outer sides of the central section of the body, and the middle of the bottom section of the upper body. After the paint has been lifted on the bristles, press the dry paper towel firmly onto each dampened section, revealing the lifted luminous highlight underneath.

Then, using the clean size 3/0 brush, mix a mid-toned solution of ivory black and water, and trace along the lower section of the body where it meets the wings. Clean the brushes.

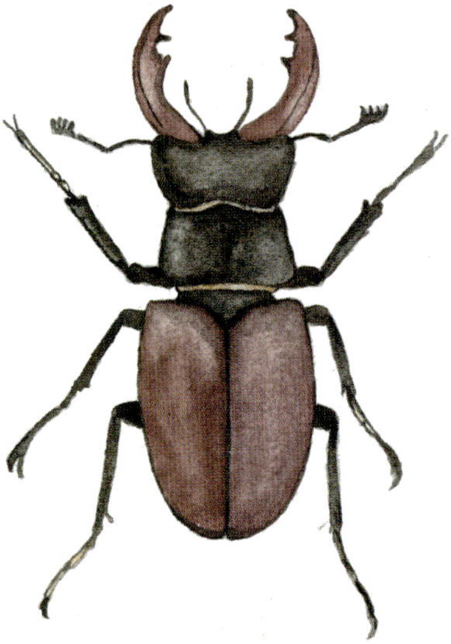

Step 6: Paint the Legs

For the legs and antennae of the beetle, we will be using a clean size 0 brush to mix a simple mid-toned solution of ivory black and water. Carefully fill in each segment of the legs and antennae. Feel free to switch to the clean size 3/0 brush if you find you need a finer tip to have more control over the lines, especially for the ends of the feet and the antennae, as they have finer and more delicate detailing. Take care to avoid painting over the sections of the feet that we painted with raw umber in step 3. Clean the brushes.

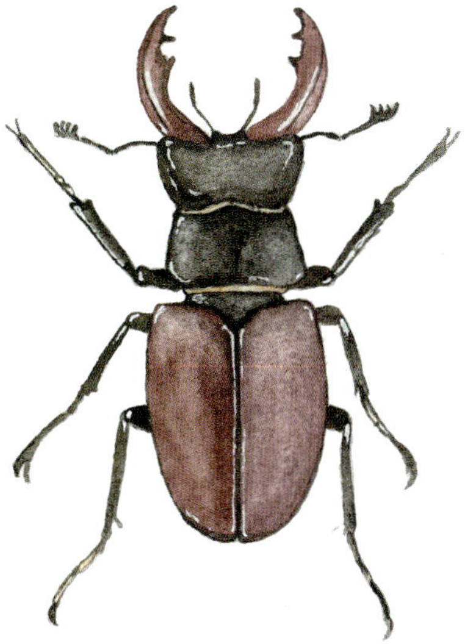

Step 7: Add Acrylic White

For the finishing touches of the beetle that will create a high shine effect, squeeze a pea-size amount of acrylic white onto your palette. Using a clean size 3/0 brush, dip the bristles into the paint and gently paint some small lines and markings along the tips and edges of the feet, the center edges of each wing, the edges of the anatomy sections, and the center of the horns. This will give the beetle a realistic high shine and glossy effect that they are well known for as they rummage around the soil in the garden!

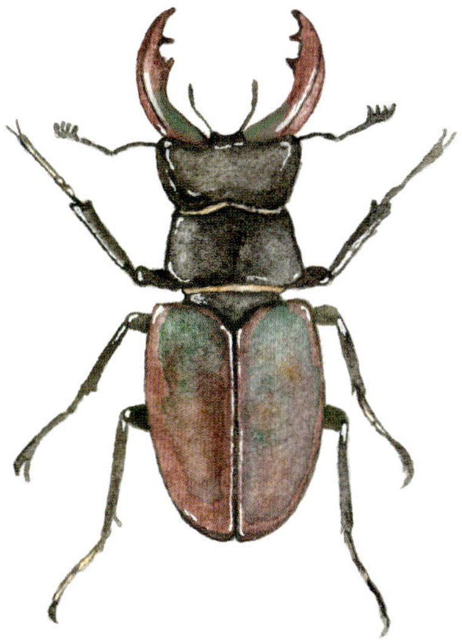

Step 8: Add Salt Effects

Using a size 1 brush, mix a mid-toned solution of emerald and water. Load this color onto the bristles and gently glaze the inner sides of the beetle's horns to the midway point. Paint a wash of this same color on the wings of the beetle, concentrating the paint at the tops of the wings, then gently dragging the paint down toward the bottom, which will soften the edges.

While these emerald layers are still damp, sprinkle a pinch of sea salt flakes onto the wings of the beetle that you just painted. As the paint is drying, the sea salt flakes will give a gentle textured effect, creating unique, organic textures and patterns that will add visual interest and depth to the wings. Once the paint layer is fully dry, gently swipe away the sea salt flakes until the surface is clear. The beetle is now complete. You did a great job!

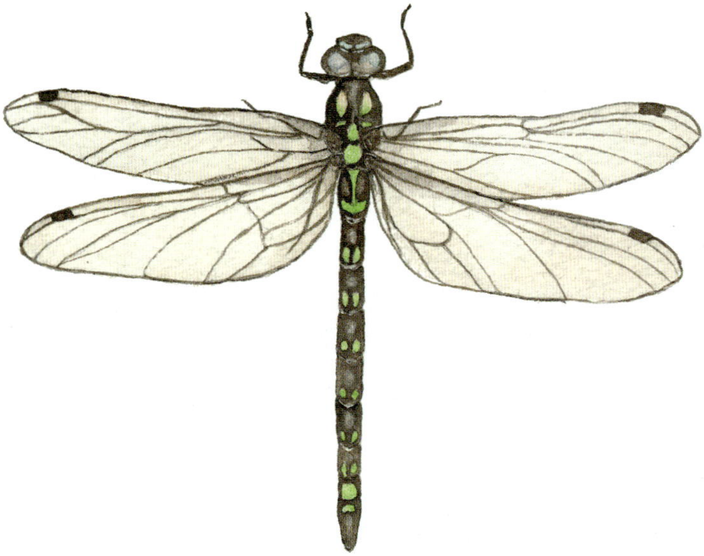

Dragonfly

It is fascinating to know that dragonflies have existed on Earth long before even the first mammals, and even before the dinosaurs! Their trembling wings upon first glance may give the impression that they are incredibly fragile or even made of glass, but they are extremely strong and agile fliers; dragonflies are among the fastest insects known!

In this project, we will explore how to balance detail with delicacy, and how a few fine lines can define a wing's structure. This will be a lesson in the fine points of a brush and how to control the bristles for the most realistic outcome that makes the finished piece feel almost ready to lift off from the page.

Materials Needed

1 sheet of cold-press 140-pound (300-gsm) aquarelle/watercolor paper

HB pencil

A piece of paper towel

Brushes

- > Size 3/0
- > Size 4
- > Size 1
- > Size 0

Watercolor paints

- > Yellow ochre
- > Sap green
- > Chinese white
- > Raw umber
- > Ivory black
- > Sepia
- > Indigo

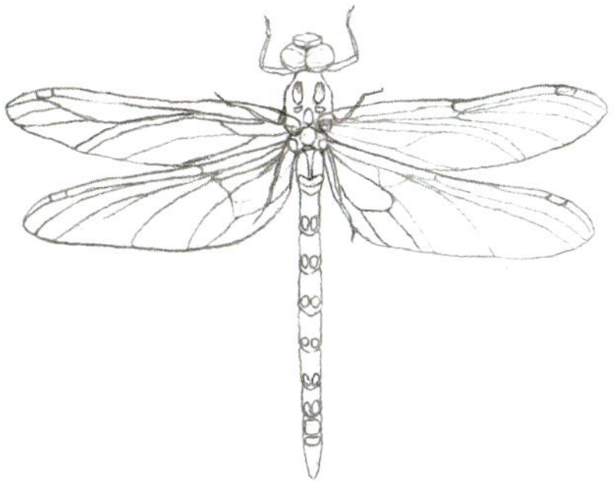

Step 1: Draw the Outline

Starting on a sheet of cold-press watercolor paper, draw the dragonfly's outline with a sharp HB pencil using the template provided on page 193. The wings of the dragonfly have many delicate lines and fine details, so do take your time in filling these areas in as they can require precision in order to portray symmetry and balance on either side.

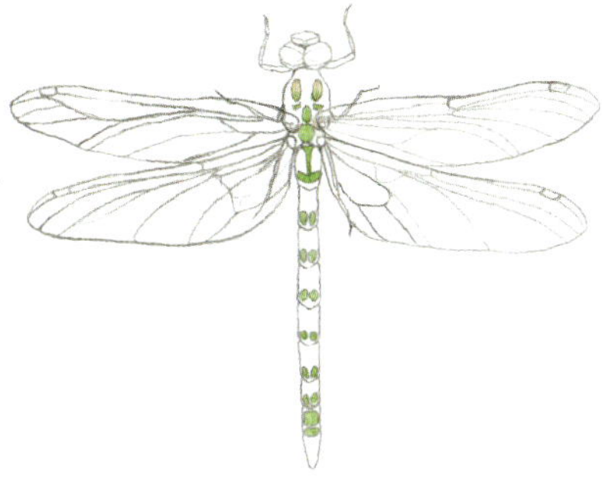

Step 2: Add Pops of Color

Using a size 3/0 brush, mix a light-toned solution of yellow ochre and water, and fill in a light layer of this solution at the very top markings on the upper torso of the dragonfly.

(continued)

While this layer is still damp, clean the bristles and use the same size 3/0 brush to mix a mid-toned solution of sap green and water. Drop this color onto the bottom of the top markings where we painted the yellow ochre. As this green layer dries, it will create a natural gradient that blends the colors from yellow to bright sap green very subtly.

Using the same size 3/0 brush and sap green mixture, fill in the remaining markings on the body of the dragonfly. Allow these layers to dry and clean the brush.

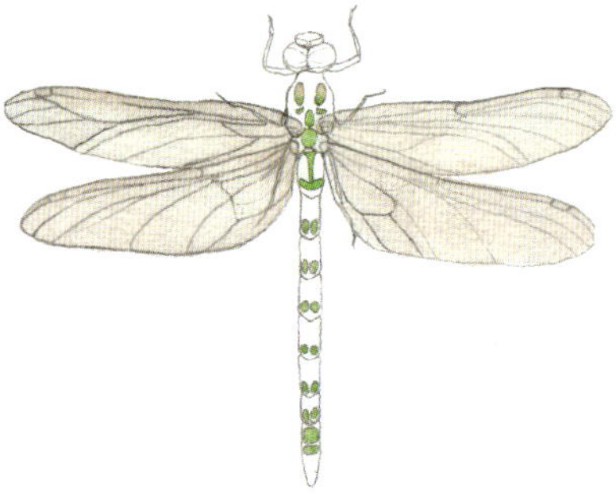

Step 3: Paint the Base Layer of the Wings

Using a size 4 brush, mix a mid-toned solution of Chinese white with a tiny dab of raw umber. We want this to be a warm cream color rather than a cool-toned pure white, but as raw umber is highly pigmented, only a tiny amount of that paint is needed. Load the bristles of the brush and glaze a layer of this cream color on both of the wings on the dragonfly. Allow this layer to dry.

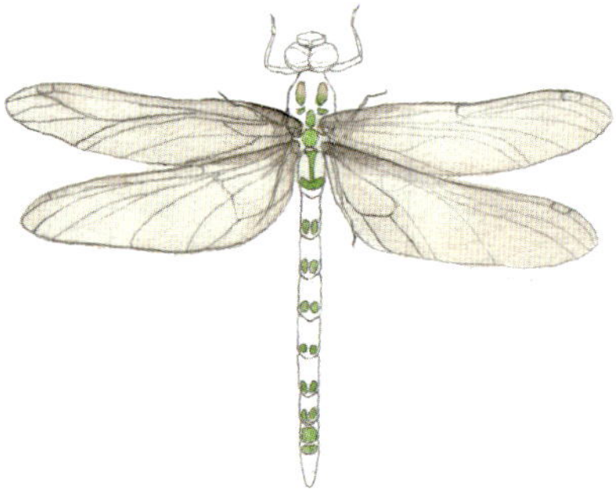

Step 4: Create Highlights and Shadows

Using the same size 4 brush, clean the bristles with water and wiggle the brush onto the center of each of the dragonfly's wings. The cream color underneath will begin to lift off the paper and onto the bristles of the brush. Then, press a sheet of dry paper towel firmly onto these dampened areas and lift off, revealing a luminous highlight underneath, which will give the wings of the dragonfly a true sense of realism and delicate translucency.

Next, switch to a size 1 brush and mix a light-toned solution of ivory black and water. We will use this color to create a sense of depth and shadow on the wing. Paint a thin layer of this pale gray on the inner section of each of the edges of the wing where they join and meet at the body. Gently push the paint outward along the upper outlines of the wings to soften any edges and to create a subtle gradient and blend into the cream base layer underneath. Allow these layers to dry.

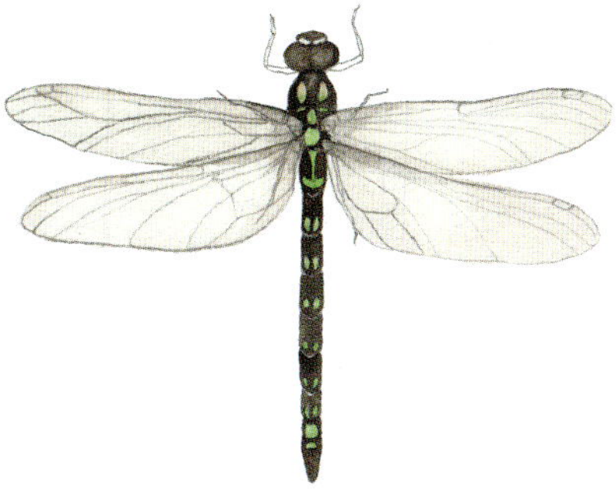

Step 5: Paint the Body

To create the rich, earthy brown color that will fill the body of the dragonfly, use a size 0 brush to mix a mid-toned solution of sepia with a tiny dab of ivory black. We want this color to still have the rich, earthy undertones of a dark brown with not too much black, which can cause it to look flat and inky.

Load this color onto the bristles and gently fill in each section of the body and head of the dragonfly with a layer of earthy brown. Be careful not to accidentally fill in any of the green markings. This is delicate work, so do take your time; the body of the dragonfly is quite minuscule. Allow the paint layer to dry and clean the brush.

When the paint is dry, take a clean size 3/0 brush and dip it in water so that it is damp, then wiggle the bristles onto the center of the head of the dragonfly, lifting up the dark brown underneath. Then, as we did in step 4, press the paper towel onto this dampened section and lift off, revealing a subtle highlight underneath.

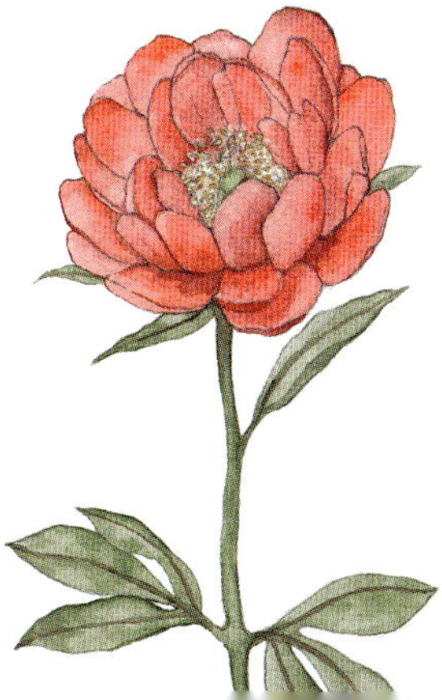

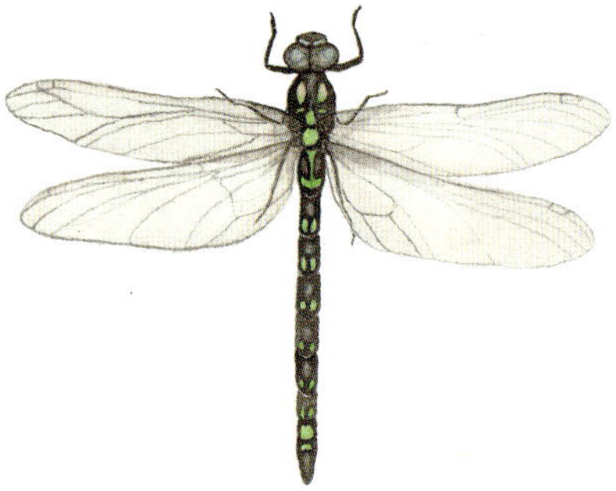

Step 6: Add Subtle and Delicate Detailing

Using a clean size 0 brush, mix a light-toned solution of indigo and water. Load the bristles with this light twilight-blue color and fill in two central circles on the top of the main part of the dragonfly's head, and two small rectangular shapes on the lower section of the top of the dragonfly's head. Allow these layers to dry.

Next, swap to a size 3/0 brush, and using the same mid-toned earthy brown color that we mixed in step 5, mix in a small dab of ivory black to deepen its pigment. Load the bristles of the brush, and holding it at the ferrule to ensure the most control over the lines, fill in and trace each of the legs on the dragonfly.

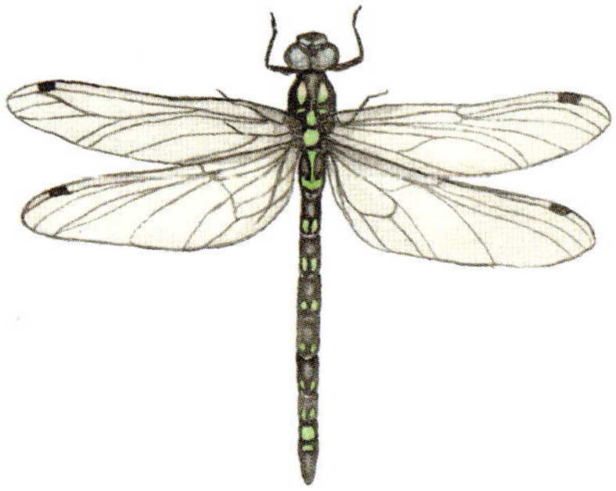

Step 7: Add Finishing Touches

The finishing touches will focus on the wings of the dragonfly, which will be a balance of detail and delicacy. Using the same size 3/0 brush and mid-toned deep brown we mixed in step 6, work from the wing's base outward, following the natural branching of the veins. Use the very tip of your brush at the ferrule and keep your wrist loose; think of it as illustrating with paint. Let each line soften and thin as it moves outward to the edges to keep a sense of variation of line and fragile realism.

Fill in the square-shaped markings on the upper edge, toward the end of each wing. Delicately outline the outer edges of each wing with the same flowing movement. Allow these paint layers to dry. The dragonfly is now complete. Well done!

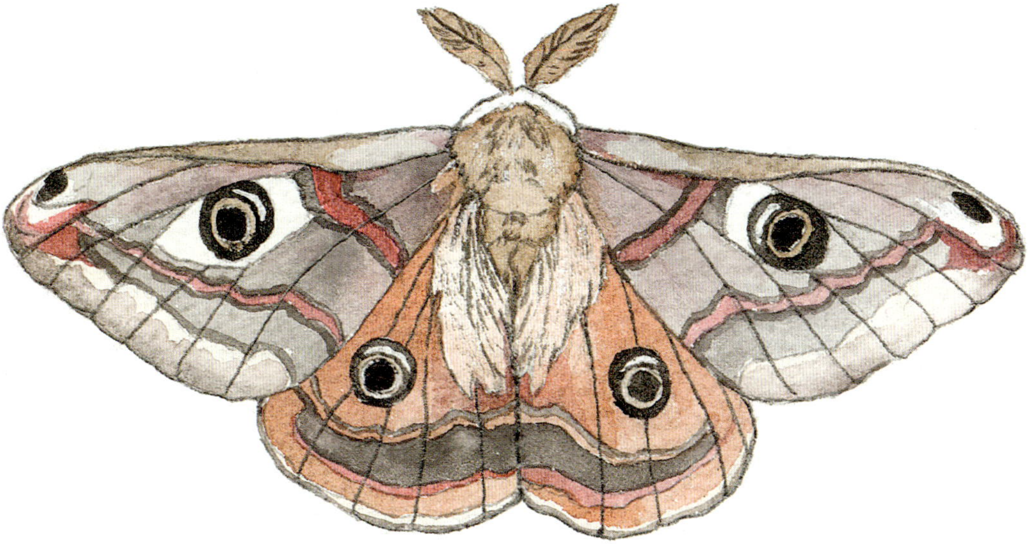

Emperor Moth

The adult emperor moth is a truly spectacular insect; with bold eyespots, feathery antennae, and soft, smoky patterning across the wings, they could be easily mistaken for butterflies due to their spectacular coloring! It is Ireland's only member of the silk moth family, and the caterpillars spin silk cocoons in which they spend the winter. So when the moths emerge in spring and summer to reveal their iconic wings, they are always a pleasure to see!

Materials Needed

1 sheet of cold-press 140-pound (300-gsm) aquarelle/watercolor paper

HB pencil

Brushes

- Size 1
- Size 4
- Size 0
- Size 3/0

Watercolor paints

- Chinese white
- Raw umber
- Burnt sienna
- Cadmium orange
- Light red
- Ivory black
- Rose madder
- Sepia
- Yellow ochre

Acrylic white

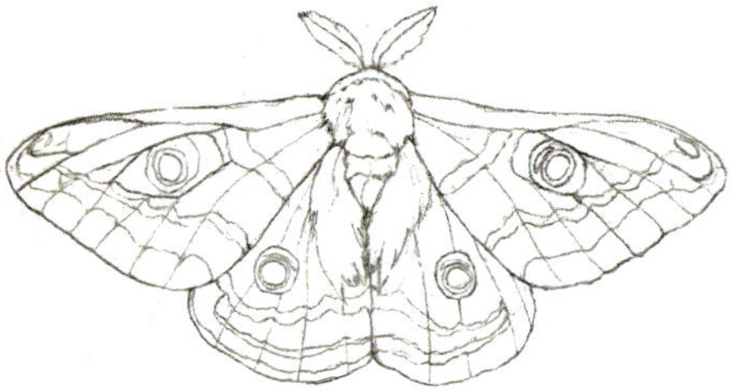

Step 1: Draw the Outline

Starting on a sheet of cold-press watercolor paper, draw the emperor moth's outline with a sharp HB pencil using the template provided on page 195.

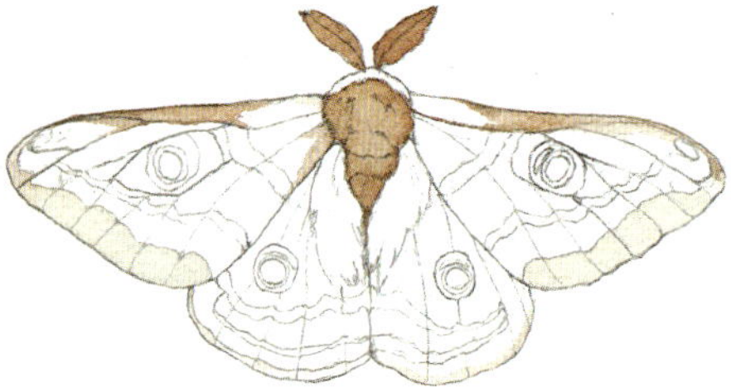

Step 2: Paint the Base Layers

Using a size 1 brush, mix a mid-toned solution of Chinese white with a swirl of raw umber to create a warm cream hue. Load this color onto the bristles and fill the sections of the wings on the lower edges, and allow these layers to dry.

Clean the bristles of the brush, and mix a mid-toned solution of burnt sienna with a small swirl of cadmium orange. Fill the mid and lower sections of the body, the antennae, and the outline of the upper wings, beginning at the upper midpoint of the upper wing and dragging the paint to the outer edges, just where the wings begin to curve. Allow these layers to dry and clean the brush.

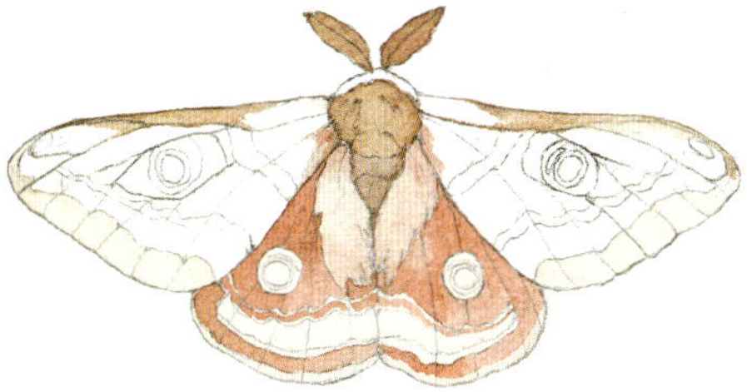

Step 3: Paint the Lower Wings

Use a size 4 brush to mix a light-toned solution of burnt sienna with a swirl of light red to create a warm, deep orange color. Glaze a thin layer of this solution onto the fluffy sections of the lower wings that are in the inner corners. While this layer is still damp, swirl the brush back into the light-toned solution and drop the pigment on the top and bottom edges of this fluffy section of the wing.

Next, use the same brush to mix in some more burnt sienna and light red into the light-toned solution to elevate its pigment and texture to a mid-toned solution. Fill the base of the lower wings with this warmer and deeper orange, being careful to avoid the eye and line markings on the central to lower parts of the wings, and the fluffy sections in the corners. Allow these layers to dry and clean the brush.

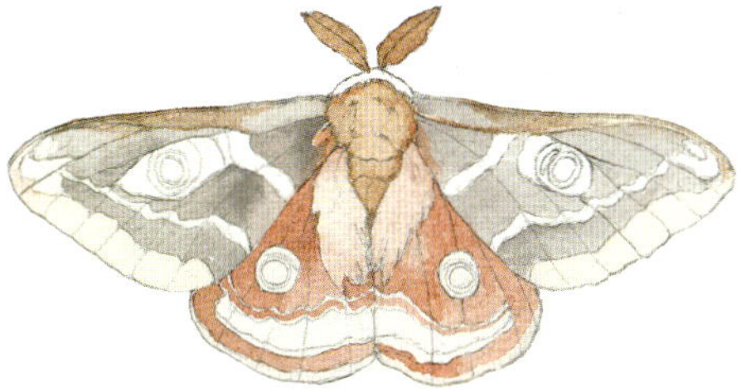

Step 4: Paint the Upper Wings

Use a clean size 4 brush to mix a light-toned solution of ivory black and water to create a watery gray hue. Load this color onto the brush and fill the main areas of the upper wing, taking care to avoid the eye markings and lined patterns that flow across the wing. Allow this light gray layer to dry and clean the brush.

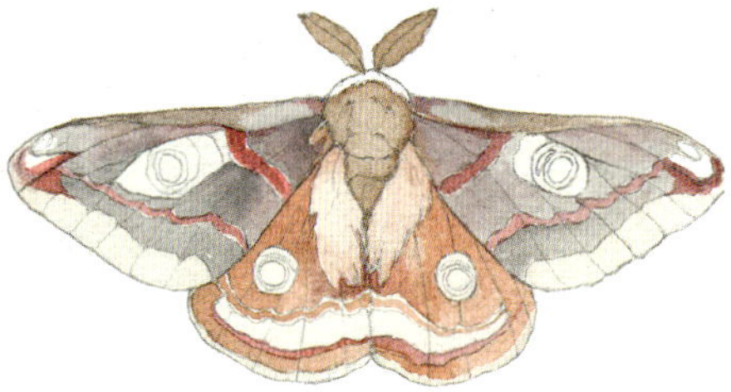

Step 5: Define the Markings

Using a size 0 brush, mix a simple mid-toned solution of rose madder and water to create a warm cerise-pink color. Load this solution onto the bristles and fill in each of the line markings that flow across the upper wings, and also a small section of pink on the curved edges of each side.

Swap to a size 3/0 brush and load the bristles with the same pink solution, and fill in the smaller line pattern on the bottom of the lower wings. Use the same brush to paint a thin layer of pink on the very inner corners of the cream upper outlines on the top wings, where the wings meet the top of the head.

Next, using a clean size 1 brush, we are going to swirl some water into the mid-toned rose madder solution to dilute it to a light-toned paler solution. Gently glaze a thin layer of this pale pink color onto the inner corners of the upper wings where they meet the central section of the body, letting the paint flow downward along the inner outline of the upper wing on the right-hand side, stopping at the second pink line design. Allow these layers to dry and clean the brushes.

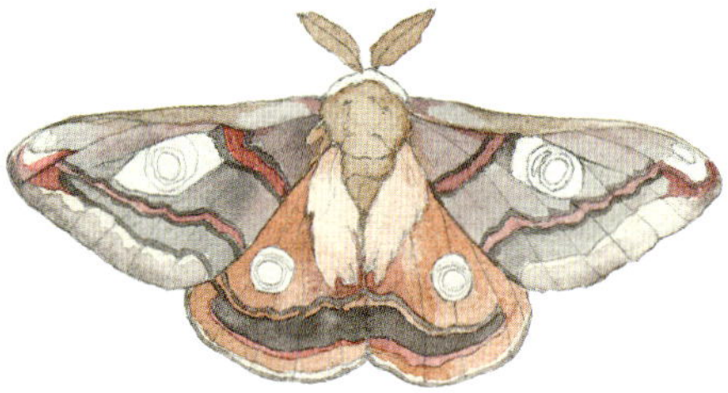

Step 6: Add More Details

Next, we will fill in the lined patterns and markings on the wings of the moth. Use a clean size 0 brush to mix a mid-toned solution of ivory black and water, making sure that this solution has slightly more pigment.

Load this color onto the bristles and fill in the line patterns on the upper and lower sides of the pink lined patterns we painted in step 5, and the larger lined markings toward the bottom of the lower wings.

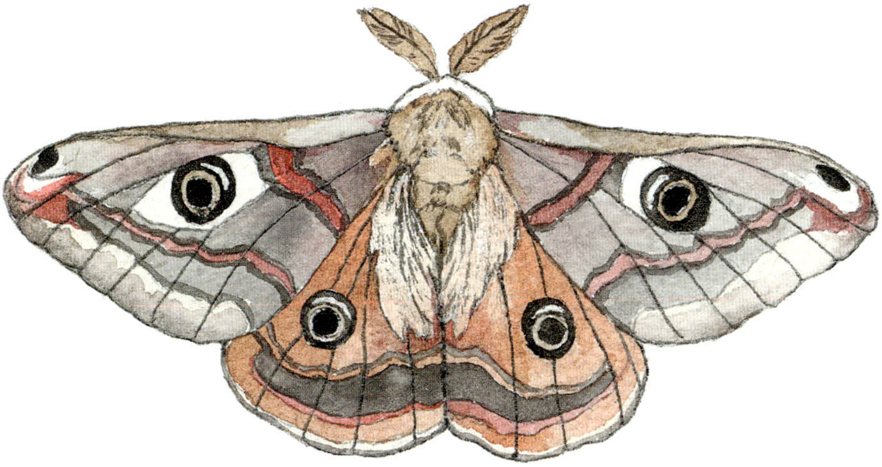

Swap to a clean size 3/0 brush and swirl the bristles into the same black mixture. Carefully glaze the outlines of the bottom of both the top and bottom wings, and fill the smaller line pattern that is closest to the eye markings. Allow these layers to dry and clean the brushes.

Step 7: Add Final Details

Using a clean size 3/0 brush, mix a mid-toned solution of sepia with a tiny dab of ivory black and water. Load this color onto the bristles and outline each of the veins on the wings of the moth with smooth, flowing lines. Outline each section of the body and paint short dash brushstrokes on the center of the body and fluffy sections of the lower wings to create a soft texture. Trace small lines coming from the soft, fluffy antennae on either side.

Clean the bristles of the brush and mix a simple light-toned solution of yellow ochre and water. Load this color onto the bristles and fill the ring section on each eye marking on the upper and lower wings. Clean the bristles and swap to a clean size 0 brush. Mix a dark-toned solution of ivory black and water, and carefully fill in the rest of the eye markings on the upper and lower wings, avoiding the small semicircle above the ring. Fill in two small oval markings at the tips of the upper wings with this black color.

Finally, squeeze a pea-size amount of acrylic white onto the palette. Using a clean size 3/0 brush, carefully fill in the semicircle marking above the ring in each eye pattern. Fill in the areas of the upper wings surrounding the eye markings, the top of the head where it meets the antennae, and the small amount of white surrounding the lower side of the black oval markings on the tips of the upper wings with the white acrylic. The emperor moth is now complete. Well done!

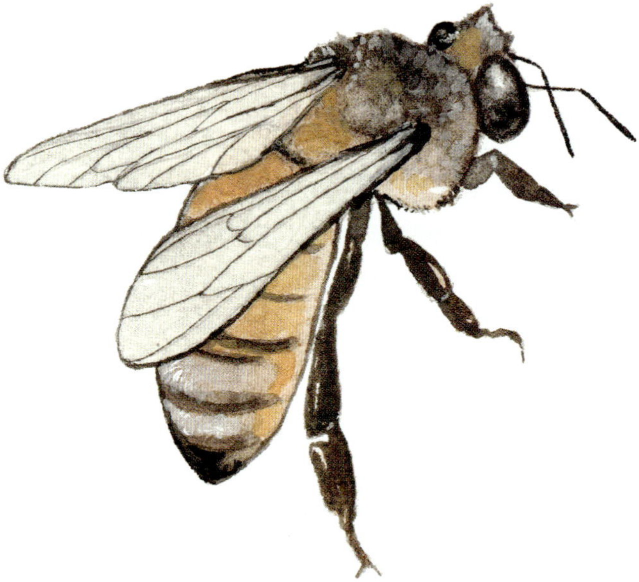

Honeybee

Honey is one of my favorite foods, not only for having an appearance essentially like liquid gold but also for how fascinating it is that it can hold the memory of the landscape it was created in: heather from the hills, clover and wildflowers from the meadows, a hint of gorse on the breeze. I wanted to create a project that was an homage to its creator, the gentle yet persistent honeybee. If you have ever been lucky enough to peer into a hive, it is impossible not to see these bees as tiny alchemists! In this project, there is a beautiful contrast from learning how to paint the translucency held in its delicate wings to the soft fuzz of its body that equally holds perfectly geometric stripes.

Materials Needed

1 sheet of cold-press 140-pound (300-gsm) aquarelle/watercolor paper

HB pencil

A piece of paper towel

Brushes

- Size 1
- Size 0
- Size 3/0

Watercolor paints

- Yellow ochre
- Burnt sienna
- Chinese white
- Sepia
- Ivory black
- Cadmium yellow

Acrylic white

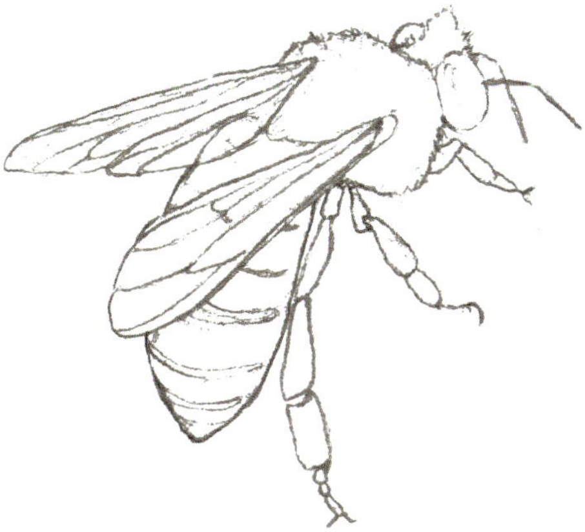

Step 1: Draw the Outline

Starting on a sheet of cold press watercolor paper, draw the honeybee's outline with a sharp HB pencil using the template provided on page 195. Note that the texture on the upper body of the bee is quite soft and fuzzy, while the lower body has smooth, confident lines.

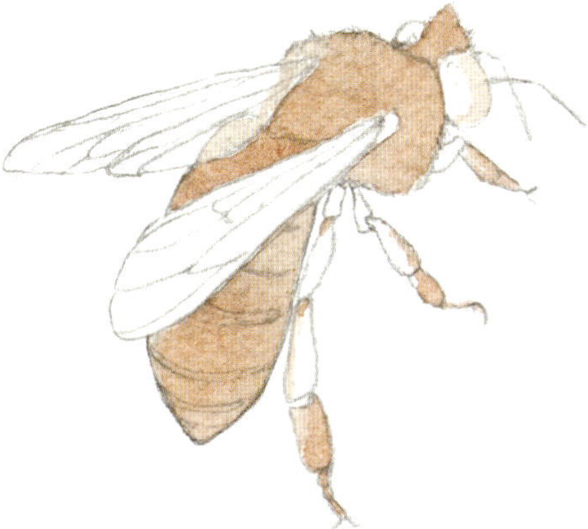

Step 2: Paint the Body

For the body of the honeybee, we want to create a warm burnt yellow. Using a size 1 brush, mix a light-toned solution of yellow ochre with a small dab of burnt sienna. The addition of the burnt sienna will give the bright yellow a deep warmth that will not be too "sunny" in color. Load this color onto your bristles and coat the body of the bee with a light glaze. Avoid the section of the body that is underneath the right wing, but do add a layer of this light glaze to the section of the body that is underneath the left wing.

(continued)

Add a small amount of this color to the sides of the legs, the entire lower foot, and the side of the right eye. Allow this layer to dry. When the paint is fully dry, add another layer to the sections of the body not covered by the wings, and to the lower sections of the feet. Clean the brush.

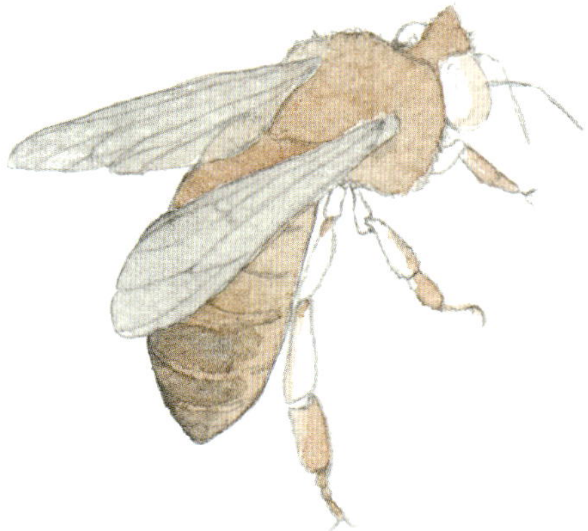

Step 3: Paint the Wings and Lower Body

Using a clean size 1 brush, mix a mid-toned solution of Chinese white with a tiny dab of sepia. We want this to be a warm cream color rather than a cool-toned white. Swirl your brush into this warm cream solution and paint both of the wings. Allow this layer to dry and clean the brush.

For the lower body of the bee, using the clean size 1 brush, mix a light-toned solution of sepia with a tiny dab of ivory black. We want this to be a watery, loose, cool-toned brown that has a slight hue of gray. Glaze this mixture on the lower part of the honeybee's body, focusing on the last three "sections," leaving a slight gap of the underlying warm yellow on the right-hand side and on the separating lines to create distinction between them. Allow this paint layer to fully dry and clean the brush.

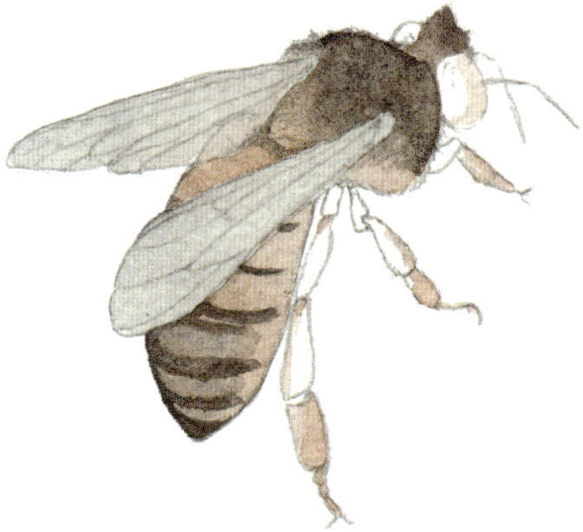

Step 4: Paint Texture and Detail

To create the color for the texture and details on the body of the bee, use a size 0 brush to mix a mid-toned solution of sepia and a tiny dab of ivory black. We want this color to be not thick but also not extremely watery and diluted, and to have a warm, dark brown hue. Glaze this color on the upper section of the body, dragging the paint downward, softening the edges until the dark brown seamlessly blends into the paper and into the yellow on the lower part of the midsection.

Repeat the same motion for the head, focusing first on the top of the head and softly dragging the paint downward until it blends seamlessly into the warm yellow base layer underneath. Allow this layer to dry.

Dip your brush back in to this warm brown solution and paint stripes along the lines of the lower section of the body, filling in the tip at the very bottom fully. Allow the paint to fully dry and clean the brush.

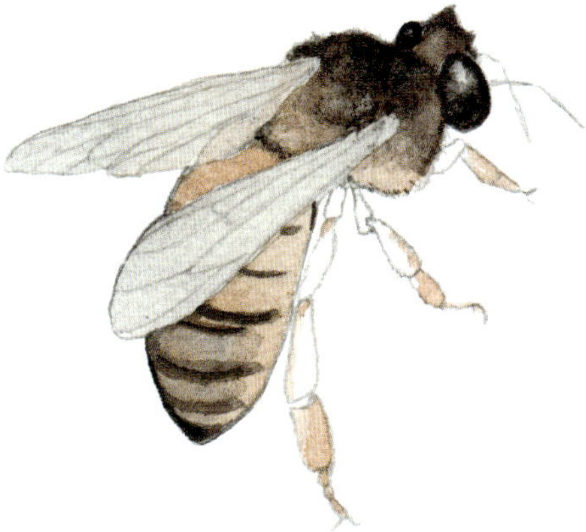

Step 5: Define Details

Using a clean size 1 brush, mix a dark-toned solution of ivory black and water. Load the bristles with this mixture and fill in the bee's eyes, and allow them to dry.

While the paint is drying, add a small amount of water into the dark-toned black solution to dilute it, creating a mid-toned solution that is more watery rather than highly pigmented. Gently drop this solution into the center of the midsection on the body of the bee, and carefully pull the paint outward so it is more concentrated in the center and softens as it moves out and downward, filling the upper three-quarters of the midsection.

Repeat this step for the head of the bee, concentrating a drop of the mid-toned black at the top center and softening it by gently pulling the paint downward until it blends seamlessly into the page. Load the bristles again with this mid-toned solution and paint along the stripes of the lower body.

Finally, load a clean size 0 brush with plain water, and agitate the paint on the upper part of the bee's eye until the dark black paint underneath begins to lift up onto the bristles. Then, using a clean, dry piece of paper towel, press firmly into this section of the eye that was just agitated and lift up, revealing a highlight underneath. Clean the brushes.

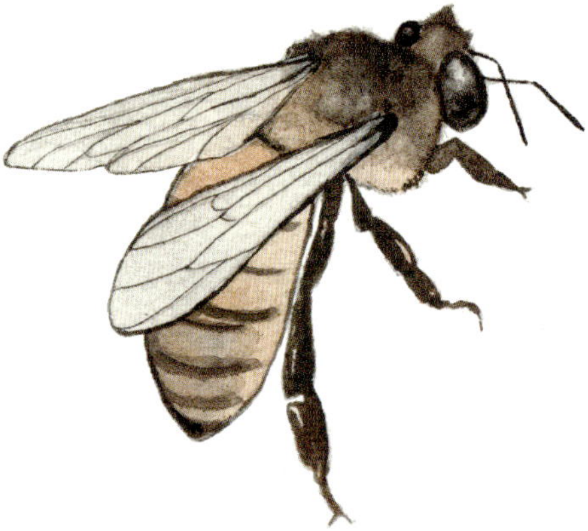

Step 6: Define the Wings and Body

Using a size 3/0 brush, mix a dark-toned solution of ivory black and water. Hold the brush at the ferrule and gently and carefully trace along the lines of the wing to create definition. Follow this same method along the entire body, defining each section, keeping note to make the midsection outlines soft and fluffy, and the lower body confident and smooth. Fill in the antennae and outline the eyes, then clean the brush. Next, swap to a clean size 0 brush and add a small amount of water to this dark-toned black mixture to dilute it slightly. Glaze this lighter black color onto the feet, leaving tiny sections on the sides of the lower two feet yellow to give the impression of a highlight. Allow these paint layers to fully dry.

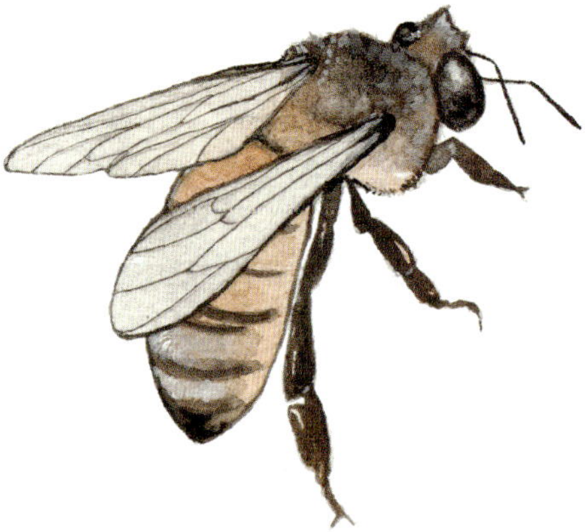

Step 7: Add Acrylic Details

Finally, squeeze a less than pea-size amount of acrylic white out onto your palette. Using a clean size 3/0 brush, load a small amount of paint onto the tip of the brush and define tiny hairs along the upper part of the top section of the body and head, using tiny downward strokes to build the texture of fur. Use this same method to create tiny fur-like strokes on the left-hand side of the lower section of the honeybee's body.

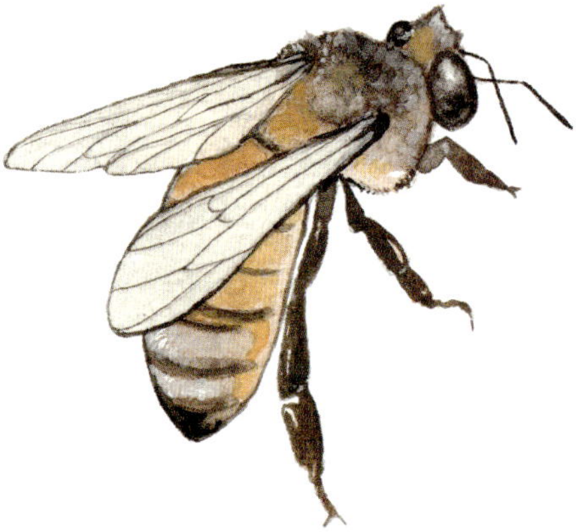

Step 8: Add Finishing Touches

Using a clean size 1 brush, mix a mid-toned solution of cadmium yellow with a small swirl of burnt sienna to create a warm, sunny yellow. Load this color onto the bristles of the brush and paint a layer of this warm yellow onto the previous layers of yellow that we painted on the body of the honeybee, making sure not to paint into the black stripes or acrylic white furry sections. Allow these layers to dry. The honeybee is now complete. Great job!

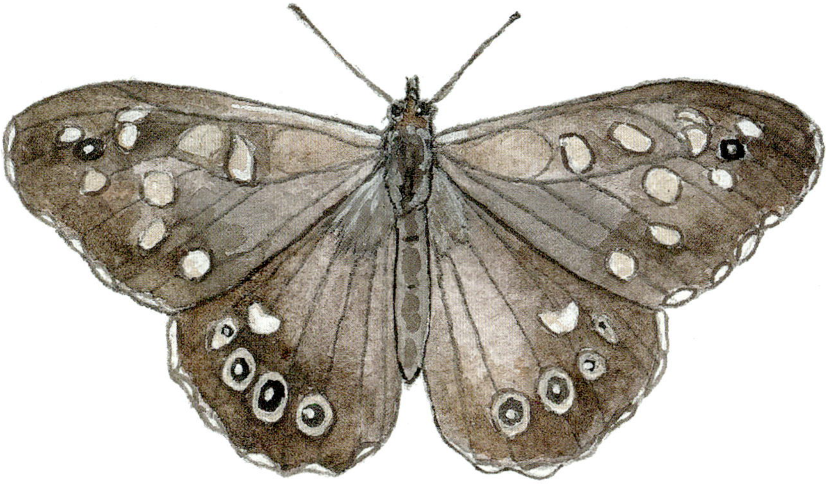

Speckled Wood Butterfly

The speckled wood butterfly is a delightful sight in the garden hedgerows. Often found perching in sunny spots, it can be a magical sight to witness them spiraling in the air as they chase each other. Although their colors are quite subdued and earthy, the scattered patterns of their wings with pale spots and deeper eye marks give you space to explore careful layering when choosing them as a subject to paint. In this tutorial, you'll learn how to build those quiet gradients that drift from warm midtones to the darker edges, how to place each marking with a steady hand, and most importantly, how to keep the wings feeling light.

Materials Needed

1 sheet of cold-press 140-pound (300-gsm) aquarelle/watercolor paper

HB pencil

Brushes

- Size 4
- Size 1
- Size 0
- Size 3/0

Watercolor paints

- Sepia
- Burnt umber
- Vandyke brown
- Ivory black
- Lamp black
- Raw umber
- Chinese white

Acrylic white

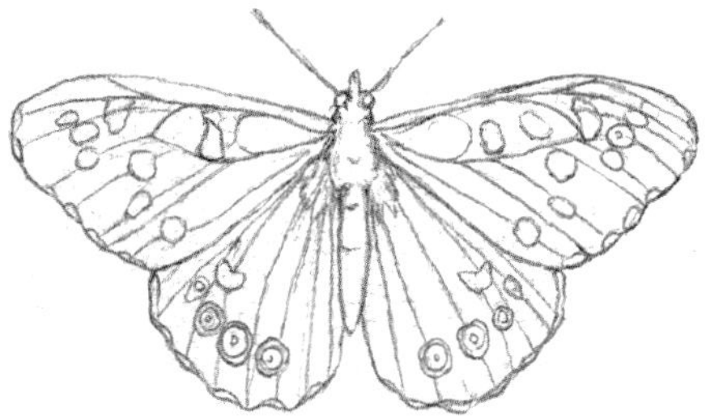

Step 1: Draw the Outline

Starting on a sheet of cold-press watercolor paper, draw the speckled wood butterfly's outline with a sharp HB pencil using the template provided on page 195. There are a lot of details in this piece, so make sure to take your time as butterflies do look their best and most realistic when the patterns of the wings are as symmetrical as possible.

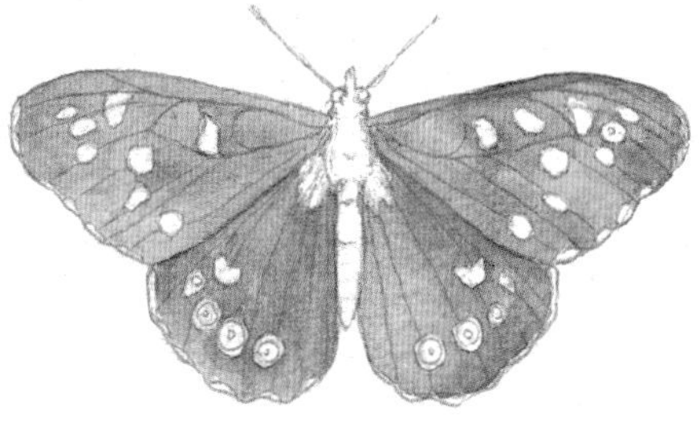

Step 2: Paint the Base Layer

Using a size 4 brush, mix a simple mid-toned solution of sepia and water to create a warm, earthy gray color. Load this mixture onto the bristles and fill in the wings, excluding the circular markings and fluffy sections on the inner corners of the lower wings. Allow this layer to dry.

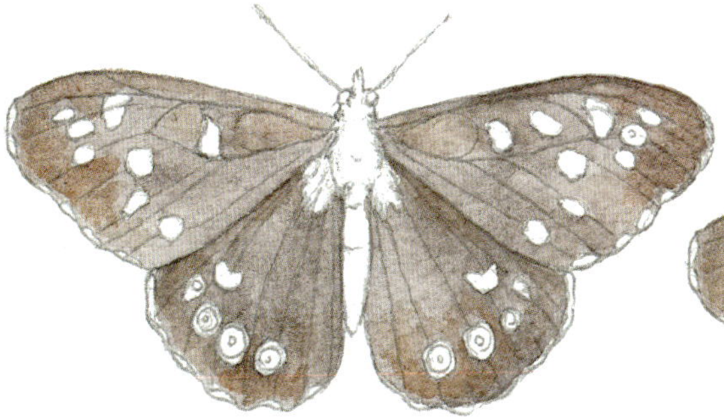

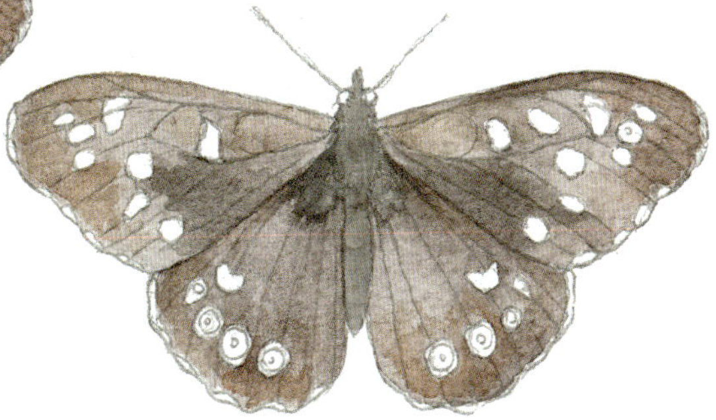

Step 3: Add Warmth

Using a size 1 brush, mix a mid-toned solution of burnt umber with a small swirl of Vandyke brown to create a warm, rusty brown. Load the bristles with this color and gently glaze the outer corners of each of the wings, softly dragging the paint inward to soften the edges and have the layers blend seamlessly into each other.

Gently glaze a thin wash of this warm, rusty brown into the inner corners of the upper wings and the upper outlines of the lower wings where they overlap in the center, repeating the same softening-edges technique. Clean the brush.

Step 4: Paint the Body

Using a size 0 brush, mix a mid-toned solution of sepia with a small swirl of ivory black to create a deep, rich earthy brown color. Load this color onto the bristles and fill in the body of the butterfly, avoiding the eyes and antennae.

Glaze a layer of this earthy brown color along the lower outline of the upper wings, gently pushing the paint upward so it disperses into the center of the wings, creating a soft blending effect.

Fill in the fluffy sections at the inner corner of the lower wings that meet the butterfly's body. Allow these layers to dry and clean the brush.

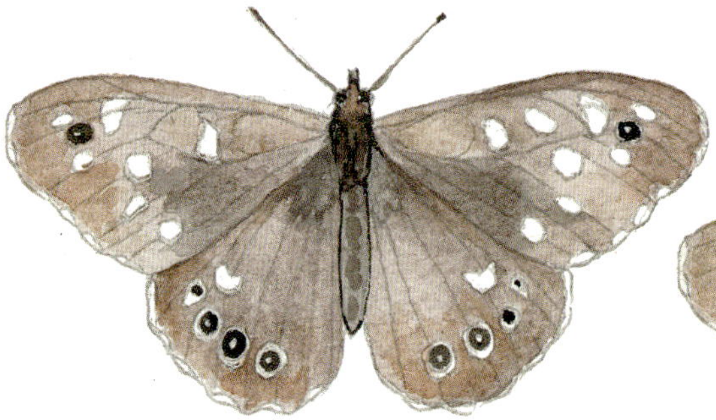

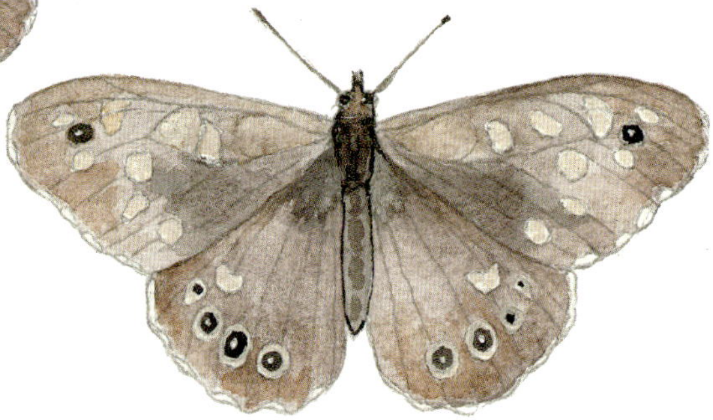

Step 5: Define the Body and Markings

Using a size 3/0 brush, mix a dark-toned solution of lamp black and water to create a thick, inky black mixture. Load this color onto the bristles and carefully fill in the circular markings on the wings; there are four on the lower wings and one on each of the upper wings. Be sure to leave unpainted a small dot in the center on each of the markings; these will be filled in later.

Swirl the brush back into the black mixture, and holding the brush at the ferrule, fill in the eyes and antennae, then trace the outline of each of the sections of the body on the butterfly. For the central section of the body beneath the head, paint short, quick brushstrokes that flow downward, stopping at the lower section of the body. This will give the central body section a fluffier appearance. Clean the bristles of the brush.

For the lower section of the body, there are small brown markings. Use a clean size 0 brush to dip back into the mid-toned sepia solution that was mixed in step 4, and paint four small, loose, square-shaped markings down the lower section of the body.

Step 6: Add More Details

For the other markings on the wings of the butterfly, use a clean size 3/0 brush to mix a mid-toned solution of raw umber with a swirl of Chinese white to create a pale, creamy sand color. Carefully fill in the rest of the markings that remain on the upper and lower wings of the butterfly. Fill in the central dots on the black markings that we painted in step 5, and paint a small circle around each of the black circles to create soft definition. Fill in each of the semicircle patterns that are sitting at the edge of each of the upper and lower wings. Allow these layers to dry and clean the brush.

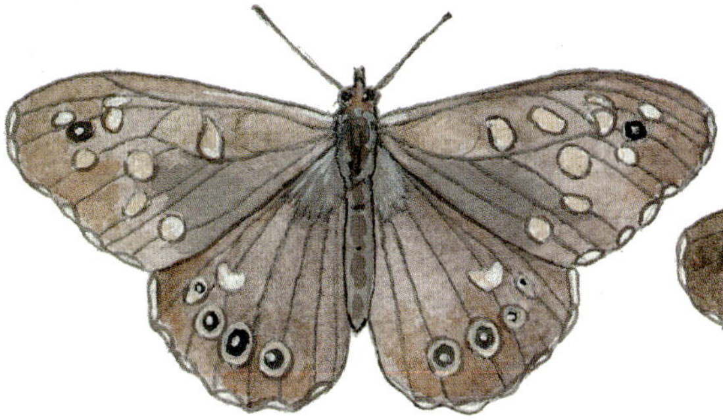

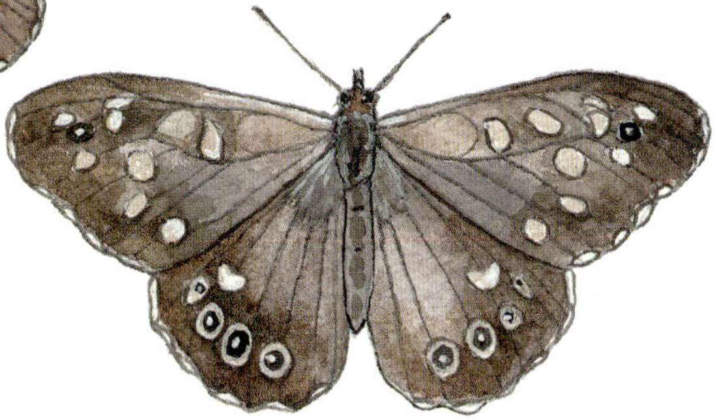

Step 7: Outline the Wings and Other Features

Using a clean size 3/0 brush, mix a mid-toned solution of sepia with a tiny dab of ivory black and water. We want this color to be a warm, earthy brown. Load this color onto the bristles and outline each of the veins on the wings of the speckled wood butterfly with smooth, flowing lines. Outline each of the markings and sand-colored semicircles that sit along the edges of the wings.

Clean the bristles, and squeeze a pea-size amount of acrylic white paint onto your palette. Dip in the tip of the same size 3/0 brush and paint some short dash brushstrokes around the inner edges of the midsection to create a furry texture, and some longer, soft brushstrokes on the inner corners of the lower wings to create a soft texture. Dab a small amount of acrylic white onto the inner outlines of each of the sand-colored markings on the upper and lower wings.

Step 8: Add Finishing Touches

For the finishing touches on the wings of the butterfly, use a clean size 1 brush to mix a mid-toned solution of sepia with a swirl of burnt umber. Load this color onto the bristles and begin by glazing along the center of each of the wings and pushing the paint to the outer edges of the wings, being careful to avoid getting paint in the markings and patterns.

Repeat the same center-to-edge motion for the lower wings but also carry the color along the upper outline to where the two wings overlap, letting the glaze gently fade and blend into the lighter brown layer beneath it as it reaches the central fluffy sections at the inner corners. Allow these layers to dry and clean the bristles. The speckled wood butterfly is now complete. Well done!

Templates

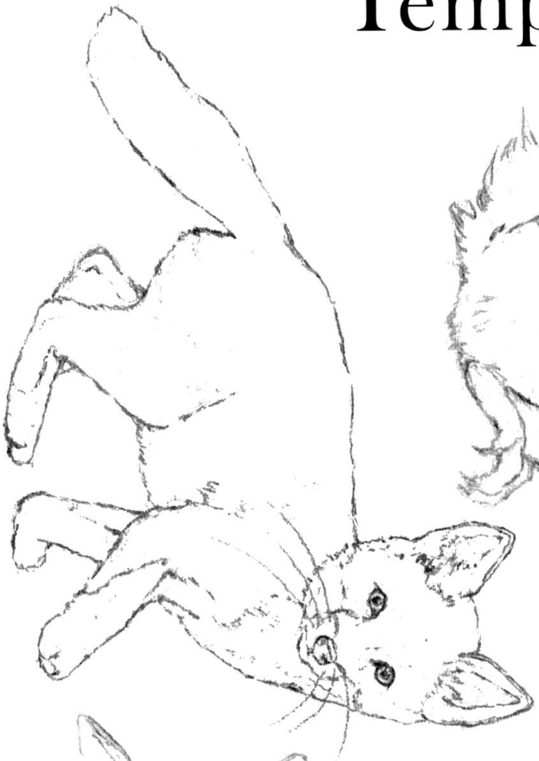

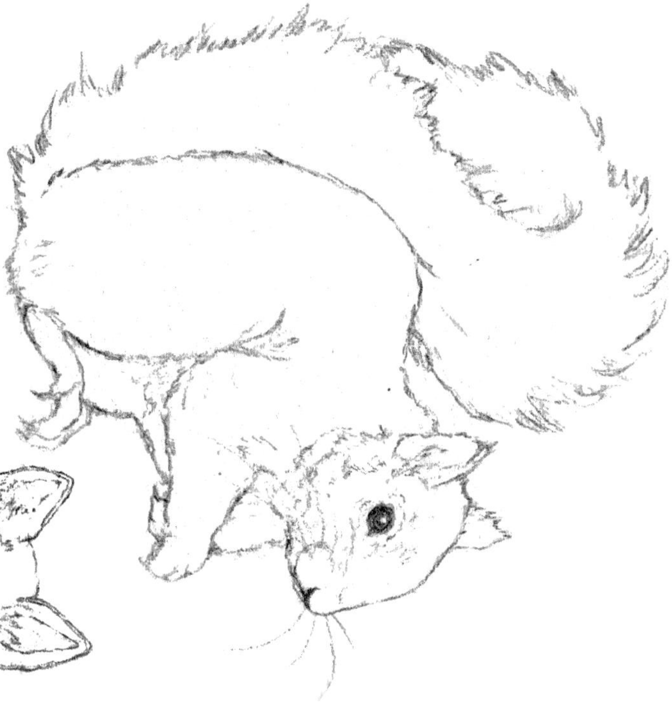

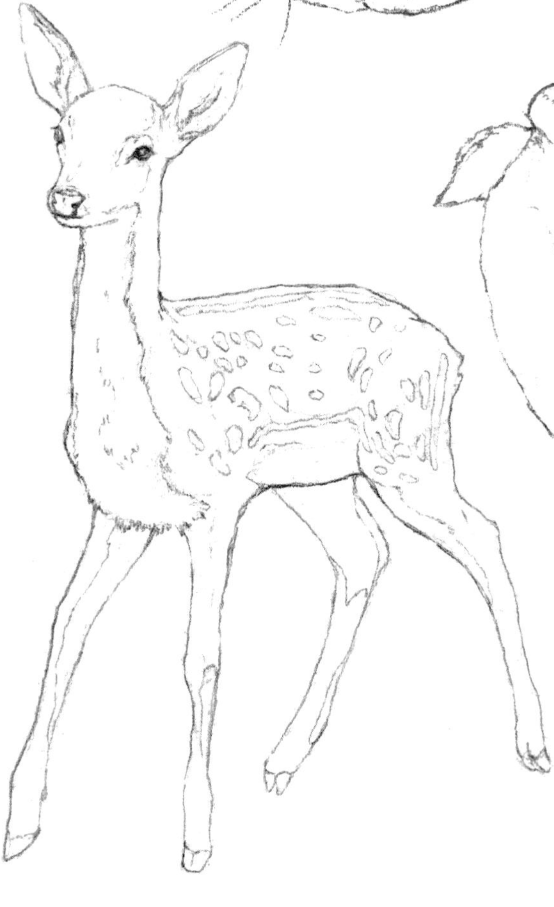

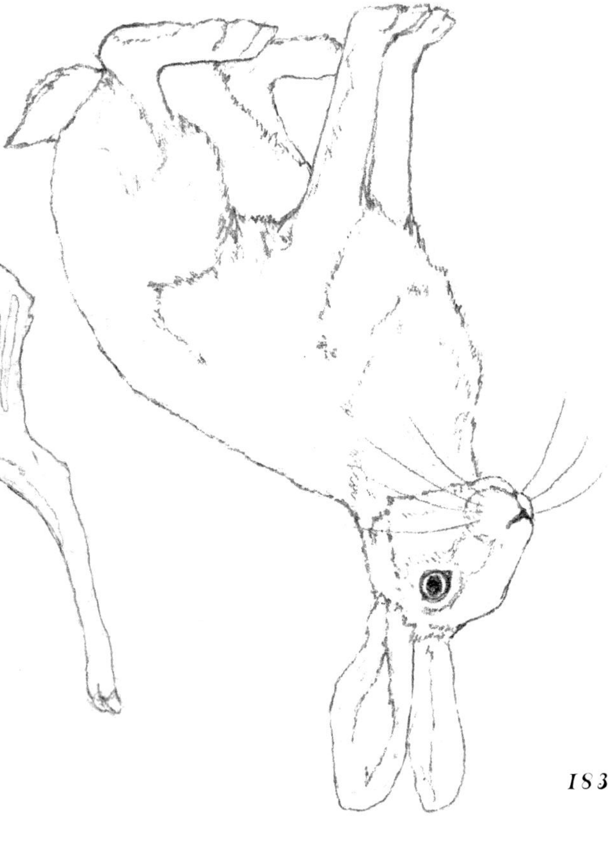

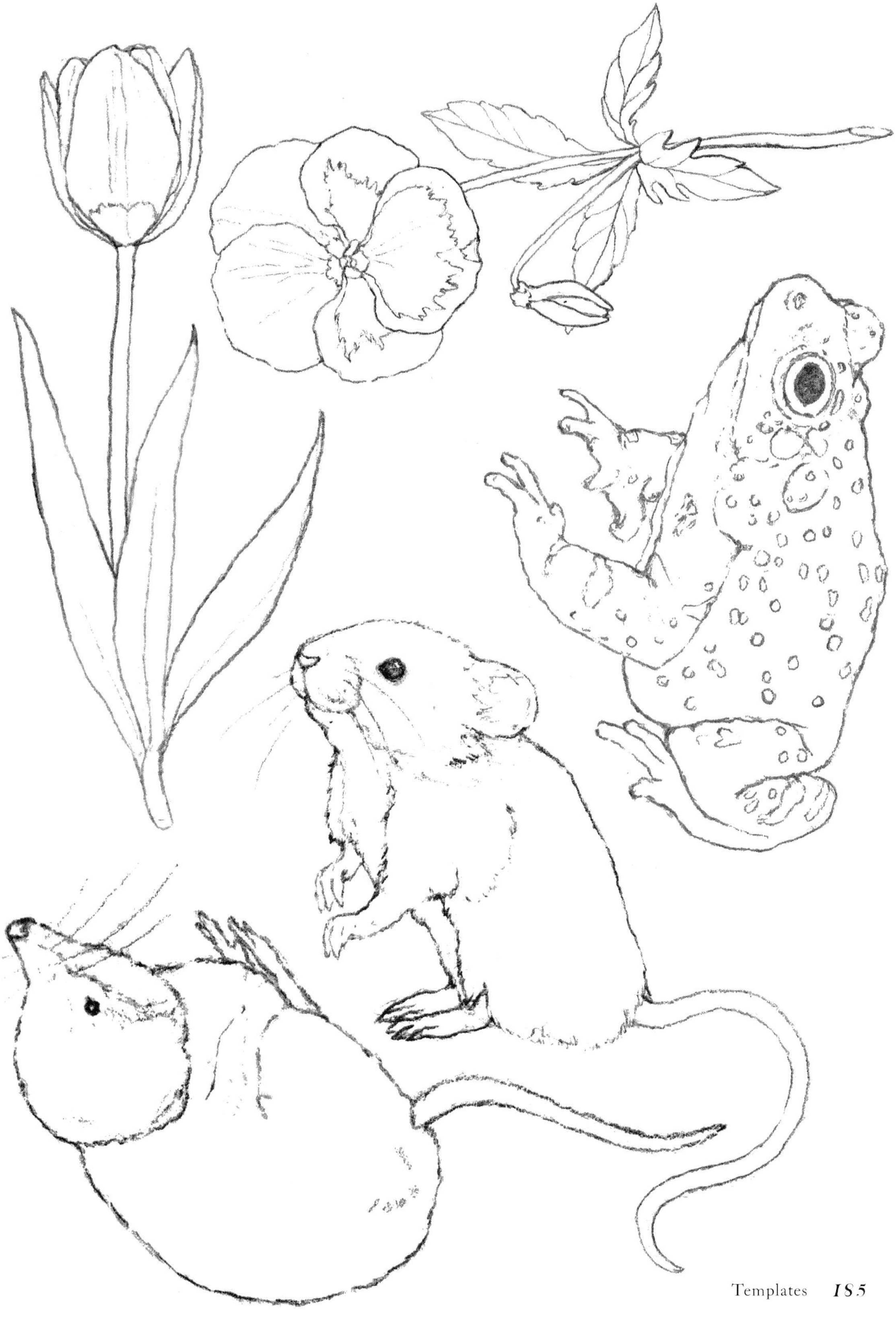

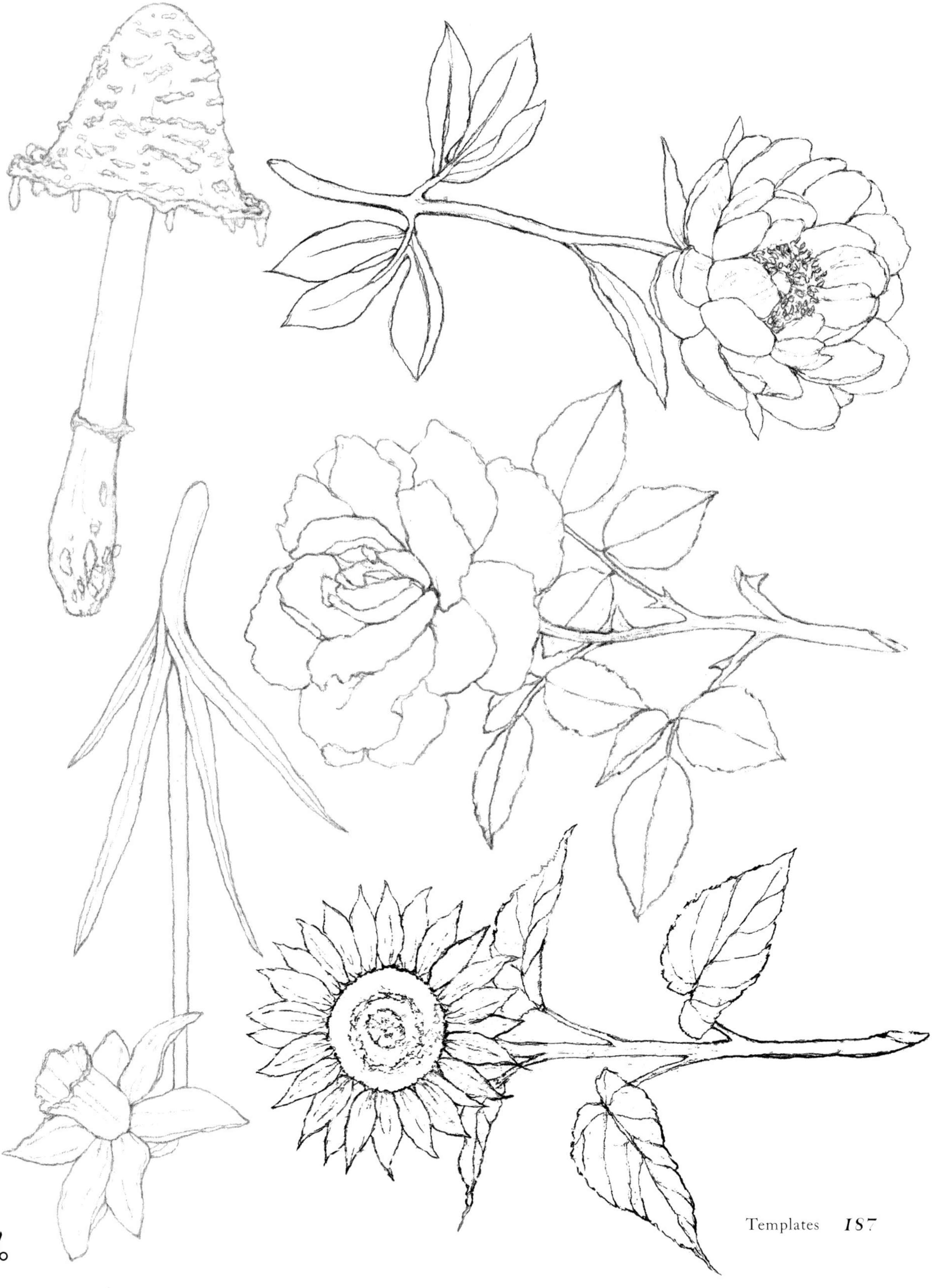

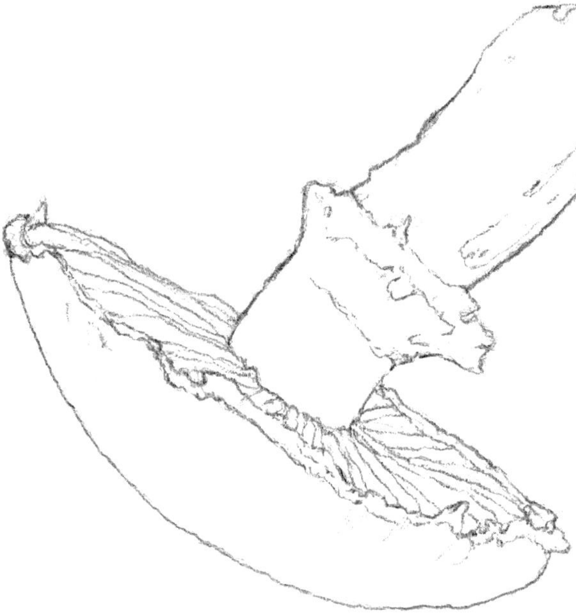

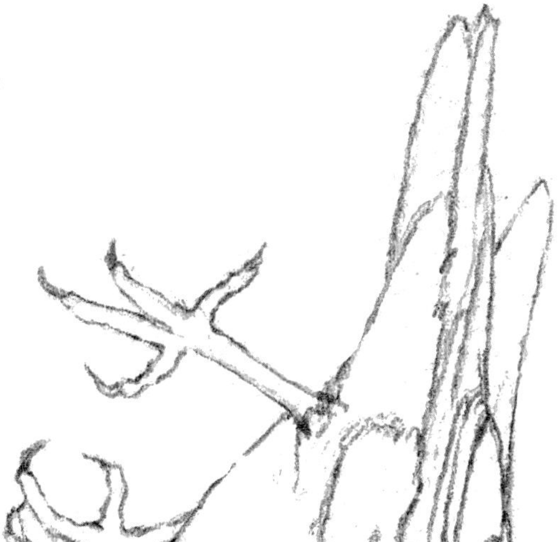

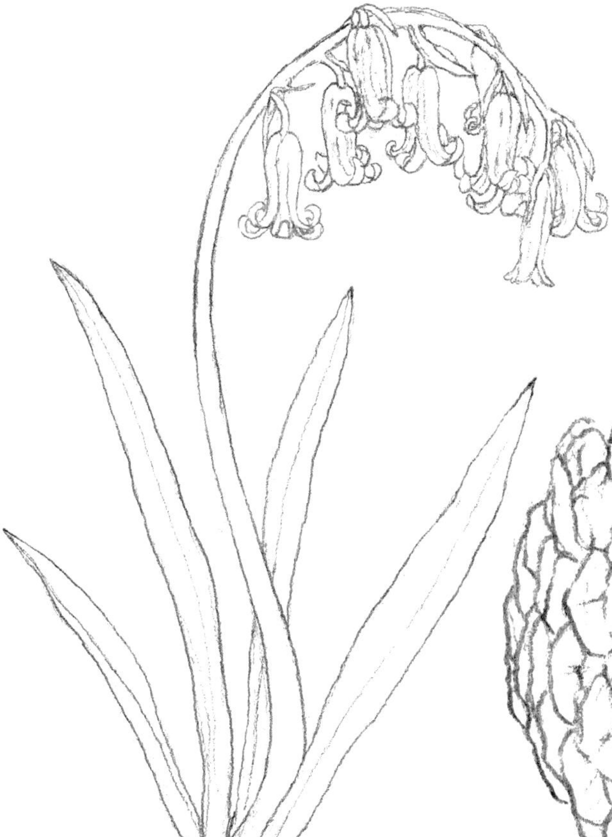

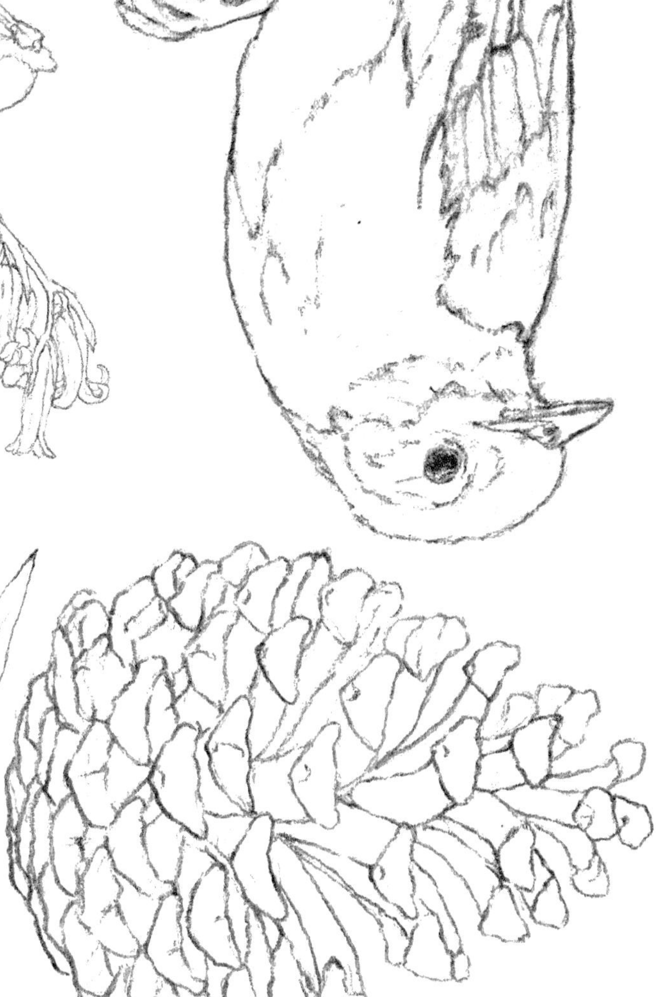

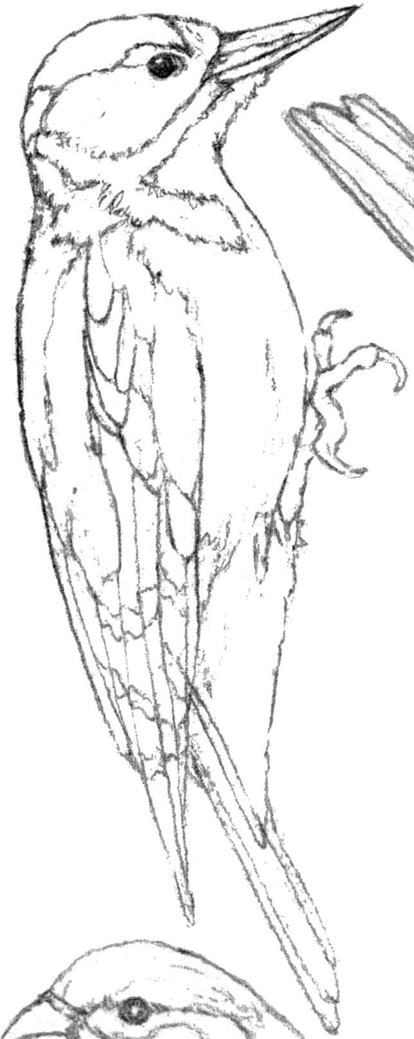

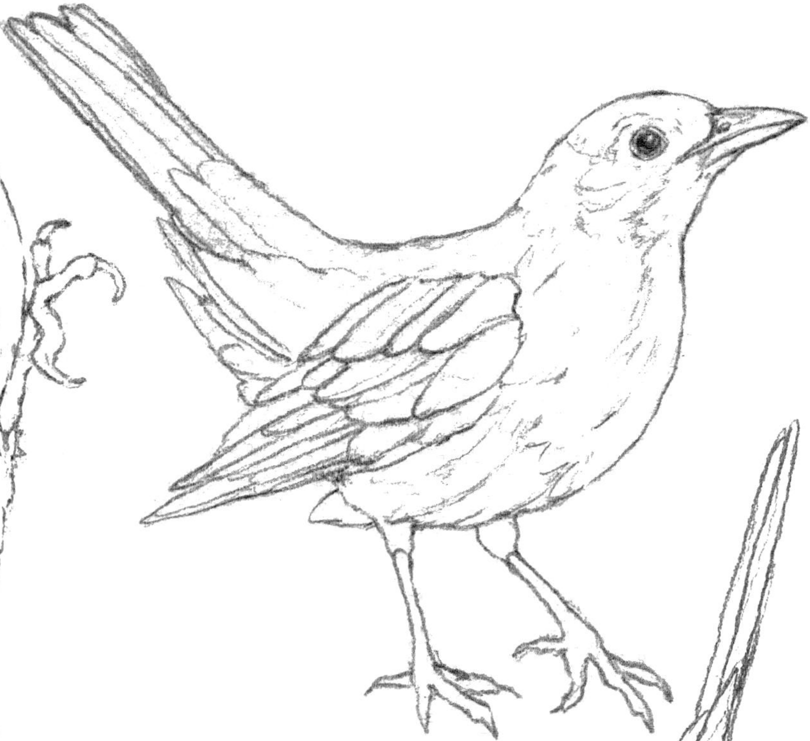

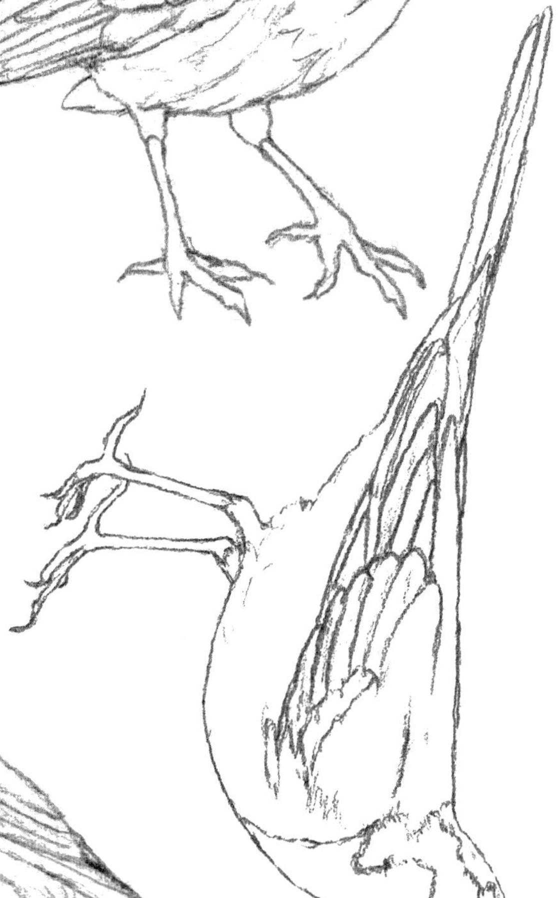

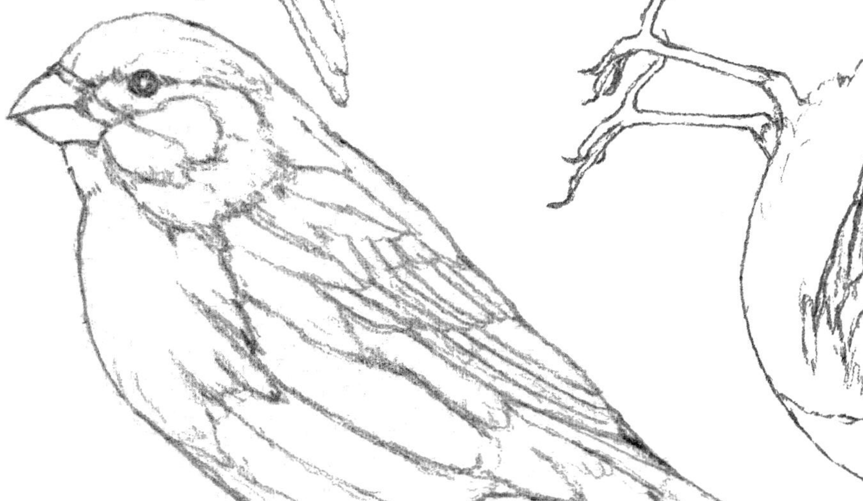

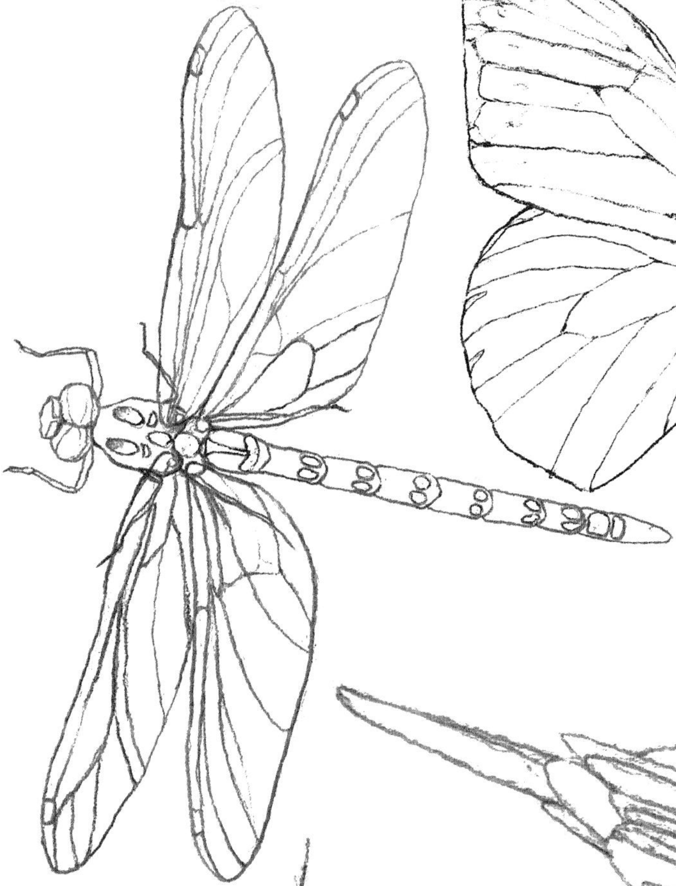

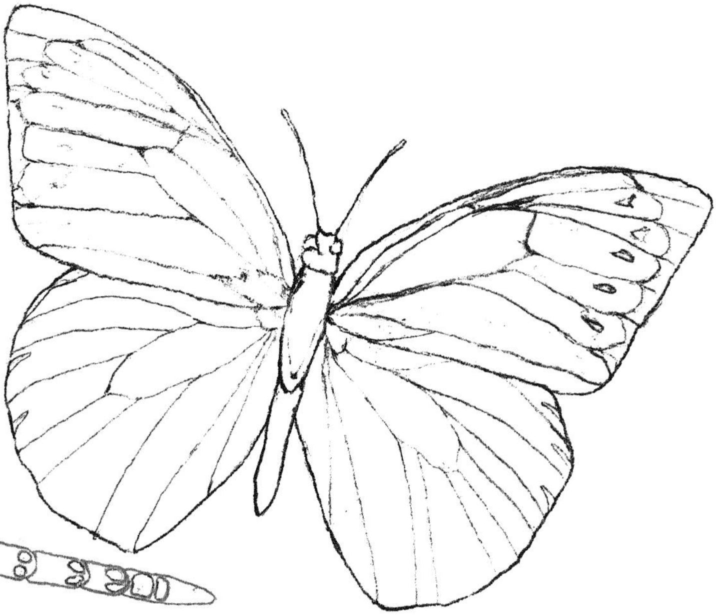

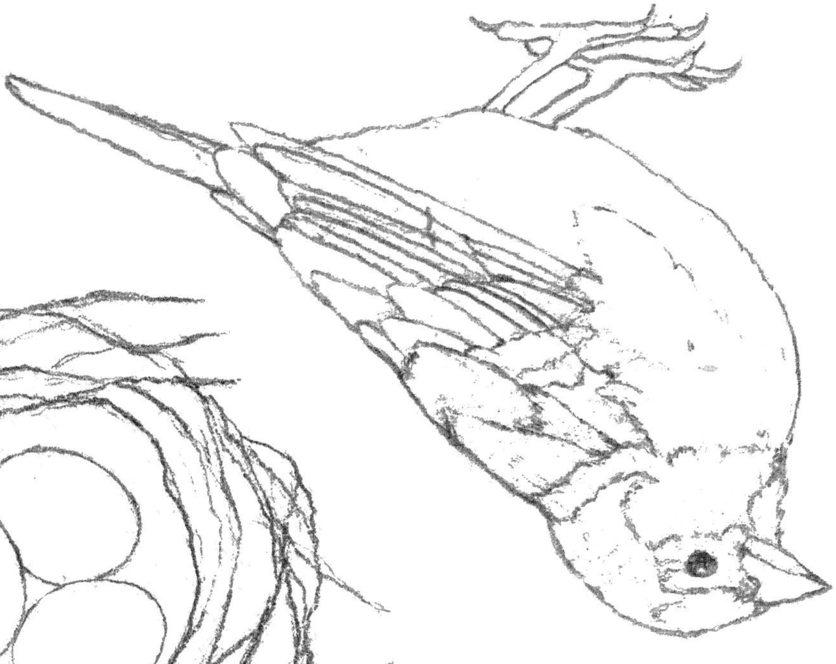

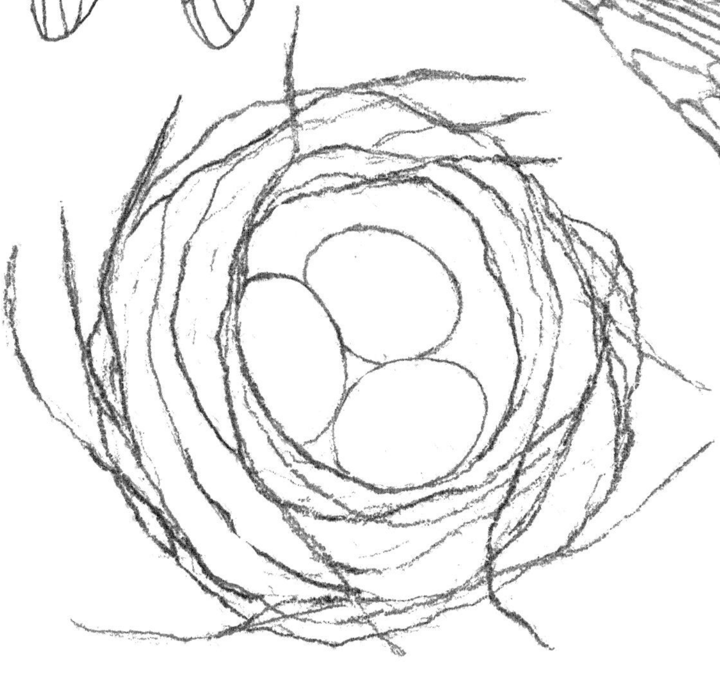

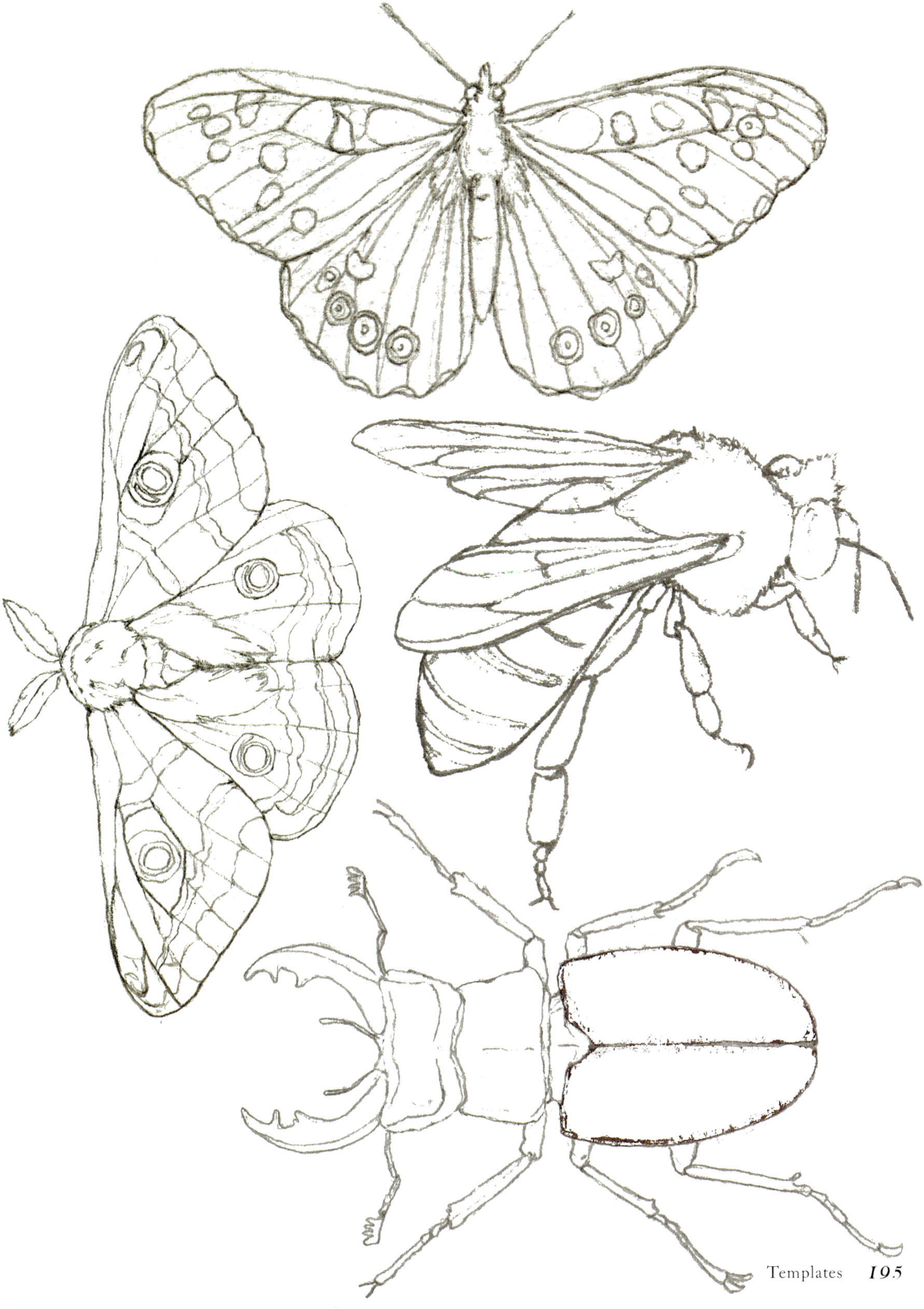

Acknowledgments

My heartfelt thanks go to my friends and family for their steady encouragement and for supporting everything I create.

I'm deeply grateful to the wonderful team at Page Street, whose enthusiasm and tireless work have brought this book to life. Your ideas, feedback, suggestions, and patience are invaluable. Collaborating with you, as always, has been a joy.

Finally, to my customers, students, and readers. Your support and encouragement mean everything. Thank you. I am so excited to see what you create from these pages!

About the Author

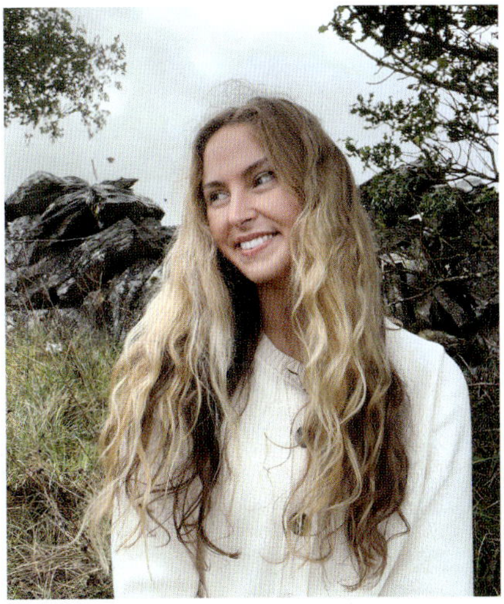

Jane Carkill is an illustrator and textile designer living in the heart of the Burren on the west coast of Ireland. She is fascinated by natural ephemeral beauty and intricate detail, and combines a love of folklore, narration, myth, and story with a precise style of illustration to capture an essence in nature that is both magical and nostalgic.

Her illustrations have been showcased in various highly acclaimed publications, including *Windfall: Irish Nature Poems to Inspire and Connect* (Hachette Books Ireland), edited by Jane Clarke; *The Hare's Corner: Making Space for Nature* (New Island Books), by Jane Clarke and Catherine Cleary; *The Keeper of the Bees: Bees and Beekeeping in Irish Folklore* (The O'Brien Press), by Eimear Chaomhánach; and *Frog Routes, Polka-Dot Newts and Other Treasures of Irish Nature* (Gill Books) and *Wild Embrace: Connecting to the Wonder of Ireland's Natural World* (Hachette Books Ireland), by Anja Murray. She is a member of the nonprofit organization Illustrators Ireland. Her debut authored book *Watercolor in the Woods: Paint a Whimsical World of Forest Animals, Botanicals, Toadstools and More* (Page Street Publishing) was published in 2024.

Index

T

W